Blackstar Theory

Blackstar Theory

The Last Works of David Bowie

Leah Kardos

BLOOMSBURY ACADEMIC
NEW YORK • LONDON • OXFORD • NEW DELHI • SYDNEY

BLOOMSBURY ACADEMIC
Bloomsbury Publishing Inc
1385 Broadway, New York, NY 10018, USA
50 Bedford Square, London, WC1B 3DP, UK
29 Earlsfort Terrace, Dublin 2, Ireland

BLOOMSBURY, BLOOMSBURY ACADEMIC and the Diana logo
are trademarks of Bloomsbury Publishing Plc

First published in the United States of America 2022
Reprinted in 2022 (three times)

Cover design: Louise Dugdale
Cover image: Eclipse © Pobytov / Getty Images

Bloomsbury Publishing Inc does not have any control over, or responsibility for,
any third-party websites referred to or in this book. All internet addresses given in
this book were correct at the time of going to press. The author and publisher
regret any inconvenience caused if addresses have changed or sites have
ceased to exist, but can accept no responsibility for any such changes.

Library of Congress Cataloguing-in-Publication Data
Names: Kardos, Leah, author.
Title: Blackstar Theory: The last works of David Bowie / Leah Kardos.
Description: New York: Bloomsbury Academic, 2022. | Series: Ex:Centrics |
Includes bibliographical references and index.
Identifiers: LCCN 2021026010 (print) | LCCN 2021026011 (ebook) |
ISBN 9781501365379 (paperback) | ISBN 9781501365386 (hardback) |
ISBN 9781501365393 (epub) | ISBN 9781501365409 (pdf) | ISBN 9781501365416
Subjects: LCSH: Bowie, David–Criticism and interpretation. | Bowie,
David–Last years. | Bowie, David. Blackstar. | Bowie, David. Lazarus. | Bowie,
David. The Next Day. | Rock music–2011-2020–History and criticism. |
Musicals–21st century–History and criticism. | Death in music.
Classification: LCC ML420.B754 K27 2022 (print) | LCC ML420.B754 (ebook)|
DDC 782.42166092–dc23
LC record available at https://lccn.loc.gov/2021026010
LC ebook record available at https://lccn.loc.gov/2021026011

ISBN: HB: 978-1-5013-6538-6
        PB: 978-1-5013-6537-9
        ePDF: 978-1-5013-6540-9
        eBook: 978-1-5013-6539-3

Typeset by Integra Software Services Pvt. Ltd.
Printed and bound in Great Britain

Series: Ex:Centrics

To find out more about our authors and books visit www.bloomsbury.com
and sign up for our newsletters.

This is for all the Kooks, still hung up on romance.

CONTENTS

MUSICAL FIGURES

TRACK ANALYSES

ACKNOWLEDGEMENTS

There are many people to whom I owe a large debt of thanks for supporting and helping me with this project. Firstly, to those who generously shared their time, expertise and remembrances in interviews: Tony Visconti, Erin Tonkon, Jonathan Barnbrook, Henry Hey, Donny McCaslin and Mark Adams. Thank you for speaking so openly and warmly about your work. Thanks also to Chris O'Leary, Paul Kinder and Andrew Wiggins for sharing research and hard-to-find resources, and to Keith Ansell-Pearson and Sean Redmond for their expert academic guidance in the places where my work strayed beyond the edges of my discipline. To the Ex:Centrics series editors Greg Hainge and Paul Hegarty, who responded to my text with the greatest of care, thank you for gently probing my meanings so that my writing could get a step closer to achieving what I set out to do. I must also thank Scott Wilson for giving me the push and Isabella van Elferen for the constant encouragement.

Writing this book would have been impossible without the help of Liz Tray, to whom I owe the greatest debt. The best sounding board and sparring partner, our long, far-reaching conversations about Bowie's work have nourished and crystallized my thinking at every stage of this intense journey. My writing would suffer so much without your discerning eye and immaculate attention to detail. I am so grateful that BowieNet brought us together.

Finally, and beyond thanks: Ben Dawson, for your endless patience and support.

PREFACE

Blackstar Theory takes a close look at Bowie's ambitious last works: his surprise 'comeback' project *The Next Day* (2013), the off-Broadway musical *Lazarus* (2015) and the album that preceded the artist's death in 2016 by two days, ★ (pronounced *Blackstar*).

These final works were among the most commercially successful and critically lauded of Bowie's career. *The Next Day* debuted at number one in the UK Albums Chart, eventually topping charts in many countries, and was nominated for Mercury, Brit and Grammy awards. It was announced by one of his most successful singles, 'Where Are We Now?' (2013). Tickets to the New York Theatre Workshop's entire run of *Lazarus* (dir. Ivo van Hove) sold out in hours. That residency was followed in 2016 by a longer production run in London (in a theatre five times the size), also completely sold out, and has since travelled to Amsterdam (2019) in addition to being produced further afield internationally with different directors at the helm. ★ won Grammy awards in all five of the categories it was nominated for and won British Album of the Year at the Brit Awards (both 2017). Debuting at number one in the UK and the United States, it would eventually be certified Gold and Platinum in both territories. Bowie's return was dramatic, mysterious and brief. This time, his return was not signalled by a new haircut or look; the final version of Bowie's star persona was conspicuous by his approach. He said practically nothing to the media by way of announcement or explanation, which naturally fuelled public fascination. Yet for all his silent withholding there was also generosity and openness in the way Bowie shared aspects of his creative process (if not the details of his private life) during the period, presenting the performance persona as a shared construction, dropping hints and puzzling clues with the public (the lists of favourite books and interesting words, cryptic press releases), making seven new music videos (all embedded with

self-reference), putting out collected B-sides (*The Next Day Extra*
2013) and sharing homemade DIY projects – a music video ('Love
Is Lost (Hello Steve Reich Mix by James Murphy for the DFA –
Edit)', 2013) and a demo track ("Tis a Pity She Was a Whore',
2014). Nobody knew he was ill outside of his trusted circle. His
death triggered a worldwide outpouring of grief not seen since
the deaths of Elvis Presley, John Lennon and Diana, Princess of
Wales. In a public statement made shortly after his passing, long-
time friend and co-producer Tony Visconti confirmed that he 'knew
for a year this was the way it would be', adding 'his death was
no different from his life – a work of Art'.[1] If this work and its
attendant sequence of events were indeed conceived as a grand
exiting gesture, then surely David Bowie was the first star to attempt
something so audacious with such precision and lucidity. Despite
his now-iconic posthumous presence in popular culture, Bowie's
creative uniqueness situates him more on the edge of mainstream
music practices than the centre. The last works of Bowie's oeuvre
enact a process of individuation for the Bowie meta-persona. The
work tackles the biggest ideas: identity, creativity, chaos, transience
and immortality. Its knotted themes entangle realities and fictions
across space and time; a catalogue of sound, vision, music
and myth spanning more than fifty years is subjected to the cut-up;
we get to the end only to find signposts directing us back to the
very start.

The last works each explore perspectives of identity, death and
surrender in the context of the Bowie star image. The catalogue
is already brimming with deathly scenes and subjects: dystopian
visions, murders and suicides, fallout and natural disasters, the
many characters made to suffer and die, if not by tragedy or hubris
then by the hand of cruel Time who waits patiently in the wings.
Whereas those past ruminations possessed something of a theatrical
or solemn intellectual distance, these last works have an at-times
messy emotionality, a 'nowness', a sense of chaos and imprecision,

---

[1] A statement published on Visconti's social media accounts on 11 January 2016,
subsequently quoted in many news stories about Bowie's death (*The Times*, *NME*,
The Guardian, January 2016): 'He always did what he wanted to do. And he wanted
to do it his way and he wanted to do it the best way. His death was no different from
his life – a work of Art.'

of thrilling wonder and scale. There's anger and outrage and longing and humour. For *Lazarus* and ★, whether by accident or design, Bowie's physical death is unavoidably written into the context. Death becomes part of the art – Bowie's finishing move.

Overview and structure

It is worthwhile from the outset to explain what this book is not attempting to do. It is not a biography.[2] Nor is it a full chronological account of the period, peeking into the behind the scenes, or a comprehensive rundown of collaborative song development, technical processes, chart performance data or associated trivia. It doesn't offer an extensive critique of the music or provide much of an account of my personal and thoughts and feelings as a fan. For anyone interested in chronology and critiques, I can recommend the comprehensive and highly detailed *Ashes to Ashes* by Chris O'Leary (2019) and Nicholas Pegg's latest revised edition of *The Complete David Bowie* (2016).

What this book does do is explore some of the interconnected webs of meaning that are observable in the work itself. By 'the work' I refer not only to the primary outputs of the period in question, but to the artistry embedded within that connects with Bowie's entire sphere of activity – his career history and the totality of his observable creative practice across time. Although *Blackstar Theory* deals with death as a subject, it is not the aim of the book to pry into the private world of David Jones. Details around the specifics of his cancer diagnosis, the realities of his treatment(s), or anything concerning any preceding health problems, are none of our business. The aim is to approach the realities of Bowie's mortality using the same terms as he used in commenting and wrestling with it through his work.

The book is organized into three parts, each focusing on one of the three main outputs during the period 2013 to 2016. My approach

---

[2] David Buckley's *Strange Fascination* (2012) and Paul Trynka's *Starman* (2011) are excellent biographies that I'm happy to recommend. Updated editions of both are reportedly on the way.

in building these sections is loosely informed by the concept of the three-part stage illusion from *The Prestige*, a novel by Christopher Priest (1995) that was adapted into a film by Christopher Nolan in 2006, in which Bowie played the role of Nikola Tesla. The structure follows (1) the setup/*The Next Day*, (2) the performance/*Lazarus* and (3) the 'prestige', or the effect/★. The book moves forward in chronological sequence, but it is not organized thematically, rather, the writing takes its cue from the swirling, associational logic of Bowie's artistry. Meaningful networks and constellations of signification will accumulate, gather focus and force as the book progresses. Recurrent themes (and familiar names, places, years, people, moments) are drawn into orbit around Bowie's late star image, a density of information pulling towards the event horizon of the blackstar.

Part 1: Last act establishes the relevant contexts of Bowie's 'late style', which I argue can be traced in the outputs from 2002 to 2016, and the remystification of his star persona in the last three years of his career. We consider the ways that late stars can exist as living archives, how creativity can become complex and self-referential as late stars age, and how they maintain cultural relevance even as they deliberately detach from contemporary aesthetics and concerns. We look at *The Next Day* and find it preoccupied by darkness and haunted by Bowie's previous works and myth, saturated with sonic and musical signification. Here we see the unveiling of Bowie's final persona, a participatory construction that draws attention to his career-long explorations of identity and the inner selves. 'Bowie' becomes a performance that we can assemble for ourselves, an image that we project on to the blank white space.

Part 2: Per ardua ad astra (trans. 'through difficulty to the stars') considers Bowie's lifelong aspiration to write and stage a musical theatre piece, which comes to pass just in time – he attended the premiere of *Lazarus* in December 2015, which became his last public appearance, a mere four weeks and six days before his death. The musical is conceived as a sequel-of-sorts to the 1976 British science-fiction film *The Man Who Fell to Earth*, directed by Nicolas Roeg, adapted by Paul Mayersberg from the 1963 novel by Walter Tevis, in which Bowie played the lead role. This section explores Bowie's connections to musical theatre, from his starting points in mime and his unfinished Ziggy Stardust stage show to the thwarted musical adaptation of George Orwell's *Nineteen*

Eighty-Four and the introduction of music theatrics to his tours
in 1974 (*Diamond Dogs*) and 1987 (*Glass Spider*). Themes of
alienation, otherness and social corruption from *The Man Who
Fell to Earth* are placed next to poet Emma Lazarus's ideation of
America as 'Mother of Exiles', as well as connecting to the biblical
story of Lazarus's miraculous revival and other recurring symbolic
imagery within the catalogue.

   Lazarus was co-written with playwright Enda Walsh and portrays
the stranded, substance-addicted alien Thomas Jerome Newton in
a contemporary setting, tormented by visions and unable to die.
Its dreamscape narrative pivots on the emotional resonances of
well-known songs and new compositions that play into and against
audience expectations. *Lazarus*'s tangle of self-reference blurs the
lines between science fiction, persona-mythology and biography.
We gain access to its interior world of archetypes and symbols with
an approach informed by Jungian dream analysis adapted from
John Izod's *Mind, Myth and the Screen* (2001).

   In *Part 3: ★*, the final album's densely packed themes are
explored: sci-fi and occult symbolism; lyrical, sonic and musical
signatures sewing up narrative threads spanning across fifty years.
We consider the existentialist's quest for wholeness; the merging
and melting of worlds: art, literature, sound, science, spirituality,
language, histories, futures, fact and fiction. We chart the features
of ★'s musical terrain, Bowie's handling of 'chaos' as a creative
force, birthing sensations and intensities, and consider the nature
of improvisation, 'liveness', ensemble creativity and the idea of
the improvising soloist (here, saxophonist Donny McCaslin) as
emotional-expressive avatar.

   ★ references and ultimately redefines Bowie's system of star
signification (the lexicon of celestial bodies – star men, shining
stars, prettiest stars, bright failing stars, new killer stars, stars that
never sleep, and so many more). Using foundational concepts from
Richard Dyer's *Stars* ([1979] 1998), where the star is a constructed
image that embodies specific ideologies and impossible tensions, and
setting these ideas in dialogue against the notion of the self-realized,
wholly unified *Übermensch*, we articulate the Blackstar Theory. The
radical potential of [black]stardom is demonstrated in the rock star
supernova that creates a singularity resulting in cultural iconicity.
It is how a seriously ill man can create art that illuminates the
immortal potential of all matter in the known universe.

Assemblage art and intentionality

Assemblage is a term used to refer to a mostly twentieth-century hybrid art movement that incorporated mixed media – often found and mass-produced objects – into painting and sculpture. A well-known example is Marcel Duchamp's *Bicycle Wheel* (1913) – a kinetic sculpture constructed from recognizable banal objects, arranged in such a way as to disrupt their function and suggest new physical possibilities, opening up new ways for us to see and understand the everyday mundanities of existence. A later, similarly notorious, example is Tracey Emin's *My Bed* (1998), a piece which blurs the lines between painting, sculpture, theatre and autobiography. The multidimensional aspect is not only present in the sculptural 3D nature of most assemblage art, it also highlights the relationships between objects and what they can represent and, in the case of Emin's example, between the assembled objects and the artist's story. This fourth dimension of creative connection between disparate elements is what lends assemblage its uniquely communicative, time-travelling, world-jumping potential, explained here by artist Betye Saar:

> I am intrigued with combining the remnant of memories, fragments of relics and ordinary objects, with the components of technology. It's a way of delving into the past and reaching into the future simultaneously. The art itself becomes the bridge.
> – Saar (*The Fragility of Smiles (of Strangers Lost at Sea)*, 1998)

Bowie's last works possess a similar sense of multi-dimensional connectedness, so it makes sense that a suitable method of musical analysis should also include the key aspects of assemblage in the frame, as we are observing musical and extramusical elements interacting – music and sound as text *and* context. Such an approach identifies the salient details revealed in the music, its locations, proximities and functions, making note of the creative connections these details afford the listener. These can be images, texts, musical elements, performance aspects, sounds and production choices and any other ideas that are suggestive or referential. What the music and lyrics suggest on the page and also how these ideas are embodied and elaborated through performance and production. How they are altered and enhanced by their proximity to adjacent tracks, signatures and vernacular, literature, history, Bowie's life and death. Throughout *Blackstar Theory*, the music analysis will employ approaches generally in line with Eric Clarke's ecological approach to musical perception (*Ways of Listening: An Ecological Approach to the Perception of Musical Meaning* 2005); starting with the assumption that musical meaning exists as a matter of perception, it is the listener who constructs meaning in response to the experience of music. This seems to be in keeping with Bowie's own philosophy on the matter, which was spelled out most succinctly in the joint artists' statement for *1. Outside* (exhibited as part of the V&A's *David Bowie Is* touring archive, which ran from 2013 to 2018):

> Taking the present philosophical line, we don't expect our audience to necessarily seek an explanation from ourselves. We assign that role to the listener and to culture. As both of these are in a state of permanent change there will be a constant 'drift' in interpretation. All art is unstable. Its meaning is not necessarily that implied by the author. There is no authoritative voice. There are only multiple readings.
>
> – Bowie and Eno (1995)

This might feel like a philosophical alignment with Roland Barthes's *The Death of the Author* (1967), where the creator's original intention, and/or the conditions of its creation, should hold no influence over any given interpretation. However, it is impossible to separate Bowie from this work because the meta-persona becomes the performance, and the material of his artistry and public life, the chosen vocabulary. Therefore we must consider the intentional and necessarily 'directorial' agency of the assemblage artist: element set beside element, 'the many qualities and auras of isolated fragments [that] are compounded, fused or contradicted ... [into] a vast repertoire of expression' (Seitz 1961, 86). Similarly, we should regard the role of intuition and choice in Bowie's intentionally dispersive and distancing approaches such as the Burroughs/Gysin cut-up method. The material we are presented with is the sum of many creative choices; our range of potential readings is based on what is 'written' and 'shown' in addition to what is already 'known'.

For listeners at varying levels of familiarity with Bowie's style, the musical elements that balance expectation, recognition and surprise will yield different reactions and individual appraisals. We can consider Bowie's collected works as a kind of ecosystem of interconnected sounds and ideas, one that listeners participate in, react and adapt to in order to search for meaning. Listeners also bring their experience to the table – what they know from culture, the ability to discriminate between music styles, references and tropes, a level of awareness of Bowie's creative vernacular. The literacy that comes from being familiar with Bowie's back catalogue and the characters, stories, cultures and shared meanings that swirl around it. Across the last works, Bowie's post-structuralist performance of himself takes place across territories of fluid space-time. The persona construction eclipses reality, with David Jones retreating from view as the final mysterious star image ascends. Here, the analysis of the artistry at play shifts from musical evaluations and textual readings to a grander exploration, looking at 'the peculiar relations that art establishes between the living body, the forces of the universe and the creation of the future, the most abstract of questions, which, if they are abstract enough, may provide us with a new way of understanding the concrete and the lived' (Grosz [2008] 2020, 3).

There are many curious and fascinating details embedded within the rich imagery of Bowie's last works (especially ★) that I have not had room to write about in this book. Like many ★ hunters, I sat through multiple seasons of *Peaky Blinders*, dug around ancient alchemical texts and spent a lot of time squinting at the images and publication dates on the 'Villa of Ormen' Tumblr account. I replayed *Omikron: The Nomad Soul* to study its soundtrack for motifs and spent days scanning Hubble's deep field images looking for the specific constellation pictured in the ★ artwork. One of the primary pleasures of Bowie's lasts works is its exquisite, barely concealed complexity, promising rich rewards for those who want to explore it at a deeper level. No doubt there is more to be discovered. This book would be much longer, and far more bloated and frustrating to follow, had I tried to resolve every puzzling detail I encountered on this journey.

I'm certainly not insisting that my reading of the last works is definitive to the exclusion of others. Nor is it my intention to strip Bowie's art of its magic by subjecting it to the rigours of academic analysis: the last thing I want to achieve is the taming of every mystery, to ruin the fabric by unpicking every stitch. I am aware that it is relatively rare to find a book about popular music that engages with music theory these days. And I know that even the idea of such a thing can set off panic alarms for certain readers who might fear being led slowly through a morass of jargon-choked text. Because I want to be accessible to as broad an audience as possible, my approach to music writing favours the use of common language over a highly specialized vocabulary; where this is unavoidable, I have included explainers in the footnotes. The notated examples are illustrative of musical features I am also describing with words, so notation literacy is not a prerequisite to understanding the contents of this book. The only aim is to demonstrate some of the beautiful networks contained in Bowie's last works by exploring what the music is, what it says and what it does. By examining these details that we can all see and hear, we can identify clusters and constellations of potential meanings that can enhance the pleasures of engaging with Bowie's music and artistry. For me, this has been a journey of discovering new ways of listening, seeing and feeling what music can be: a vivid sensation of the beauty, complexity and intensity of existence; a way to dream big for our selves, transcend limiting circumstances and penetrate the mysteries of the unknown.

PART ONE

Last act

1

Lateness

Lateness, late style and late-period work are terms associated with a concept originally articulated by twentieth-century theorist Theodor W. Adorno (1903–69), describing the characteristics of the work made by composers, writers and artists who are approaching the end of their lives. Adorno, who coined the term 'late style', explored the idea in a series of essays about Beethoven's last works (1964, and the posthumously published *Essays on Music*, 2002). He found that the music held a disruptive 'catastrophic' essence that agitates against prevailing aesthetics and foreshadows something new; in the case of Beethoven, hinting towards the atonal modernism of Schoenberg and the Second Viennese School. Adorno's ideas about late style suggested that, as time runs out, the mortal limits of life create special conditions that can allow art to reach its fullest potentials.

This concept was further developed by Palestinian writer Edward Said (1935–2003) in his final publication *On Late Style* (2006), written while he himself was dying of leukaemia and published posthumously. Said considered the last works of a range of 'great' artists, not only composers (Beethoven, Richard Strauss, Bach) but also performers (Glenn Gould) and writers (Jean Genet, Thomas Mann), and uncovered the conflicts and complexities that distinguished these outputs in contrast to what was popular at the time, revealing them as forerunners of what was to come in each artist's discipline. Both Adorno and Said point out that late-period work can often be characterized by a complex, contrary and questioning spirit, more agitated and restless than serene or reconciliatory, going against what one might expect from artists of advancing age.

There is also a sense in these writings that an awareness of diminishing time can lead an artist to shed any concerns about being liked or necessarily understood. This idea was echoed by Eve Kosofsky Sedgwick in her book *Touching Feeling: Affect, Pedagogy, Performativity* (2003, 24), when she described the 'senile sublime' quality of the work of 'old brilliant people, whether artists, scientists, or intellectuals where the bare outlines of a creative idiom seem to emerge from what had been the obscuring puppy fat of personableness, timeliness or ... coherent sense.' A feeling that the difficult, knotty quality of late Shakespeare, Beethoven, the irascible final writings of an Alzheimer's-suffering Iris Murdoch, somehow possess an uncanny brilliance, finally free of self-consciousness.

Yet lateness is a quality ascribed retrospectively, usually only to the oeuvres of 'exceptional', renowned individuals. More often than not an artist isn't aware that their final work will indeed be their last, so the concept cannot be applied universally. Wrapped up with this idea is the post-mortem reappraisal of something that might have been missed and under-appreciated in its time; for example, it was only after Picasso's death, when the rest of the art world had moved on from abstract expressionism, that art critics came to see his last works as prefiguring neo-expressionism. It is only after Bowie's death that the mainstream music press rewrites its appraisals of those 1990s outputs that they once scoffed at.[1] The discovery and designation of 'late greatness' allow cultural commentators to engage in historical revisionism.

There is a danger that the romance surrounding these ideas of lateness and greatness taints our discourse with undue reverence, constructing fantasies that perpetuate cultural bias. 'Genius' is a descriptor that can be lazily applied to artistic works and creative processes. It blesses entire oeuvres with specialness and implies preternatural ability, erasing an individual's hard-won achievements and the gradual refinement of one's process by way of struggles, failures and breakthroughs. It is also worth noting that the retrospective labelling of the 'great' and 'genius' artists is determined by collective assumptions and biases, which can lead

---

[1] See *Rolling Stone, Uncut, The Observer/The Guardian* positively reviewing music they once eviscerated (Greene 2016a, Hughes 2019, Petridis 2020). Also see Jonathan Dean's conciliatory *Sunday Times Magazine* cover story 'He Fell to Earth: How David Bowie Dealt with a Decade of Obscurity' (2020).

to a more grievous kind of erasure: history's 'greatest' and most venerated geniuses are overwhelmingly white and male. It is easy to say an artist is good and their work is special, especially when the artist is popularly loved. It is unhelpful if one of the reasons we cite something as being 'great art' is simply because the artist was at the end of their life and the piece was complex or 'difficult'.

Despite these tensions, and acknowledging the dangers of romanticizing art and the artistic process, identifying the material attributes of lateness within the catalogue of outputs from a long career remains a useful exercise. It need not predict the future trajectory of an art form; it can simply be the arrival at a state of artistic being. It might be marked by an apparent detachment from contemporary concerns with trends, scenes, peer groups, audiences or industries. We may observe shifts in the texture and syntax of a creative language – sounds and musical devices, lyrics, voices, images and references. The nature, quality and rhythm of late-life creativity could be influenced by tangible late-life circumstances such as citizenship, family, financial pressures, access to collaborators, technologies and ways of working, bouts of illness, periods of treatment and convalescence. For Bowie, lateness can be observed in his arrival at a stable and autonomous creative process; his compositional practices that consciously reach back into the past to connect it with the present, using his catalogue and star image as lexicon. Bowie's lateness is evident in the finessing of those details that complicate, encapsulate and complete the long-running themes of his oeuvre.

A taxonomy of Bowie's late style

Up until the end of the twentieth century, Bowie's pop career was characterized by frequent surface reinventions exploring different music styles, looks, lyrical perspectives and ways of working. He would restlessly seek creative reinvigoration through change and became known for this mercurial energy. Changes in the sound and style of Bowie's music were often (though not always) brought about by the arrival of new musical collaborators or producers, sometimes a radical geographical relocation (London, Switzerland, France, Germany, America), and were quite often announced with a new look. Some of these reinventions took form around the construction of a new 'Bowie' persona – a character in costume associated with a specific album from which listeners could perceive the lyrics and ideas as being from that persona's point of view (Ziggy Stardust, the Thin White Duke). Sometimes Bowie's performance personas became linked to a time and place (Beckenham Arts Lab, Berlin) or associated with a particular manner of public engagement (blond, tanned, mainstream-ready in the early 1980s; paint-splattered art-polymath in the mid-1990s). Towards the very end of the twentieth century Bowie would change his costume one final time – seemingly retreating from the frontiers of the new and away from restless reinvention, he 'made himself more ordinary than ever before' (O'Leary 2019, 451), performing a public version of himself that seemed in closer alignment with the 'real' David Jones. Roughly coinciding with the new millennium and the birth of his daughter, Alexandria (Lexi), Bowie's late style begins with his reunion with producer Tony Visconti, marking the start of the final period where we can observe his songwriting perspectives and compositional processes stabilizing into a consistent approach.

Tony Visconti and ISO

When Visconti reunited with Bowie for the 1998 one-off track 'Safe' (co-written by Reeves Gabrels for *The Rugrats Movie* (1998), of all things, and not released publicly until 2016), they hadn't worked together in fifteen years. Before this, the last Visconti production credit had been on 1982's soundtrack EP to Bertolt Brecht's *Baal*, which accompanied a televised version of the play for the BBC and starred Bowie in the title role. *Baal* became Bowie's final release of new material for RCA Records, freeing him from his unhappy contract with them; the following year he signed with EMI and released *Let's Dance*, unceremoniously ditching Visconti in favour of hiring Chic guitar legend Nile Rodgers as his co-producer.

Up until that point, Visconti and Bowie had enjoyed a long-standing and successful creative relationship. Beginning back in the late 1960s with production and arrangement on early Bowie single 'In the Heat of the Morning'/'London Bye Ta Ta' (1968) and producing his breakthrough second album *Space Oddity* in

1969 (title track aside), Visconti would be Bowie's bandmate in glam outfit The Hype, produce and play on *The Man Who Sold the World* (1970) and collaborate on 1974's *Diamond Dogs*. From there, Visconti co-produced an impressive run of legendary releases with Bowie, from 1975's *Young Americans*, the 'Berlin Trilogy' (*Low* and *"Heroes"*, both 1977, and *Lodger* in 1979) and *Scary Monsters (and Super Creeps)* in 1980 – the album commonly held up by rock critics as a high point in Bowie's career, his 'last great album' against which every subsequent release would be compared.

After 'Safe', Bowie released *Hours...* in 1999, his final collaboration with guitarist and co-writer/co-producer Reeves Gabrels, with whom he had been working consistently since the late 1980s (with the exception of 1993's *The Buddha of Suburbia*). It was around 2000/2001 when Visconti was called on again to create string parts and help finish the ill-fated *Toy* album project – a mixture of new and re-recorded old songs from Bowie's pre-fame years, produced by Mark Plati, planned for 2001 but never released. Their professional relationship now rekindled, Visconti went on to co-produce 2002's *Heathen* (widely praised as a return to form upon its release), in the process salvaging what could be saved from *Toy*, with a few tracks refashioned and revised ('Slip Away', 'Afraid') and others relegated to B-sides and extras.

From here on Visconti remained in the co-producer's chair on every release until the end of Bowie's life, bringing his uniquely intuitive sense of musicianship and the weight and wealth of their shared history and proven working methods to the table. The sound of Bowie and Visconti in the 1970s was dramatic and boldly coloured, often with a sharp, weird edge. By contrast, their sound in the late period is more expansive, filled from top to bottom, highly detailed and atmospheric. Visconti's gilded string arrangements and characterful, hard-hitting drum production became a permanent feature throughout the period, along with richly detailed reverbs and large-scale ambience, the velvet backdrop behind everything. The Visconti reunion created opportunities for Bowie's songwriting to reference and converse with the past through the reprisal of signature sounds (Stylophones, recorders, vintage synths, *Low* drum effects, varispeed vocals, Hansa-era mic techniques), a trend that was echoed sometimes in lyrical references ('Slip Away', 'Bring Me the Disco King', 'Like a Rocket Man', 'Where Are We Now?').

Perhaps most importantly of all, Visconti could still reliably coax winning vocal performances from Bowie – the kind of takes that came close to matching the dramatic range and intensity of previous pinnacles: *"Heroes"*, *Lodger* and *Scary Monsters*. At all times the production choices are in service of the songwriting, not the other way around and, for the first time since *The Buddha of Suburbia*, the new material was primarily written by Bowie alone. That trend would continue throughout the late period. Returning to, and building upon, a signature Bowie/Visconti sound became a source of inspiration:

> [*Reality*] would be identifiably kind of a Bowie/Visconti production, and it would just have that special thing that we have when we work together. I can't really articulate it, but when we work together, we do seem to produce really good quality stuff that has a sense of integrity and is interesting. It's just right, and it's very exciting.
> – Bowie (Orshoski 2003)

The timeliness of this reconnection found the two musicians particularly compatible – both being of the same generation and, handily, living quite near to each other in Manhattan. Common interests that bonded them in the late 1960s were still present: an eclectic appreciation of music, fondness for British-style humour, continued interests in Tibetan Buddhism and newfound sobriety – both men were/are card-carrying members of Alcoholics Anonymous. In fact, Bowie had quit all his vices, even smoking, by 2001. That same year he set up his own record label, ISO (departing from EMI/Virgin after they shelved *Toy*). The ISO/Columbia agreement would be in place until his death, eliminating unwanted contractual obligations and granting Bowie the freedom to make and release music whenever and however he liked. This meant he could design an album with a world tour in mind (*Reality* 2003) or time a surprise release to occur on his birthday ('Where Are We Now?' 2013), retaining complete autonomy in all matters of creative control and public engagement.

Sound engineer Erin Tonkon was hired to assist Visconti's sessions from 2013 and subsequently spent a lot of time working in close quarters with the co-producers. I asked her what it was like seeing Bowie and Visconti working together:

There were a lot of inside jokes, a lot of references to obscure British comedy shows. They had their own little secret language as well ... You know it's that thing when you have an old friend and you can just pick up where you left off? They really did that creatively and musically.

– Tonkon (interview with the author, 2020)

New ways of working and new musicians

The late 1990s/early 2000s was a time when digital recording became standard practice in professional studios and, for the first time, was an affordable option for home recording setups too. Writing more on his own, Bowie's home-studio work and early demoing sessions with Visconti became integral to the creative process during this period. Bowie prepared song demos that contained sketch performances of top-line melodies and 'scratch' (placeholder) keyboard, bass and guitar parts. The demo would be built upon, with some parts replaced and more layers added to construct a final, complete arrangement. Sometimes they decided to keep elements of Bowie's rough demos in the final productions because they had the right energy and attitude:

A lot of it [on *Reality*] we didn't replace ... And I left my own guitars on most of the tracks. Most of the rhythm tracks, I'm plunking away in there. So it has a quasi-demo feel to a lot of the tracks, which is really good – a demo energy.

– Bowie (Orshoski 2003)

Rather than bury Bowie's playing in the mix, Visconti more often spotlighted it; he can be heard on lead and rhythm guitars, keyboards and synths, saxophone, harmonica, drums and percussion – the kind of diverse instrumental playing that had been prevalent in projects like *Diamond Dogs* (1974) and the 'Berlin Trilogy' (1977–9). Bowie's self-described 'pretty basic home setup' (Buskin 2003) was built around a Korg Trinity synthesizer workstation, a Korg Pandora effects unit and a vintage ARP Odyssey, alongside a collection of guitars and small amps. The unique sound of the Korg Trinity, in particular, became a recognizable signature of late-period albums; its tones are present on *Hours...* (1999) (and the *Omikron: The*

Nomad Soul game soundtrack of the same year) and *Reality*, and appear again on *The Next Day* and ★. The co-producers worked together to design interesting and original sounds, Bowie exploring the range of tones available with the synthesizer's tools and Visconti processing the resulting sounds:

> He loved that [Korg] keyboard. He'd tweak the sounds and then I'd process them with the [Eventide] Harmonizer and other special effects. He was comfortable with it and it gave him a songwriting tool which prior to that was only a piano or a guitar. So now he could dial up brass and string sounds and all that. It really inspired him to write.
> – Visconti (interview with the author, 2020)

Bowie's home studio setup was connected to a Zoom R24 digital multitrack recorder, which came with an on-board drum machine, bass synthesizer, audio loop editor and a step/real-time sequencer. Even as home recording practices quickly evolved in the early millennium towards software applications like Logic and Pro Tools, Bowie preferred to stick with his Zoom hard disc recorder, a relatively limited and old-fashioned piece of kit by the time he used it to produce the 2014 version of "Tis a Pity She Was a Whore' (the B-side to the 2014 single version of 'Sue (Or in a Season of Crime)'). Because they were lifting takes from it to use in their final productions, Visconti bought his own R24 unit: 'Sometimes David would say, "I like the way I did it, I don't see why I have to do it again." So it became important, and I bought one to understand how it works.'

Bowie brought in some new players for the *Heathen* sessions, many of whom would become mainstays of this period (up until 2013 at least). Guitarists David Torn and Gerry Leonard, each known for their atmospheric, effects-heavy playing styles, had connections with the Allaire Studios complex in the Catskill mountains in upstate New York. Torn originally recommended the facility to Bowie for *Heathen* and Leonard himself lived in nearby Woodstock. Bowie would eventually purchase a sixty-four-acre plot in the area, electing to live there part-time from 2011 onwards. In 2002 he claimed that the mountain atmosphere inspired his songwriting in a particular way: 'I don't know what happened up there, but something clicked for me as a writer. I've written in the mountains before, but never with such gravitas' (Sischy 2002).

Drummer and percussionist Matt Chamberlain (Tori Amos, Fiona Apple, Soundgarden), with a wide background spanning rock, classical, jazz and avant-garde styles, was another newcomer, appearing on *Heathen* and *Reality*. Session pro bassist Tony Levin (King Crimson, Peter Gabriel, John Lennon, many others) appears on *Heathen* and *The Next Day*, and his studio bandmate from Lennon and Ono's *Double Fantasy* (1980), Earl Slick (who played on *Young Americans* and *Station to Station*), returned for *Reality*, the subsequent *A Reality Tour* and *The Next Day*. Long-standing members of Bowie's touring bands throughout the 1990s would also be variously called upon during the period up until 2013: bassist/vocalist Gail Ann Dorsey and drummers Sterling Campbell and Zachary Alford returned for *The Next Day*; Mike Garson and Mark Plati returned in 2003 for *Reality* (and Garson would join the *A Reality Tour* band alongside bandleader Leonard, Campbell, Slick, Dorsey and background singer Catherine Russell). Bowie also invited past collaborators The Borneo Horns (*Tonight* 1984, *Never Let Me Down* 1987) to feature on *Heathen*, and member Steve Elson played on *The Next Day*.

The only new musician recruited for *The Next Day* was pianist Henry Hey, who performed overdubs for a handful of tracks (notably the piano part for surprise 2013 single 'Where Are We Now?'). In 2014, Bowie chose him to be the musical director for *Lazarus*. Also in 2014, Bowie actively sought out new musical collaborators who were skilled in jazz, a search that first led him to bandleader Maria Schneider and her orchestra and, through her, to Donny McCaslin and his band, who appeared on ★. Even though the personnel would change, shift and refresh over the late period, the way Bowie and Visconti managed the productions from start to finish remained consistent.

In the studio, they encouraged players in the core rhythm section (drums, bass, guitar) to improvise and develop their own parts in the arrangements, which would then be rehearsed and tracked together, a process that Leonard described as having a 'greasiness to it' (Leonard 2013). With an appropriately energetic foundation captured and in place, overdubs were laid on top – strings, synths, guitar effects, horns, backing vocal arrangements and, finally, the main vocal. This approach, going from a home demo to live jam-outs and then constructed to full scale with layers of overdubbed detail, became the standard template for productions throughout this period. Even though Bowie was writing more often at home on his own, the process created space and opportunities for his musicians to contribute in ways that could take the material in different directions. Henry Hey told me how working with Bowie as a collaborator in this way made him feel:

> He loved to see what people would do with his ideas, where things could go. He was a great guide, and he gave me a lot of room to do what I wanted. And then he would say, 'I like this' and 'What about this?' He rarely said negative things. It was a fascinating lesson in leadership for me. Everybody wanted to give him their best because he made us feel included.
> – Hey (interview with the author, 2020)

During the late period we also see Bowie engaging in self-sampling, taking elements from older recordings to form starting points for new song ideas. This technique can be heard on 'Bring Me the Disco King' from *Reality*, a stark arrangement based on a loop cut from Matt Chamberlain's performance on *Heathen* B-side 'When the Boys Come Marching Home'. The same technique is found on *The Next Day Extra*'s 'Plan' and 'The Informer', and Bowie's 2014 version of ''Tis a Pity'. In addition to using old drum takes as rhythm beds for new songs, Bowie was also programming his own electronic drum parts on the Zoom R24, for example the loop that opens ★'s 'I Can't Give Everything Away'. Reflecting on their history of co-production and arrangement, Visconti told me that Bowie's 'arranging skills [had] quadrupled over those years, and he was already a great arranger. I remember for "I Would Be Your Slave", he wrote the string parts and I transcribed them. I turned to him afterwards and said "You could make a living as an arranger", and he joked, "Yeah, but why would I?"'

Voice(s)

Richard Elliott, in his 2015 book *The Late Voice: Time, Age and Experience in Popular Music*, defines the late voice as something that contains time, age, authority and authenticity: 'A voice of authority is also a voice of authenticity and a voice that authenticates experience' (104). This idea of vocal authentication is picked up on by Thomas Jones, who points out that Bowie's 'self', insomuch as we perceive and understand it, exists and is identifiable inside his voice – it being the one continuous reliable thread that connects such a diverse oeuvre of vastly different sounding music (Jones 2012). Shelton Waldrep notes how Bowie's voice is readily identifiable by its distinctive grain, even as he demonstrates its malleability through wide-ranging performance techniques and characterizations, '[Bowie's voice] is always recognisable on a song, and he calls a lot of attention to it by the many ways he manipulates it' (Waldrep 2015, 105). Bowie's late voice holds a different colour and weight from the tight-sounding tenor he started with in the late 1960s. After developing his vocal technique during the 1970s, patterned after Scott Walker, Elvis and Little Richard, and after a lifetime of smoking, his voice became deeper in pitch and broader in tone and vibrato swell; although it grew heavier, it never lost its precision, nor its elasticity for characterization. According to Visconti, Bowie's voice was powerfully dynamic, a quality that did not diminish with advancing age: 'He was loud! I couldn't stand next to him when he was singing it was so loud.' Visconti's approach to capturing Bowie's voice favoured spirited performance and the preservation of natural expression 'as standard, a bit of 3:1 compression on his vocal just to cut about 3dB from the peaks. I didn't want to have him slam into full compression because I didn't want to lose his dynamics' (Visconti, interview with the author, 2020).

When performing his late voice, Bowie plays multiple versions of himself, like a guitarist might do through a range of different special effects. These vocalizations can range from the seemingly unaffected to dramatic histrionics, with unique gradients in between: solemn (or what Chris O'Leary describes as 'ashen', the opening tones of 'Sunday', 'Heat'), childlike ('A Better Future'), frail ('The Loneliest Guy', ''Tis a Pity She Was a Whore'), aggressive ('Pablo Picasso', 'The Next Day'), melodramatic ('You Feel So Lonely You Could Die') and many more. These voices sometimes point back to Bowie's former selves, using subtle reminders of sounds past – the smooth 'Wild Is the Wind' that seems to inhabit the opening tones of 'Bring Me the Disco King', the 'It's No Game (Part 2)' flatness of 'Fall Dog Bombs the Moon', the tightening excitement of 'The Supermen' creeping in as verse builds to chorus in 'The Next Day'. Complementing these performances are characteristically detailed Bowie/Visconti vocal production signatures: call and response, rich block-style harmonies, counterpoint lines, double-tracking at both unison and the octave, reverse and varispeed pitch modulations.

Particular to Bowie's late voice is a naked, vulnerable-sounding characterization, heard on songs that touch on themes of old regret and melancholy. From the cusp of the late period with *Hours...*-era cuts 'Survive' and 'Thursday's Child', *Heathen*'s 'Afraid' and 'Everyone Says Hi' through to *Reality*'s 'Days' and *The Next Day*'s 'Where Are We Now?', it's an almost waterlogged sound, subtly warped by time and memory with a strangely loose vibrato, like the wow and flutter of ancient tape. It's a remarkable vocalization, heavy with knowing but also spread thinly, both large and feeble at once. Bob Dylan once described Frank Sinatra's voice on the song 'Ebb Tide' as if he could 'hear everything in his voice – death, God and the universe, everything' (Dylan 2004, 81). Bowie's late voice also possesses a kind of accumulated grandeur in its signification. A singular voice inhabited by a cast of characters, loaded with history.

Lyrical themes

In many ways the lyrical themes of the late period are continuations of Bowie's career-long explorations of alienation, otherness and the existential anxieties of the human condition, only now with added recurrent meditations on family relationships, ageing and the terrors of knowing.

Around the time of *Heathen*, Bowie spoke in interviews about how his writing was about coming to terms with transience, attempting to untangle the conundrum of loving life despite knowing it will soon end: 'It's a head-spinning dichotomy – of the lust for life against the finality of everything. It's those two things raging against each other, you know?' (Sischy 2002). In the same interview, he revealed that *Heathen* contained a quartet of songs modelled in part on composer Richard Strauss's *Four Last Songs* (the incomplete cycle of five, written at the end of the composer's life and published posthumously in 1950), end-of-life meditations called 'Spring', 'September', 'Going to Sleep' and 'Sunset'. Bowie's corresponding compositions are understood to be album opener 'Sunday', '5:15 The Angels Have Gone', 'I Would Be Your Slave' and finale 'Heathen (The Rays)'. *Heathen* can be read in the context of Bowie musing on his own mortality; it could also be understood in the context of a midlife reckoning – losing your parents, living long enough to see friends die, worrying for the future of your children. Bowie was working on *Toy* in 2000 while Lexi was yet a newborn; she was only eight months old when Bowie's mother Peggy died at a nursing home in England (at age eighty-eight, though the death itself was sudden and unexpected). Shortly after, his old friend Freddie Burretti (a fashion designer responsible for some of Bowie's iconic glam-era looks) died of cancer. In that difficult space between familial joy and grief, the *Toy* project, a revival of aspirant songs from his teens and early twenties, transformed into *Heathen*. Visconti described the album concept to Dave Simpson for *The Guardian*: 'The concept … is a godless century. He was addressing the bleakness of our soul … and maybe his own soul.' Another dimension of loss would manifest in the wake of the 9/11 terrorist attacks in Manhattan, which unfolded while Bowie and Visconti were working on *Heathen* at Allaire, 100 miles away from home in upstate New York. Visconti described the impact that the events had on their work:

> For that whole day we lost contact with our loved ones. Iman [Bowie's wife] was very close to it … My son lived very close. His business partner lived across the street and managed to get out five minutes before the building collapsed. All of us have stories like that. Did it influence the album? Undoubtedly, but a lot of those lyrics are very prophetic. I swear to you only a few lines were amended after September 11.
> – Visconti (Simpson 2002)

The impact of 9/11's trauma would be felt in a deeper way on *Reality*. After its release, Bowie spoke in interviews about his disenchantment with the twenty-first century and his concerns about the kind of world his young daughter would inherit.[2] The misfits and strangers of *Reality*'s song worlds are now older and sadder, cast as depressed parents; a father holding in his despair,

---

[2] '… the advent of a new child in my family, my daughter, really sort of focused my fears and apprehensions. I mean, what a disappointing twenty-first century this has been so far. I had, personally, really quite high expectations about "the future". I had no idea it would sort of capitulate into this awful mess.' – Bowie (Wilson 2002, 11:50)

crying in his car ('Fly'); a mother fantasizing about crashing her car into the Hudson River and taking her family down with her ('She'll Drive the Big Car'). The petulant boomer in midlife crisis, promising himself that he'll never get old, yet wholly preoccupied with being comfortable and looked after by others in his old age, or, worse still, 'The Loneliest Guy', pathetically telling himself he's actually the luckiest guy because he has a hard drive full of pictures from the past. All the lonely people, all the errors left unlearned.

There is a lingering temptation to read the songs of the late period as semi-autobiographical, if only for the coincidences: David Jones was also now in his midlife, processing death and questioning the future despite/because of his newfound domesticity. References to New York's roads, rivers and skyline remind us that he lives there too; so is he singing about his real life? The apparent realness of his persona at the time, the absence of obvious theatrical devices and disorienting cut-ups, and the use of frank and introspective language all implied something of a vulnerable reveal.

As Fremaux and Usher note, Bowie's early career personae, Ziggy Stardust and the Thin White Duke, were stand-alone fictional characters, whereas others deployed later in his career, for example the ones that appear on *1. Outside* (1995) and *Earthling* (1997) are semi-fictional constructions, 'magnified parts of his inner self and inspirations. Bowie's image ... becomes a pure simulacrum; they rely on blurring the lines between Bowie and [*1. Outside*'s detective Nathan] Adler and Bowie and the "Earthling" to intentionally distort' (Fremaux and Usher 2015, 69). The songwriting in the late period turns this distortion up a notch; in the context of the wider late-style performance of 'Bowie' as an ordinary ageing human being, the close-proximity entanglement of reality and fiction results in song constructions that draw attention to the man behind the mask and raise the possibility that Bowie may be revealing something private and troubling about himself. On *The Next Day*, songs like 'Where Are We Now?' sit within this blurred space, where the singer is presumed to be the Bowie of 2013, questioning and contextualizing his current existence in terms of a past that exists both in Jones's reality and in Bowie's myth. On the album's first track, 'The Next Day', Bowie sings 'Here I am/not quite dying', couching it within a decidedly non-autobiographical narrative context (a song about religious hypocrisy and mob violence, presumably based on an obscure story plucked from history (O'Leary 2019, 581)). The line draws attention to itself as a connection to the real – his voice angered and energized, putting to bed the public speculation about his retirement and rumoured ill health. The closing refrain of *The Next Day*'s 'Heat' – 'I am a seer/I am a liar' – resonates with similar possibilities of knowing self-reference and semi-fictional autobiography. *Lazarus* also plays out in a realm of authenticated illusion, with 'David Bowie', both the private, mortal man and immortalized star image, being self-consciously projected into the fictional world of the stranded alien on Earth.

Waldrep identifies one of the dominant riffs in Bowie's oeuvre as being a self-consciousness in performance, the sense that 'Bowie has always been performing himself – as Davy Jones performing David Bowie performing one of his many personae ... the self-consciousness of his performances, which call attention to themselves as performances, threads through his work' (Waldrep 2015, 13–14). He goes on to place Bowie's artistry within the traditions of avant-garde theatre and performance art, those artists who were interested in 'removing barriers between media, and creating an art that was a new form of total theatre' (ibid., 15). The late period sets up the conditions for Bowie to push the limits of such a 'total' theatrical form, exploring his maturation and possible redemption as a star image and meta-persona. In the past, his experiments with identity had taken place within the space of a single artwork; Bowie's creative autonomy in the late period grants him the freedom to complicate, develop and test the limits of identity as a construction through time, encapsulating and completing the 'Bowie' project from across the catalogue. Long-running themes play out not only on the stages of his songs in a narrative sense but also inside the deeper, psychological realms of the meta-persona – shadows, animas, sublimated anxieties and desires. In the last works, Bowie subjects his whole career performance to the cut-up, assembling references and signs in such proximities as to draw attention to complications and confrontations with the self.

2

Remystification

The return to solo songwriting craft and a more personable demeanour in the early years of the new millennium could have been seen by some as a final unmasking of Bowie. Without an obvious theatrical device at play, the songs from *Heathen* and *Reality* felt relevant to what people could presume were his real-life experiences. *A Reality Tour* featured a chatty and relatable David, a man at ease, cracking dad jokes, looking and sounding normal and human enough. This sense of accessibility and personableness also came about from his active involvement with the official online fan club. It might seem quaint now, but back in the late 1990s BowieNet was a groundbreaking idea: a social network predating Myspace, Facebook and Twitter that allowed fans to interact and engage with the artist and the creative process. Its promise of engagement and access foreshadowed the direction fandoms would evolve towards in the burgeoning internet era. For BowieNetters during this period (he was most actively engaged from 1998 to 2004), it was not uncommon to have the odd encounter with the man himself online in real time. It seemed as if he was very much like we were: wasting time on the internet, posting about how much he loved Arcade Fire's new album, recommending books to fans who asked what he was reading.

As already touched upon, the late period is when we can observe more frequent gestures looping back in time to former selves and past sounds. The *Toy* project (intended for release in 2001 and leaked online in 2011), conceived as a revival of some of his earliest songwriting, reached all the way back to the late 1960s and brought about a reconnection with Visconti, who he first met and befriended in that era. Also in 2000, Bowie took the Sunday headline spot at

Glastonbury, performing a set that has now been critically lauded as one of the best performances in the history of the festival.[1] This would be another full-circle moment, returning to Worthy Farm in Somerset for the first time in twenty-nine years, having last performed there in 1971 as a relatively unknown folk singer, when he took to a small stage at 6.00 am. The choice to include Bowie's Stylophone, an instrument that he had not played on record since 'After All' from 1970's *The Man Who Sold the World* and, before that, 'Space Oddity' in 1969, on new Bowie/Visconti collaborations 'Safe' (1998), 'Your Turn to Drive' (2001) and 'Uncle Floyd'/'Slip Away' (2001/2002), felt like nods to their shared legacy, drawing attention to and historicizing their professional relationship.

Space Oddity is an especially meaningful reference, being the proverbial lift-off moment of Bowie's career. Major Tom, who we saw for the first time in 1969 onscreen in the promotional showcase *Love You Till Tuesday* wearing a cheap plastic visor, would once again return during the late period, in corporeal form as the astronaut in the music videos for 'Slow Burn' (*Heathen*) and 'Blackstar', where he ended up as a bejewelled skull relic. The unreleased video for 'Slow Burn', directed by Gary Koepke, which surfaced online in 2011 around the same time as *Toy*, shows Bowie dressed in white, confined to a recording studio control room, like Major Tom's symbolic studio spaceship that featured in Mick Rock's 1972 video for 'Space Oddity'. In the video, Bowie peers through the window into blackness and paces like a caged animal. He also mimes the 'flying eagle', a gesture that he often performed on stage as Ziggy and reprised multiple times in live shows throughout his career. The move originated from an early solo mime piece called *Jetsun and the Eagle* (1968).

Another noteworthy backwards glance finds first-time performances of *Low*, in order and in its entirety, incorporated into the short 2002 *Heathen Tour*. Even after promising to never perform his greatest hits again after the *Sound+Vision Tour* in 1990, 2003/2004's *A Reality Tour* would feature a rotating set list of sixty potential songs drawn from between 1970 and 2003. Every concert concluded with an encore of 'Ziggy Stardust'. These

---

[1] Pronounced 'the best headline slot at any festival ever' by Andrew Trendell for *NME* (2018).

self-conscious references and reprisals are conspicuous in this period, especially in the context of Bowie's career up to that point, which had always embodied a ruthless and restless search for the new. In embracing aspects of his past in this way, some might have seen an older artist finally acquiescing to his status as a heritage act, tending to the desires of his older fans. Even after his 2004 heart attack, when his active music career was put on hold, the thirtieth anniversary reissues, special and deluxe editions of his 1970s era records rolled on through the decade. Across Bowie's quiet years frequent 'new' releases continued to emerge – remasters and remixes in 5.1 surround sound, bonus and live tracks. 'Bowie' had become an automated creator of content; David Jones could effectively retire at this point and let the legacy continue working for him.

After the summer of 2004, our friend David receded from view. Far less engaged with BowieNet while in recovery, his last personal interaction with the online fan community as 'sailor' (his username) happened in 2007. He chose to adopt a low profile during a time when the appetite for celebrity access was in its ascendancy. In the new twenty-first century school of celebrity, stars are seen trading their privacy (and often their dignity) for the oxygen of public attention on programmes like *Big Brother*, writhing amongst bugs and worms on *I'm a Celebrity Get Me Out of Here*, inventing petty dramas to sell to tabloids and courting their followers on social media by trading personal access to their daily lives. Maybe he sensed it coming. Maybe playing the relatable, accessible pop star and living up to our expectations was exhausting.

Bowie's unwillingness to participate in twenty-first-century celebrity culture was the silent non-compliance that would help remystify the Bowie brand. The release of *The Next Day* coincided nearly perfectly with the launch of the V&A's *David Bowie Is* exhibition in 2013 (the album came out twenty days before the exhibit opened), both projects seeming to be of a shared spirit, contextualizing the Bowie of 2013 against the objects and ephemera of his history. Both invited the audience to construct their own image of who and what Bowie is, and the exhibition was able to tour the world in his stead. Running for five years, *David Bowie Is* travelled from London to Toronto, São Paulo, Berlin, Chicago, Paris, Melbourne, Groningen, Bologna, Tokyo, Barcelona and New York, with more than 2 million tickets sold. It contained audio and video projections, lyrics, stories, props, interviews, mannequins in full costume, even a tiny silver cocaine spoon. 'Bowie' was present, in deconstructed form; all you had to do was put the ingredients together like a Michelin-starred meal kit.[2]

Lazarus was another live performance of Bowie that David Jones didn't need to personally appear in. On 17 December 2015, Michael C. Hall performed 'as' Bowie on *The Late Show with Stephen Colbert* to promote the new single, 'Lazarus' (released the same day), and the musical, which had at that point been open for more than a week (though all performances were already sold out). Hall performed a skit that acknowledged and made light of Bowie's obvious absence: 'Hello, it's me, David Bowie. Ziggy Stardust, the Thin White Duke, and now, in my most outlandish persona yet, acclaimed actor Michael C. Hall.'

Throughout the late period and into the last works, David Jones recedes and Bowie's mythic figure looms larger. Bowie becomes a text, a role, a fashion, a signifying language. A blank square. *David Bowie Is.*

Late stars, living archives

Once predicated against the idea of longevity, rock 'n' roll has at least one final frontier for those post-war music stars that survive into old age. The business of popular music matured from youth culture to nostalgia trade as the industry transformed under market pressures, changes in media consumption and monetization structures over time. The industry also needed to adapt after the disruption caused by streaming and reorient its priorities to consider the ageing music fan. Cycles of nostalgia show up in waves, in generational obsessions with the ephemera of people's formative childhoods – such as 1950s culture represented in the 1970s like George Lucas's *American Graffiti* (1973), the TV show *Happy Days* (1974–84) and the Jacobs and Casey musical *Grease* (1971) all the way through to the 2000s house music sound of Lady Gaga's *Chromatica* (2020).

---

[2] Bowie: 'I'm an instant star. Just add water and stir' (1975, as quoted by Halliwell and Walker, 2003).

Loving what has gone before us is embedded in the creative process, too. The evolution and development of a musical style is a mechanism of assimilation: copying, paraphrasing and imitating your heroes, like the great composers studied the older masters before them. Older music stars of influence would live to see their 'children' passing the torches down through the decades. The DNA of even the strangest and most bizarre music today leads back to common ancestors that emerged in the mid-twentieth century. The currency of artistic legacies can appreciate in value over time, especially as nostalgia markets continue to dominate. Bowie's iconic status as one of rock 'n' roll's elder statesmen was finally established during the late period, perhaps helped along by the self-conscious referencing of his early history, promoted by waves of nostalgia and further exacerbated by his conspicuous absence from public life. Anyone whose work was influential enough, and who was lucky to live long enough to see themselves canonized as living nostalgia, had to contend with the monster of their own making: living alongside a legendary legacy. A relatively new phenomenon, music fans got to witness their boomer music heroes grow old and become mythic.

The latter music career of Scott Walker is often characterized as a stubborn and enduring enigma, despite the fact that the artist was forthcoming in interviews about his process, and not so secretive and mysterious to deny a film crew access to his recording sessions for Stephen Kijak's film *30 Century Man* (2006), for which Bowie was an executive producer and interviewee (with a rare, for the time, onscreen appearance). Best known for his chart-topping balladry with The Walker Brothers in the 1960s, Walker's late style was characterized by a complete rejection of formal pop song structure and a radical departure from conventional lyrical themes. Walker was an inspirational figure to Bowie, particularly his shimmering dark baritone and the austere production aesthetics of his late-period outputs, qualities Bowie attempted to emulate on occasion (see 'The Motel', 1995, and 'Heat', 2013). Walker's creativity was singularly expressive, not only through performance but by lyrically deploying dream imagery and refracting his points of view through a collage of rich visual tableaus. His avant-garde approach to sound and text in his sprawling nightmare trilogy (*Tilt* 1995, *The Drift* 2006, *Bish Bosch* 2012), with its 'interest in totalitarianism and its discontents; in the banality of evil and an insistence on portraying the perpetrators of cruelty as human beings' (Young 2012), could be another Walkerism that Bowie would fold into his own songwriting practices towards the end. Walker lived long enough to see his legacies publicly celebrated, not only with Kijak's film but also with tribute performances from the likes of Jarvis Cocker and Damon Albarn in *Drifting and Tilting* at the Barbican Centre, London in 2008 and a special BBC Prom in 2017. He attended both events. The last record he released, *Soused* (2014), a collaboration with a new group of musicians, the avant-doom metal group Sunn O))), saw drones and elongated melodies punctuated by severe walls of noise, cracking whips and the smashing of concrete blocks. Bowie's final works would also align, in a way, with Walker's late work, with the complicated and troubling representations of violence in *The Next Day*, the surreal dream journey of *Lazarus* and a final collaboration with a new group of younger musicians associated with a different style in ★.

Another stubborn and enduring enigma, fellow twentieth-century icon and one of the last legendary boomers left standing, Bob Dylan is also curating his late career in a similar spirit to Bowie. There are several interesting parallels. His late period kicked off with the thoughtful meditations of *Time Out of Mind* (1997), finished just prior to a heart-and-lung-related health scare. He continued to detach from contemporary music cultures and attendant expectations, exploring his artistry across a range of diverse activities and decoupling his star image from the linear discographic narrative. Dylan could be found dressing like Hank Williams and playing old-time music on his own radio show (*Theme Time Radio Hour*, 2006 to 2015, with a brief return in 2020 to promote his own whisky), making a Yuletide album (*Christmas in the Heart* 2009) or reinventing himself as a Sinatra-style crooner (*Shadows in the Night* 2015, *Fallen Angels* 2016, *Triplicate* 2017). Dylan and Bowie share extracurricular interests in visual art, both men showing preference for expressionism with paint. They both dabbled with writing: Dylan's autobiography *Chronicles: Volume One* came out in 2004; Bowie was known to be working on his own book projects around this time, though none would be completed – an autobiography and a novel that he was reportedly busy writing in 2003. Dylan would be the first of the two to have a musical use his songs, the circus-themed flop *The Times They Are a-Changin* with choreographer/director Twyla

Tharp in 2006, then Bowie's *Lazarus* with Irish playwright Enda Walsh in 2015, followed by Dylan again with 2017's acclaimed *Girl from the North Country* with another Irish playwright, Conor McPherson. Both artists would latterly, finally, top the American Billboard charts for the first time in their careers, Bowie with 2016's ★ and Dylan with 'Murder Most Foul' from *Rough and Rowdy Ways* (2020).

The pair were not known to be friends – after Bowie started out by appropriating Dylan-esque details into his early folk style on *Space Oddity* and *Hunky Dory*, which also contained a tribute, 'Song for Bob Dylan', they met a few times during the 1970s and 1980s and it was alleged that Dylan was rude, telling Bowie that he hated the song 'Young Americans'. In what could be seen as a grudging acknowledgement of respect, he had a habit of nicking Bowie's musicians over the years – Mick Ronson, Charlie Sexton, Matt Chamberlain, G. E. Smith and Stevie Ray Vaughan. According to Clinton Heylin's book *Behind the Shades*, Dylan once approached Bowie about co-producing an album, *Infidels* (1983), as he 'felt that technology had passed him by [and he] needed an artist at home in the modern recording studio' (Heylin [1991] 2011, 550). Bowie's response to this suggestion is unknown (he'd finished *Let's Dance* three months before the *Infidels* sessions started) and in the end Mark Knopfler was installed as co-producer. Both men would be accused of magpie behaviour, if not outright plagiarism, and both would be associated with extensive archives – while not conceived for a single exhibition like the V&A's *David Bowie Is*, a Bob Dylan archive would materialize in Tulsa, Oklahoma, in 2016, with the express aims of serving music researchers and future public exhibitions.

Scott Walker's surreal lyrical refractions flashing back and forth through time and space feel like kin to Dylan's late lyrical style, which also seems to easily swell into sprawling rhizomatic collage. The music writer Carl Wilson described this quality in his review of *Rough and Rowdy Ways* as 'specific to his work in the twenty-first century as a senior citizen. This is Dylan less as irreverent magpie than as artfully dodging archivist. An archivist of himself ... an archivist of the world that made him and the world he's helped to make, under the sign of his own mortality ... ' (Wilson 2020). Like Bowie and Walker, Dylan's songwriting at the tail end of his long career similarly enfolds multitudinous references, deploying disparate characters from divergent timelines flashing through moments of anger, violence, grotesquery and humour. Wilson goes on to suggest that elsewhere on the record Dylan might have been inspired by the late style of another contemporary ' ... a song like "Mother of Muses", ... remind(s) me distinctly of Leonard Cohen in "Sisters of Mercy" – one of several times I wondered if Dylan was thinking of Cohen, perhaps spurred on by the extraordinary albums the Canadian poet (a couple of years his senior) recorded in his late infirmity.' Wilson is referring to *You Want It Darker*, Cohen's 2016 album, released nineteen days before his death, and the posthumously released *Thanks for The Dance* (2019). Both records are meditations on mortality, transition, God and the afterlife. The single 'You Want It Darker' was released on Cohen's eighty-second birthday, echoing Bowie's preference to announce and release new music on his birthdays towards the end of his life. *You Want It Darker* and ★ were shared in 2016's year of collective cultural mourning; both works were, seemingly, impeccably stage-managed stunting from two late stars who were very unwell indeed.

Though different in form and with a wholly unique candour, Cohen's late style still incorporated the curation of his own legacy into the work. In *The Late Voice* (2015, 124–5), Richard Elliott identifies an implicit shared knowledge between artist and audience as a feature of Cohen's lateness: 'In the same way that [late] Sinatra performances were clearly staged with an understanding that listeners knew about the singer and could therefore connect song to persona, so Leonard Cohen has often made direct appeal in his songs to his listeners' knowledge about him ... ', pointing to 'Tower of Song' and how the lyric that contains a knowing self-deprecating reference to Cohen's limited vocal range would transform into a charming in-joke at live performances later in his career, becoming a kind of shared empathetic pleasure.[3] This mutual knowing and understanding creates an intensifying intimacy in the reading of his final works, an aspect that Cohen actively leans into with his creative decisions.

---

[3] 'As he pronounces the word "golden" he closes his eyes: he knows that the audience will explode, he knows that his audience feel with him. And so it happens. A highly visible shudder runs down his back; watching the video you can almost feel it, through a magical empathy' (Maruffa 2015).

An important influence on the work of Cohen, Walker and Bowie was Belgian singer-songwriter, actor and director Jacques Brel. A young Bowie was introduced to Brel's world via the translated cover versions that Scott Walker had recorded for his 1967 solo debut *Scott*. In 1968, Bowie saw a London performance of the musical *Jacques Brel Is Alive and Well and Living in Paris* and, for the next four years, would regularly perform his own version of 'Amsterdam' (released by Brel in 1964) in his sets. In 1973 on the *Ziggy Stardust Tour*, he began performing a version of Brel's 'My Death' ('La Mort' 1959) – a song that he later reprised on the *Outside* and *Earthling* tours in the mid-1990s. Bowie's 1999 live album was called *LiveandWell.com*, the title a likely reference to Brel's 1968 revue. Bowie also namechecked Brel in the lyrics to 'Reality' (2003).[4]

Beyond admiration for the repertoire, Bowie would have been inspired by Brel's theatrical style of performance, which often involved elaborate props, careful choreography and moments of intense emotive acting. Brel's public persona was entangled with the subjects of his songs, which were often by turns morbid and idealistic, and, towards the end of his life, existential. Coincidentally both artists decided to spend a decade away from the limelight; Brel put his own music career on hiatus at the height of his fame in 1967. What's more, both artists organized their 'comebacks' in secret; Bowie's *The Next Day* was sewn up tight with non-disclosure agreements, while Brel's *Les Marquises* (1977) was protected by an elaborate locked box with a timed electronic mechanism that only allowed reviewers to open and listen to it after its intended release date. *Les Marquises* was Brel's swan song; already very ill with terminal lung cancer, the songs are meditations on mortality and memory. He died a year after it was released, aged forty-nine.

The songwriting of *Les Marquises* at times deliberately evokes Brel's performance persona of the 1960s era, blurring the boundaries between art/artifice and the authentic. The song 'Vieillir' (trans. 'to age') asserts the narrator's preference for death over the prospect of old age and infirmity. At one point in the song Brel pictures with disdain an image of his future elderly self 'spitting out his last tooth' singing 'Amsterdam' ('Cracher sa dernière dent

---

4 'Now my death is more than just a sad song' ('Reality' 2003).

en chantant "Amsterdam"!'). It is a moment of collision where the narrator is revealed to be Brel himself. Is it authentically revealing and autobiographical, or is the song merely furnishing lines for the completion of the 'Brel' persona's narrative? It could be read as both, and neither, of these things. The only certainty is that Brel is capitalizing on the indefinite aspects of his constructed identity to complicate and enrich the reading of his final work, as Chris Tinker puts it: 'Without doubt, Brel exploits his public persona in his [last] songs', making space and possibility for a 'public expression of private grief' (Tinker 2005, 27–8).

Non/sense-making and the edge work

The cut-up, one of Bowie's favourite writing techniques, provides an efficient way to circumvent the obvious and reveal the unseen connections and meaning-making potentials that already exist within a text. It has links going back to the 1920s, to the Dadaists, who enjoyed making a mockery of earnest traditions, and the Surrealists, who were trying to tap into the unconscious in order to free the imagination. The modern literary version, where a razor blade is taken to an existing text and the pieces are reshuffled into a new arrangement, was attributed to artist Brion Gysin in 1959 by his friend William S. Burroughs, who used the technique in works such as *Naked Lunch* (1959), *The Nova Trilogy* (1961–4) and *The Third Mind*, a collaborative text with Gysin, published in 1977. Bowie embraced the method too, adapting the technique into his songwriting in the early 1970s, hastening the evolution of his star image from intimate pop singer to something more alien and remote. In the 1990s Bowie co-created the Verbasizer with digital pioneer Ty Roberts (co-founder of Gracenote) (Smith 2013). A bespoke software application that improved the speed and scope of Bowie's cut-up methodology, the program had the capacity to randomize longer texts and generate a larger range of permutations. By processing something ordinary and banal through the cut-up, Bowie 'manufactured … a porousness, allowing for multivalent readings and associations to arise', surrendering a portion of creative decision-making to chance and chaos; rather than creativity flowing out from within, Bowie 'takes his cues from outside himself'

(Naiman 2015, 182). The cut-up puts distance between the heart and its utterances, transforming something concrete into something malleable, and it put a veil of abstraction between David Jones and his audience. Handily, it also provided a quick Warholian cheat to 'originality', spinning meaning from impulse and accident. And there was more: the cut-up created nonsense as well as new kinds of sense, a simultaneous act of assembly, discovery and destruction. An oracle that offered a new way of seeing; now everything could be juxtaposed, subverted, rearranged. Even the self could be subjected to the cut-up: the man, the star persona and the living archive in rearranged pieces, the virtuoso fact and fiction entanglements of *The Next Day* and *Lazarus*.

Waking up every day to a world of pieces and bits we spend the remaining hours putting it into some kind of form we can deal with. No order, no function. Basquiat takes a cursive swipe and re-establishes the disorder that is reality. The pure joyful chaotic miasma of it all. Goo-goo-ga-joo. Refracting fact fractions facting refact.

– Bowie (1996)

In his capacity as editorial board member and occasional writer for *Modern Painters* magazine, Bowie eulogized the expressionist painter Jean-Michel Basquiat and spoke about art's propensity for creating beautiful chaos. A coping strategy for the absurdity and cruelty of life can be the deliberate, joyful re-establishment of disorder. Bowie collected Basquiat pieces and clearly felt an affinity with the artist and his way of seeing things: joyfully turbulent in exploring the expressive potentials of distressing ideas, Basquiat applied a corrective rewrite to harsh realities like racism and poverty by refracting truths and appropriating texts – poems, histories and news stories – and combining them with images, abstract figures, colourful painted shapes. Sometimes it's better, in the face of impossible cruelty, to deny the existence of any sense at all. The non/sense, the chaotic miasma of it all, is where the really interesting things are happening.

Living longer allows for more detail to be painted into the scene of a life. With ageing comes complexity, the accumulation of memories, with doubts and experiences creating a nexus of psychic debris, tissues of vague truths growing into webs. Existence gets complicated and art can be complex. And popular music can be art. Maybe the remystification of our late pop stars is simply an attempt to re-introduce a healthy amount of disorder and new possibility into an otherwise settled scene. To twist potentials in new directions, bend the light so that we might see things differently. Scott Walker's alternative reality in 'Jesse' (*The Drift* 2006), where the destruction of the Twin Towers is a dream that Elvis (still alive) is having about his dead twin and his own survivor's guilt makes almost as much sense as the horrific reality played out. What Bowie alliteratively described as the refraction of fractions of facts, the cut-up language that correctively reorders of 'the disorder that is reality', Walker would refer to as 'edge work': ' … a way to talk about the unsayable things of existence, the unnameable. You're working around it, it's a lot of edge work. You're using language to discuss things that are beyond language' (Irvin 1995).

Bowie enjoyed and favoured complexity, not only in the art he loved but also in the art that he made, commenting at the press conference for the European leg of his 1995 *Outside Tour*: 'I think I like complications. I like things that tend to be endless puzzles … I like thickly textured things.' Self-expression subsumes the cut-up, and it is present in the deliberate invocation of the past, made-up truths, fictions and dreams, looping back to the start of things to bring the whole confusing journey into view. Searching for Walker's elusive unnameable. In the full remystification of his final three years, we see Bowie creating pop music artefacts that might seem on the surface like frustratingly hard work – knotty, tangled up, possessing of frightening depths and full of complications. But this is the work that I believe achieves something the closest to Bowie's artistic ideals.

3

The Next Day

The Next Day (released on 8 March 2013) was recorded in secret. It has the distinction of being the longest Bowie production-in-progress ever, stretching over two and a half years – the first batch of demos were being worked on as early as November 2010 and overdubs for B-sides and extras ran up to August 2013. The raw material that would become the sprawling *The Next Day* project might have been cooking for many years; Gerry Leonard told interviewers he was sent at least one song idea dating back to the 1970s (Sweeney 2013) and Zachary Alford said *The Next Day Extra* cut 'Born in a UFO' was a discarded track from 1979's *Lodger* sessions (Greene 2013a). We know from previous form with 'Tired of My Life'/'It's No Game' and 'Bring Me the Disco King' that the notion of Bowie hoarding song ideas across decades is not unusual. The album was announced with no warning, only the surprise drop of lead single 'Where Are We Now?' and its video on 8 January 2013 (his sixty-sixth birthday). It was Bowie's first new album in nearly a decade.

Visconti confirmed to the press that a total of twenty-nine songs were developed for the project. Of these, twenty-two would be released in some form or another across *The Next Day*'s official and deluxe editions and in a final 2CD/DVD box of B-sides called *The Next Day Extra*, released on 2 November 2013. The remaining seven songs were left unfinished.[1] After 'Where Are We Now?' came four follow-up singles 'The Stars (Are Out Tonight)', 'The Next

---

[1] Visconti told Nicholas Pegg that they were only instrumental sketches without proper titles, lyrics or fully developed melodies, just 'la la la' placeholders (Pegg 2016, 467).

Day', 'Valentine's Day' and 'Love Is Lost (Hello Steve Reich Mix by James Murphy for the DFA)'/'I'd Rather Be High (Venetian Mix)', each accompanied by a music video in which Bowie makes an appearance.

Rhapsodic and breathless media coverage did the work of promoting the project, pushing it to the top of the charts. 'Where Are We Now?' hit number one in eight countries on the day it appeared, his biggest singles chart success since 1986's 'Absolute Beginners'. *The Next Day* became a number one record in nineteen countries and was nominated for Mercury, Brit and Grammy awards. It was included in the 2014 revision of Robert Dimery's *1001 Albums You Must Hear Before You Die*.

The album was met with near-universal acclaim from critics,[2] though many writers who rated it highly also noted that the record was difficult to penetrate: 'thought-provoking, strange' (Alexis Petridis, *The Guardian*), 'beautiful and baffling' (Neil McCormick, *The Daily Telegraph*), 'dense, angry, complex' (Kitty Empire, *The Observer*), 'Bowiephiles will have fun picking over the themes and sub-themes here for ages' (Chris Roberts, The Quietus). The arrival of *The Next Day* became a story less about the music itself and more a celebratory expression of relief felt by music fans that Bowie was back after being away for so long.

The Bowie-mania of 2013 was further bolstered by the opening of the *David Bowie Is* exhibition at the Victoria and Albert Museum in London in March of that year. The retrospective displayed a collection of roughly 500 objects relating to Bowie's life and career. It would run for five years and travel to twelve museum locations around the world, attracting more than 2 million visitors.[3] Bowie had returned to the cultural consciousness; in addition to the magazine covers in the music press, iconic imagery from his career was used to promote the exhibition with billboards and tube-station advertisements appearing all over London. Francis Whately's *David*

---

[2] Metacritic is a website that aggregates all available reviews for cultural products like albums, films and games to reach a single rating based on average consensus. *The Next Day*'s score is 81 ('universal acclaim').

[3] The exhibition lives on in the form of an augmented reality *David Bowie Is* app for iOS and Android platforms, introduced and narrated by Bowie's longtime friend Gary Oldman.

Bowie: Five Years documentary was broadcast on the BBC in May, the first in a trilogy.[4] Bowie was back, but he remained elusive – there were no press statements, no interviews, no BowieNet blog. The closest thing to an explanation for *The Next Day*, actually the only direct transmission from the man himself concerning the matter, came in the form of a list of forty-two words – a 'sort of workflow diagram' sent to novelist Rick Moody (*The Ice Storm*), who had written to the artist asking for assistance in getting a grip on the album's 'lexicon'. The list was published on The Rumpus on 25 April 2013 and it took a while for people to figure out that every group of three words in the sequence correlated thematically to each of the fourteen tracks of *The Next Day*. Another mysterious list, 'Bowie's top 100 must-read books', appeared later in the year as a new addition to the V&A exhibition when it moved to Ontario in October 2013 (Bury 2013). A chronological index only, it seemed to be another clue from the artist about how his new work could be approached; there was the sense that Bowie was challenging his audience to connect the dots for themselves. Reflecting on his manner of engagement during the period, Nicholas Pegg observed 'his long years out of the spotlight had, in effect, forged Bowie a new media persona. The voluble, witty chat-show guest of ten years earlier had been eclipsed by the silent, enigmatic recluse … ' (2016, 468).

Everybody involved behind the scenes on *The Next Day* – co-producer Visconti, the musicians, studio personnel and graphic designer Jonathan Barnbrook – had signed non-disclosure agreements (NDAs) that forbade them from speaking about the project before its surprise announcement. During the years of silence that this secret demanded of them, some musicians wondered if the project would ever come out. On the night of the surprise 'Where Are We Now?' release, Visconti and Bowie excitedly waited online for it to drop:

> It was going to hit at a certain time [5am GMT, midnight New York time, 8 January 2013]. We were both online together, waiting for the countdown. We were so excited, making jokes

---

[4] It was followed by *David Bowie: The Last Five Years* (2017) and *David Bowie: Finding Fame* (2019).

and texting each other. Then when it hit, we said 'Okay here we go' and we both went silent. We watched Facebook light up, Twitter light up. Just like that, he was back. I couldn't believe it. My heart was pounding.

– Visconti (interview with the author, 2020)

Once the secret was out, Bowie's continued media silence created an information vacuum that only intensified everyone's appetite for more insider knowledge. Unique to this period in Bowie's career, it fell upon his collaborators to speak to the press on behalf of the work – how, when and where it was created, and what it might mean.

Bowie's silent approach played against the trend for heavy-handed promotion that had become the norm for popular music by 2013. A lot had changed since *Reality*. Everyday cultural discourse had largely migrated to online spaces. Reorganized digital media markets driven by clicks and 'likes' had given rise to marketing and promotion practices that had essentially become shouting competitions focused on whipping up enough hype to catch the attention of consumers already spoiled for choice. 'Where Are We Now?' and its music video simply appeared on YouTube and online music services without a word. It caused such a sensation that it was reported as breaking news on the BBC. Bowie had orchestrated the perfect surprise release, a highly effective music marketing strategy that was soon adopted by other major artists at the highest echelons of pop.[5]

Beyond the idea of Bowie's secrecy and silence being a successful marketing stunt for the album, it also contextualized the years of absence and presumed retirement that had gone before, connecting the period into something of a continuing, mystifying performance. He was back, but was he really? Or was he ever gone? People were desperate to know what he'd been doing all that time. Were the rumours of his ill health really true? What Bowie offered by way of explanation was an enigmatic, densely layered, at-times-bewildering presentation. Lists and literary references, musical

---

[5] Notable surprise releases that turned into huge commercial successes include Beyoncé's self-titled LP in 2013 and *Lemonade* in 2016, Jay-Z's *4:44* in 2017, Ariana Grande's 2019 hit single 'thank u, next' and Taylor Swift's twin releases *Folklore* and *Evermore* in 2020.

quotations embedded in the fabric, a star image subverted and obscured. Carefully assembled layers of signification.

The Next Day functions as a stand-alone project without qualification, yet much of the knowledge which allows it to make more sense is situated within Bowie's extended universe. At the surface level, it works as a suite of angry, atmospheric, slightly eccentric rock songs; it becomes a deeper, more rewarding experience when considered within the context of Bowie's identity and idiolect. A density of information presented without a clear guiding structure or obvious map, the listener is obliged to assemble something coherent and meaningful for themselves. These ideas are supported in the graphic themes carried through The Next Day cover, where an iconic Bowie image is defaced and obscured by a simple white square. Designer Jonathan Barnbrook (who previously worked on 2002's Heathen and 2003's Reality) worked closely in secret with Bowie to develop the visual theme.

The cover art of The Next Day appropriates the cover of 1977's "Heroes", an image by Masayoshi Sukita that pictures Bowie in a pose inspired by Erich Heckel's 1917 Roquairol paintings, arguably one of the most recognizable album images of Bowie's oeuvre. Here, the "Heroes" title is crudely scratched out and a white square is positioned in the centre covering Bowie's face. Inside the square, 'The Next Day' is written in plain sans-serif font. According to Barnbrook, the concept of subverting an iconic image was Bowie's idea:

> It started with a picture he sent me, of him in the 1970s [a concert photo from Radio City Music Hall, 1974, which ended up being used on the cover of 'Where Are We Now?']. He said, 'I feel very isolated in this picture. I want it to be on the cover somehow.' But I really couldn't do anything good with the image. It was his idea to turn it upside down … and it took him to do that for me to understand how we could play with his history.
> – Barnbrook (interview with the author, 2020)

The choice to play with "Heroes" was based on Barnbrook's assessment of The Next Day: 'When I first heard it, I thought, he sounds like he's happy being David Bowie, he's in his own idiom. It felt right to use the "Heroes" image' (ibid.). For the CD and vinyl packages, Barnbrook's approach was continued on the back sleeve

– the back of the original "*Heroes*" LP was pasted over with another white square containing the new tracklist. Printed on the inserts, the lyrics and credits for *The Next Day* are presented as a single block of unformatted text. A new portrait of Bowie is shown twice; one is covered by a white square, the other revealing Bowie's face to have a pursed-mouth grimace.[6]

The white square concept came from Barnbrook's special interest in constructivism, the use of symbols in communist propaganda in the early twentieth century and the idea of anti-advertising – covering over the very thing you're trying to sell. The concept also has direct connections to Kazimir Malevich's *White on White* (1918), a painting of a white square set at an angle inside another larger white square; a seemingly impersonal geometric abstraction, except for the way it draws the eye to the artist's hand, which can be sensed in the texture of the paint and the subtle differences between the shades of white. In a 2013 interview, Barnbrook explained, 'We understand that many would have preferred a nice new picture of Bowie but we believed that would be far less interesting and not acknowledge many of the things we have tried to discuss by doing this design' (Tuffrey 2013). The denial of access to the artist's face mirrored the silence that his public had been subjected to. There was a time when every Bowie album had a new visual style to match – this dimension is refused here. In its place is a riddle about the artist's identity, the white space functioning both as a cover of privacy to hide behind and a blank surface prepared for some new creative act. The idea that 'Bowie' was a construction by forces of imagination outside of himself – a 'shared constitution' between artist and fanbase (Palmer 2013) – was something that he himself intimated in a 1999 interview: 'I guess I am what the greatest number of people think I am. And I have no control over that at all' (quoted in Roberts, 1999).

The obscuring of Bowie's face, combined with the impersonal design and strong focus on Bowie's past, creates mystery and uncertainty around Bowie's present. If the album covers of his catalogue serve as reliable evidence of transformation across multiple representations of identity, *The Next Day* stands out for

---

[6] Barnbrook: 'He called it the "lemon lips" picture' (interview with the author, 2020).

its conceit – it's not a new Bowie, but a new way of seeing and understanding who Bowie is/could be. The artist has been fully eclipsed by his star image. The Bowie of 2013 is sidelined and the larger construction takes centre stage.

Several rejected drafts of *The Next Day*'s cover art were included as last-minute additions to the V&A exhibition: *Aladdin Sane* and *Pin Ups* (both 1973) were two other images subverted and defaced with crude digital 'paintbrush' markings in red, large black circles and five-pointed stars. Barnbrook explained that the presence of a black star in the roughs was purely coincidental: 'It looks like Blackstar was one of the prototypes, but it is just a coincidence. I use lots of basic forms and symbols; the star was one of them.' It was Barnbrook's choice to include *The Next Day* roughs in the exhibition, a decision that Bowie gently questioned:

David phoned me up and said, 'The covers in the exhibition. Are you sure?' I kind of panicked as I thought he was upset about it, but then he said, 'I'll let you put them in if you want, because I wouldn't tell you what to do, but just be aware that you change the final object when you present the roughs.' And I think with that cover maybe he was right.

– Barnbrook (interview with the author, 2020)

If seeing the drafts of the artwork detracts from the elegance and simplicity of the final version, then the arrival of *The Next Day Extra* on 4 November 2013 might also subtly destabilize *The Next Day*'s sense of confidence and refinement. This new 'B' material brought even more puzzlement and density to the already crowded and lengthy project; the hazy overarching structure implied in the list of forty-two words was disturbed and complicated by the presence of new compositions that were quite unlike the rest. Visual themes were extended in the package design for *The Next Day Extra*'s CD/DVD boxset. Again, Barnbrook adapted Sukita's *"Heroes"* imagery, only here it is glitched and ruined, as if it were a corrupted scan or photocopy error. The content is presented in white, square booklets and the sleeves are identified by generic labels: 'Tracks' (*The Next Day* CD), 'Extra' (B-sides CD), 'Light' (DVD of music videos), 'Frame' (music video stills, stylized with glitches) and 'Language' (lyrics and credits presented once again as a single block of unformatted text). There is also an empty booklet (only containing pages of blank white squares) labelled 'You'. The generalized labelling suggests the detachment of intent with the multimedia contents of the package identified merely by format category. Here is a portfolio of objects, a box of things: whatever it means to you, you can write it down in the blank white spaces provided.

> It was extra. Literally extending *The Next Day*. The extension of the image was a practical solution to the fact that we had only the one image to work with. And the original point of what I was saying was that the relationship you have with an image of a pop star is also a relationship with yourself. That's why the white square is on there and that's why you have the blank page, the blank booklet that is 'you'.
> – Barnbrook (interview with the author, 2020)

The extended design of *The Next Day Extra* doubles down on Bowie's strategy to force his audience to create coherence from his materials and construct the star image for him. The star construction that is also an image of your reflected self. As Barnbrook discovered, Bowie is giving us permission to play with his history.

Music

The musical arrangements of *The Next Day* were built up from Bowie's early demos in the usual way, with musicians developing ideas together on the spot in the studio, responding through jamming and improvisation. Gerry Leonard explained 'He likes to work fast so the pressure is on … You just trust your instincts and allow the inspiration to come forward' (Line 6 2013). The sound of *The Next Day* is guitar-based and rock-centric, a continuation of the late-period sound of *Reality*, an aesthetic quality attributable in part to the already existing chemistry and muscle memory instincts shared between these players, many of whom were long-time tour and session regulars in Bowie's employ. Visconti's co-production is spacious and dynamic, similarly building in the same direction that *Heathen* and *Reality* were travelling. Many of the players were previously members of the *Reality* touring band – Gerry Leonard,

Earl Slick, Gail Ann Dorsey and Sterling Campbell. Other musicians included drummer Zachary Alford, guitarist David Torn, bassist Tony Levin, pianist Henry Hey, saxophonist Steve Elson and singer Janice Pendarvis. Visconti contributed some bass and recorder parts, as well as string arrangements, which were performed by a quartet: Maxim Moston, Antoine Silverman, Hiroko Taguchi and Anja Wood. Bowie played keyboards and twelve-string guitar.

Leonard spoke in interviews about how the long gaps in production led him to suspect the project was being shelved: 'When the line went dead for a few months I figured "Oh well, he's not digging the stuff"' (Line 6 2013). The album's long gestation period suggests an element of uncertainty on Bowie's part, or else betrays the amount of time it took him to figure out a suitable way to frame the project, which in the end had adapted a diverse range of sources and styles – unused song materials from as far back as 1979 alongside brand new songs crisscrossing a wide range of styles, from doo-wop and piano ballads to sunshine pop, Scott Walker-style dark atmospherics and more varieties of rock than you can count on one hand. He took more than a year to complete his vocal parts and spent further months tinkering with the track selection and order. Visconti told *The Hollywood Reporter* that, while they were working on it, Bowie refused to call it an album until the point where it obviously became one; for much of the time it was referred to only as an 'experiment' (Halperin 2013). In the same interview, Visconti added the qualification that *The Next Day* wasn't really a rock album, rather it was a 'David Bowie album', supporting the idea that the artist's identity and idiolect is the cohering concept that glues the piece together. Bowie and Visconti embedded signature motifs and sounds throughout the production, and there are also references relating to specific musicians in the band with whom he has history (note Gail Ann Dorsey's 'Dead Man Walking'-style vocalise at the start of 'If You Can See Me' and the energetic breakbeat drumming from Zachary Alford, who played similar styles on *Earthling* (1997)). Such details can trigger sensory/memory recall and reveal connections between the present assemblage and elements from the past – other places, other song meanings, other iterations of Bowie's personae. A sensory, cognitive, historical refraction forcing disparate ideas into proximity; an invitational space for ghosts to haunt the scene.

Prior to the late period, Bowie's artistry had been characterized by his synthesis of outside influences; rarely did he reference or directly quote himself in his work. When he did, it was usually in a manner of shared knowing, 'winking at the audience' – for instance, in the 'ch-ch-ch' reference to 'Changes' in the lyrics of 'You've Been Around' (1993) and riffs taken from 'Space Oddity' and 'All the Madmen' in the title track from 1993's *The Buddha of Suburbia*. On *Heathen* and *Reality*, Bowie and Visconti mostly avoided overt references to their shared production legacy ('Slip Away' Stylophones aside). By contrast, *The Next Day* is packed with their vernacular: the Eventide Harmonizer-processed drum sounds famously innovated on *Low* (1977), varispeed vocal effects from *Scary Monsters* (1980), recreating whole outros from *Lodger* (1979), quoting snatches of Ziggy tropes in 'You Feel So Lonely You Could Die'. As Waldrep also notes about the album, 'Bowie references only himself, by now having become his own repertoire of musical history' (2015, 13).

A number of song compositions on *The Next Day* share distinguishing features that reveal Bowie's structural approach to songwriting. There are big juxtaposing moments between sections, often coupled with dramatic key changes ('If You Can See Me', 'You Feel So Lonely You Could Die', 'Like a Rocket Man') and jolting metric shifts ('Dirty Boys', '(You Will) Set the World on Fire'). Visconti said that Bowie had been composing more often on a keyboard and less with a guitar, and it shows in the harmony choices on tracks such as 'Where Are We Now?' and 'So She'. Another songwriting device that shines through is the choice to use upbeat arrangements to underscore dark lyrical themes, for example in 'Valentine's Day' and 'Dancing Out in Space'. People who expected Bowie's voice to be battered by illness and age (perhaps based on their impressions of lead single 'Where Are We Now?' and its particularly fragile delivery) would have been surprised by his vocal range and muscularity throughout *The Next Day*. From a ferocious opening command, 'Listen!' (an echo from 1977's 'Breaking Glass'), his voice moves with agility between songs from fury to fragility, with soaring, crooning, growling brio. The background vocal arrangements are extensive and ornate, for instance the 'wall-of-Bowie' effect that builds towards the end of 'Love Is Lost' and the contrapuntal detail woven through 'The Informer'.

Aside from the piano parts on 'Where Are We Now?', 'You Feel So Lonely... ' and 'God Bless the Girl' (which were contributed by newcomer Henry Hey), Bowie performs all other keyboard parts on his trusty Korg Trinity workstation. Something of a 'vintage' instrument from the late 1990s (it was discontinued in 1998), it contributes startled organ sounds to 'Love Is Lost', the pillowy string pads in the background of 'Where Are We Now?' and the strange slippery mono lead in 'Dancing Out in Space'.

Visconti's string arrangements are characteristically lavish in 'The Stars (Are Out Tonight)' and 'Heat', and his drum production across the board stands out for its dramatic power and heft. The unique drum sound was attributable in part to a sound engineering trick that Visconti had learned from his mentor Denny Cordell:

> Denny told me, 'Always record the room, the room is the sound.' So I would aim the microphones at the glass surfaces. That's what gives it more depth, the sound is travelling from the drum to the glass and bouncing back into the microphones, it gives it extra distance to travel. Another secret was mixing in some of the drum bleed coming from David's live mic.
> – Visconti (interview with the author, 2020)

The album is thick with guitars, lowdown and crunchy ('Boss of Me'), atmospheric and fluid ('Dancing Out in Space'), sleazy ('Dirty Boys'), cranking ('The Next Day') and monumental (the guitar solo section of 'How Does the Grass Grow?'). It is also given to extended cinematic details: the oceanic coda of 'If You Can See Me', the unexpected 'Five Years' drum pattern at the end of 'You Feel So Lonely... ', the space-radar slides at the start of 'The Informer'. These details, when they appear, are slightly separated from the main body of the songs, offering new information, transitional glimpses or points of departure.

Words

The lyrical mood of 'Where Are We Now?', nostalgic, melancholy and apparently personally revealing, was not an accurate indication of what to expect from the song themes on *The Next Day*. The stories implied within the album are often disquieting – killers and tyrants revelling in their wickedness ('Valentine's Day', 'If You Can

See Me'), victims of abuse denied salvation ('The Next Day', 'God Bless the Girl'), people suffering the traumas of war ('How Does the Grass Grow?', 'I'd Rather Be High'), alienation and loss ('Love Is Lost'). The narrators of 'You Feel So Lonely… ', 'Heat' and 'The Informer' feel somewhat united in their capacity for treachery. Then there are seemingly more obvious references to the Bowie legacy: not only in 'Where Are We Now?' but also in 'Atomica', 'Born in a UFO' and 'Like a Rocket Man' from *The Next Day Extra*, which sit uncomfortably in the vicinity of the main album's cruelty, the collective lyrical themes that Tanja Stark vividly describes as ' … a bleeding beehive of blood, a honeycombed-catacomb of cryptic mystery, rage and resignation' (Stark 2015, 61).

The Next Day is by no means the only album in the oeuvre to have a taste for cold-hearted violence. Serial killers and mass shooters have existed in Bowie song worlds since 1967's 'Please Mr Grave Digger' and 'Running Gun Blues' (1970). The presence of such nastiness is a challenge to the broader popular consensus of Bowie's lyrics offering a safe haven for outsiders and the alienated.[7] Tiffany Naiman, in her exploration of the gratuitous violence of *1. Outside* (1995), positions its brutality in the context of what she refers to as 'Bowie's "narrative of decline" – his musical discourse convened with the deterioration and fall of civilisation', as evidenced in those albums that explore dystopia and the dark sides of humanity, of which *The Next Day* is certainly one (2015, 183).

In observing the violence and suffering contained on *The Next Day*, it is worth noting the album's particular interest in toxic and fragile male masculinity. Men lost in time: perverted priests and dirty boys toting cricket bats, a puny man guided by sinister voices to perpetrate a school massacre, traumatized young soldiers aiming their weapons at each other, tyrants, spies and sneaks and liars whose fathers ran the prison. It is also present in the background of gentler-seeming assertions in 'Boss of Me' ('who'd have ever dreamed that a small town girl like you would be the boss of me?') and 'God Bless the Girl' ('I don't want to hurt you/I just want to have some fun'). Waldrep writes about how Bowie's work has historically sought to unravel and make sense of gender through

---

[7] Summarised by Jon Pareles in his obituary for *The New York Times*: '[Bowie's] message was that there was always empathy beyond difference' (2016).

performance, identifying the artist as one 'who has tried to give us a vocabulary for talking about masculinity – and femininity – in terms of the male body' (Waldrep 2015, 33). Alec Charles makes similar claims, that Bowie's work (throughout his career) 'pose(s) a more powerful and influential challenge to the forces of toxic masculinity and heteronormativity than any other mainstream male musician of the postmodern period' (Charles 2021, 233). From this viewpoint, what are we to make of the problematic men of *The Next Day*, who seem light years away from Ziggy's promised gender utopia? One possibility is that the work challenges toxic masculinity by exposing it to the air. Rather than addressing the problem from an external moral high ground, the artist can embody villainy and challenge their audience to recognize it – what Charles refers to as a 'post-quietist … quasi-Orwellian' approach that locates the artist in an appropriate setting to indirectly confront the audience with the 'horrors of its age' (ibid., 246). How is the genuine murderer outed? The play's the thing. If you can see him, he can see you too.

During the first rounds of media questioning that asked 'So, what's it all about?', Visconti helped steer people towards the idea that Bowie was not singing about himself, but from the point of view of various characters from history. According to him, Bowie had been spending much of his spare time over the past decade reading big history books – about wars, tyrants, dark stuff – and many of these themes made it on to the record (Graff 2013). When the V&A's list of 100 books emerged in October, it seemed like listeners were being given the same big hint. A popular consensus found that many of the lyrical subjects on *The Next Day* could possibly be linked to ideas and stories from history and/or literature.[8]

Bowie's bibliophilia has been known to filter into his songwriting, from 'We Are Hungry Men' (1967) to '1984' (1974) to 'Seven Years in Tibet' (1997) and beyond. Sometimes the borrowing of references is subtle, as in the case of '"Heroes"' rendering an impressionistic and oblique lyrical quality, one that philosopher Simon Critchley believes makes Bowie's songwriting especially compelling, as it invites the listener to fill the gaps in information with their own imagination and longing (Critchley [2014] 2016, 154).

---

[8] The literary connections evident on *The Next Day* are well covered in Chris O'Leary's *Ashes to Ashes* (2019).

The final word on Bowie's list of forty-two is 'mystification'. The confusion is artful and deliberate. The claustrophobia of working in an elaborate assembly of self-reference is tempered by the distancing and detaching of troubling allusions by pinning them on obscure literature and world history. It creates a tension between constructions of realities and fictions, what is signified from within and without the Bowie persona; a gap that the listener must bridge, as Critchley suggests, by projecting upon the music our own versions of the truth.

Projection

Biographer Nicholas Pegg observes that 2013 'saw Bowie returning to the cutting edge of rock video, an area in which he had shown every sign of losing interest after the millennium' (Pegg 2016, 467). Each of the videos from *The Next Day* is different in tone. After 'Where Are We Now?', the next two were directed by Floria Sigismondi (who also helmed the videos for 'Little Wonder' and 'Dead Man Walking'). In 'The Stars (Are Out Tonight)', Bowie appears alongside Tilda Swinton, with models Andreja Pejić and Saskia de Brauw playing their celebrity doppelgängers. This was followed by the darkly funny and controversial play on religious imagery of title track 'The Next Day', with Gary Oldman and Marion Cotillard playing a corrupt priest and 'stigmatized' woman. 'Valentine's Day' (dir. Indrani Pal-Chaudhuri and Markus Klinko, returning for the first time since they photographed the artwork from *Heathen*) is a simpler representation, featuring Bowie alone in an abandoned grain mill, his G2T Hohner guitar at times resembling a semi-automatic weapon in his hands as images of bullets and a horned shadow flash across the screen. Two videos for 'Love Is Lost (Hello Steve Reich Mix by James Murphy for the DFA)' exist, the most well known being the one that Bowie wrote, shot and edited himself for the total cost of $12.99 (the price of the flash drive he needed to save the footage). The other is an animated visualization, directed by Barnaby Roper, for the full-length remix (10:26), featuring morphing vector graphics and glitched imagery. The final video to surface was 'I'd Rather Be High (Venetian Mix)' (dir. Tom Hingston), splicing historical First World War-era footage with song lyrics and shots of Bowie lip-syncing. A month later, a one-minute Louis Vuitton ad set at a masked ball, shot in Venice, used the same song (dir. Romain Gavras). It was after this shoot was over that Bowie made his final trip to England.

The first video to appear, out of nowhere, was 'Where Are We Now?', directed by multimedia artist Tony Oursler. Set in an artist's studio stuffed with surreal objects that could be Bowie career memorabilia, the singer's face is projected on to one of the heads of a small two-headed rag doll, propped up on a pommel horse (the other face is Oursler's wife, abstract painter Jacqueline Humphries). The rag doll figure was one of the Oursler pieces that featured on stage during Bowie's fiftieth birthday celebrations at Madison Square Garden in 1997.[9] On a screen behind there are images of Berlin with a focus on the streets and neighbourhoods that Bowie references in the lyric, which we presume he knew well when he lived there from 1976 to 1978. Towards the end of the video Bowie appears, standing in Oursler's studio, wearing a T-shirt on which is written 'm/s Song of Norway' – a reference to the musical film that Hermione Farthingale, his girlfriend in the late 1960s, appeared in; her taking the job ended their relationship. In Bowie's career mythology, this was a pivotal heartbreak that preceded his first commercial breakthrough in 1969.

The video contains many Easter eggs – symbolic elements that link to significant aspects of Bowie's life and career. Oursler spoke afterwards about how he and Bowie had latched on to the idea of creating a 'kind of memory palace':

> I think David was attracted to the mounds of junk, which are either from past projects or to be potentially included in future projects. The studio is a kind of memory palace, which we tapped into ... There has been much discussion about why David wanted a pairing or a doppelgänger. My personal feeling is that the video is all about the border between the present and the past, the east and the west, the self and the other.
> – Oursler (quoted in Santos, 2013)

---

[9] Oursler met Bowie in 1996; in addition to contributing pieces for the fiftieth birthday concert, his unique face and eyeball projections were featured in 1997's *Earthling Tour* and, in the same year, Sigismondi's 'Little Wonder' video. Bowie made occasional cameos in Oursler's video pieces from around this same period.

The song builds to a climax as it asserts that what really matters is purely elemental: sun, rain and fire; artist and audience; me and you. Bowie's presence in the video is multiplied; he is the projected image performing to the camera, the puppet conjoined with the other, and a silent body observing from the sidelines. The presumed personal effects and images that fill the scenery and background could be nothing more than junk; the meanings that you can possibly assemble from the clutter are wholly reliant on your own ideas about who and what David Bowie is. In this way, the 'Where Are We Now?' video illustrates the assemblage artistry of *The Next* Day, connecting to and extending the V&A show. The Bowie camp denied any official connection with the exhibition, but in an interview in 2016, Oursler revealed that, at least at one point, Bowie was actively engaged with its planning: 'I sat with him and looked at the material … We kicked around a lot of ideas about presentation' (Kachka 2016). Music writer Paul Morley, part of the V&A's curatorial team, came up with the title for the exhibition, which is also an unfinished statement: 'David Bowie Is… '. Much like Bowie's difficult lyrics, which require a measure of creativity to engage with, and like Barnbrook's blank space, the question is an invitation to consider Bowie's star image in its totality. In this way the audience becomes active participants in the creation, co-ownership and preservation of the star text.

In *Lazarus*, Thomas Jerome Newton builds a rocket out of junk and makes his final attempt to return home. In *The Next Day* Bowie is assembling something interesting and potentially confronting from the mounds of junk in the memory palace, drawing disparate ideas into proximity. Bowie sets up a dummy and screens his face upon it. Bowie writes songs that sit in tension between the self and the other. Bowie paints his productions with the signature sounds of the past. He's watching from the sidelines. What will you project into this empty frame?

4

Assemblage

'Love Is Lost' (*The Next Day* track 4)

Tempo: 102 bpm.
Tonalities: B♭ minor in the interludes and verses, B major in the bridge.
Song form: ABABACABBA (interludes/verses (A/B), with a single bridge (C)).

The first salient feature of the composition is its distinctive combination of rhythms. An 8th note pulse shared between the bass and muted rhythm guitar cuts anxiously like a strobe light, with a single-step variation in every second bar. Another rhythmic feature is the driving, syncopated drumbeat – 8th notes in the hi-hats and with an anticipated second backbeat, which gives the track a stunted, tripped-up energy (Figure 4.1). This syncopation is accented by a familiar timbre, the Eventide Harmonizer pitched drum effect that Visconti innovated on 1977's *Low*.

The effect is achieved by sending a copy of the drum sound to the Harmonizer effects unit, which is programmed to detune the pitch after a very slight delay; the resulting lower sound is fed back into the machine, creating a feedback loop that sends the sound spiralling downwards in pitch until it fades away. This thicker, sloping drum sound can be heard on 'Breaking Glass' and 'Speed of Life', on *Low*, and on other albums such as *"Heroes"* and Iggy Pop's *The Idiot* (all 1977). The effect has been much copied since and it has become a signature sound of Bowie and Visconti's Berlin era. The *Low* effect is announced in the opening moments of 'Love Is Lost' and returns for a brief showcase in the exposed four-bar drum solo at 2:28. These spiky rhythms persist throughout the

FIGURE 4.1 *'Love Is Lost', opening rhythmic texture (the bass and muted guitar pulse, and the drum pattern underneath).*

track, pushing it relentlessly forward. Zachary Alford's playing is muscular and disciplined until the final back-to-back verses, when the intensity spills over to crashing cymbals.

A startled organ figure, played by Bowie across on the black notes (pentatonic 4ths) of his Korg Trinity, cuts sharp lines across the shuddering texture and has a judgemental, religious tone. An ill omen. Gerry Leonard's distorted guitar growls and whines menacingly in the gaps between Bowie's vocal in the verses. In the interludes between sections, it barks like an angry dog. Double-tracked and positioned far left and right, the listener is surrounded.

The interludes and verses (A and B sections) are differentiated by arrangement, texture and the presence of Bowie's lead vocal; the organ and Leonard's hectoring rhythms counterbalance the texture of the interludes against Bowie's singing in the verses. The basic architecture underneath both sections is the same, with a chord progression that begins in muddy Bb minor, sinking down and down to Ab, Gb and Eb minor before returning to repeat. The interludes create spaces between his singing and allow the track to spread out and exert its atmospheric menace. As it progresses, there is an accumulation of tension and stress.

One brief moment of respite arrives at 1:55 when a bridge (C section) introduces a new ascending chord progression in B major, sounding lifted and more hopeful. For the first time all of the textural elements can be heard together – the organ, guitar riff and Bowie's vocal, along with new backing harmonies. After the exposed drum solo leads out with a snarling fill, the last two verses are delivered with no gaps between, no room to breathe like before. The threatening texture is stacked with layers of call-and-answer backing vocals, leading to a final instrumental interlude, the heaviest and most intense moment of the piece. It ends with Bowie repeating the last lines of the verse dramatically: 'What have you done?'

Bowie's three clues from his list of forty-two that relate to this song are 'hostage', 'transference' and 'identity'. The lyric begins with a description of a young person in their darkest hour and moves through their life in scenes of mounting trauma. The narrative details offered from the outset – a 22-year-old whose 'voice is new', lamenting a lost love – connect to Bowie's age and situation in 1969, heartbroken and on the cusp of fame. As the song progresses, physical and cultural transformation, emigration, new wealth – all seemingly lead to futile ends. This sets up the possibility of a (somewhat bleak) semi-biographical reading, though this is complicated by the reveal in the bridge suggesting the central 'you' character being addressed by the song's narrator is or has become 'a beautiful girl'. The bridge also introduces the idea that a Faustian pact has been made; they have chosen shallow perfection over a chance to experience love. The repeating lyrical hook 'Love Is lost/lost is love' echoes John Lennon's similarly mirror-reflected 'Love is real/real is love' from 'Love' (*John Lennon/Plastic Ono Band* 1970). Bowie's tragedy proves Lennon's point: our main character's problem is that they aren't real. And no amount of reinvention or material success can fix that.

The central character's life is ruined by knowing and the lyrics imply that guilt has driven them to mental illness, necessitating therapy. The final two verses introduce new background voices intoning call and response/counterpoint against the main part. Here Bowie engages deliberately varied vocal tones that, together, suggest a multitude speaking at once; like the motley chorus that chimes in with 'oh by jingo' in 'After All' (1970); here also with the uncanny dorian[1] twist that snakes down the end of 'The Bewlay Brothers' (1971), 'Lay me place and bake me pie I'm starving for me gravy'. In the final climactic verse, the background voices converge into a

---

[1] Dorian mode is a tonality that sounds like a minor scale, but with a sharpened 6th degree; the dorian effect in a melody can sound reminiscent of sea shanties and Irish/English folk music (e.g. 'Drunken Sailor' and 'Scarborough Fair').

united crowd in reproach: 'You know, you know, you know, you know, you know... '.

'Love Is Lost' says you can never escape or outrun the knowledge of what you have done, and what has been irreparably lost as a result. In the album sequence it is followed by 'Where Are We Now?', which continues on themes of loss and knowing, carrying over in similar semi-biographical intimacy. The Berlin-era sounds in 'Love Is Lost' connect to the lyrical descriptions of Berlin in 'Where Are We Now?', leading us back in time to walk the dead. The crowd's bullying chant at the end of 'Love Is Lost' ('You know, you know, you know... ') is balanced by the more compassionate faith in self-awareness we hear in 'Where Are We Now?': 'The moment you know, you know, you know'.

The homemade music video that Bowie created for the extended 'Love Is Lost (Hello Steve Reich Mix by James Murphy for the DFA)' draws even more self-reference to the surface. In the video, Bowie observes two of his character creations in marionette puppet form – the Thin White Duke (c. 1975–6), a dark performance persona associated with fascist politics, and Pierrot the sad clown/everyman, a costume related to a specific representation of Major Tom from the video for 'Ashes to Ashes' (1980) and also a reference to Lindsay Kemp's theatre piece *Pierrot in Turquoise or The Looking Glass Murders* (1967–8). The puppets act out a scene where the victim/antagonist role-play script is flipped. The one we presume to be dangerous is the only one who can see the situation clearly; the one we presume to be innocent might be concealing his malice. Bowie lingers in the background and anxiously washes his hands. The audience is left to decide which identity wins in the end, and at what cost.

Through its music, production, text, use of self-reference and the video's narrative expansion, 'Love Is Lost' explores the effects of estrangement on identity through a lens of guilt and regret, and situates those ideas in a production atmosphere of harsh judgement, mounting anxiety and mental unwellness. The semi-biographical traces from 1969 – heartbreak and 'darkest hours' – are directly juxtaposed with the pummelling rhythmic sound of *Low* and Bowie's self-exile in Berlin, a hiding place and starting point for recovery after acute personal crisis. Implicated in this narrative is Bowie's choosing fame over a potentially very different life, one that might have avoided so much suffering and isolation.

The composition suggests that a loveless life leads to alienation and eventual madness and incapacity. Alienation from one's youthful aspirations, culture, social circle, even one's own reflection and sense of self. The resultant isolation traps our character in a frightening echo chamber with menacing, barking dogs surrounding, a stern organ casting erosive judgement, the bullying voices multiplying from within.

'If You Can See Me'
(*The Next Day* track 7)

Tempo: 142 bpm.
Tonalities: F minor in the verses, C# major in the chorus.
Song form: ABABA (chorus/verse).

The song structure has two opposing ideas taking turns, each with its own unique metric device that dominates and cheats time. The A section (the opening vocalise and the chorus sections thereafter) is a polymetric[2] ascending theme. The drumbeat, guitar and percussion rhythms are in 4/4, but the bass and changing harmony is in 5/4. This creates a phase relationship where downbeats only come into alignment after five bars (counting in 4/4, see Figure 4.2), or four bars (counting in 5/4).

The ascending A section theme starts from F# and for the first four bars suggests lydian mode,[3] but eventually arrives to establish a C# major tonality once it reaches the top of the phrase. The polymetric interplay between these elements is disorienting and cumbersome, cogs of uneven size turning at different speeds. This effect, when combined with the resolute ascension up the scale, moves in a spirit of grim, lumbering inevitability. The 5/4 bass line

---

[2] Polymetre is when two or more time signatures that share a common subdivision can be detected within a musical texture occurring at the same time.
[3] The lydian mode is like a standard major scale, only with a sharpened 4th degree – the characteristic lydian modal effect is famously heard in the opening notes of the themes to *The Simpsons* and *The Jetsons*. Bowie uses it surprisingly often and I talk about this more in Chapter 9.

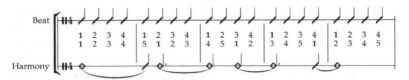

FIGURE 4.2 'If You Can See Me', showing polymetric alignment of beats and harmonies in the A sections (shown as five bars of 4/4).

and chord progression conquer the frenetic 4/4 drum and percussion loop with large easy strides to the top.

The opposing B section is a tonally ambiguous riff starting on E (the contour of the riff plays on the augmented 4th – the so-called 'devil's interval'),[4] a goading musical question. It is answered with an abrupt resolution to F minor at the end of the phrase, a quick, dark riposte. The B section motif also cheats time; after six measures of 4/4, it resolves with two clipped measures of 3/4. This creates a sneak-effect inside the music, stealing pulses, cutting the natural rhythm of the phrase short (see Figure 4.3). The themes of sections A and B are connected chromatically. The verse's ambiguous chord leading from E (Esus2 or $C^{7(b5)}$/E, depending on whether your analysis favours the underpinning chord resolution or the melody) to F minor, then steps up to the next section, the ascending scale from F# towards that triumphant C# resolution, as though it has just climbed a summit and planted a flag.

The bass is a central character in this composition. The lyrical 'chutes and ladders' are illustrated in its straight lines and trailing movements; either striding towards the ascent (in the A sections) or sliding off its perch (in the opposing B sections). The bassist here is Tony Levin, shadowed by the conspicuous presence of another well-known Bowie bassist: Gail Ann Dorsey's wordless singing across the introduction summons memories from the live shows she appeared in, particularly the *Outside* and *Earthling* tours in the mid-1990s. A faint essence of the live duet version of 'Under Pressure'

---

[4] In music theory, an augmented (sharpened) 4th or diminished (flattened) 5th (effectively the same thing) is commonly referred to as a 'tritone' because it's an interval made of three whole steps. It is also known as the 'devil's interval', *diabolus in musica* in Latin, due to its unsettling dissonance and ambiguous nature.

FIGURE 4.3 *'If You Can See Me', showing an example of the B section riff (1:58) and the metric shift to 3/4 at the end of the phrase.*

(her vocalise part inspired by Freddie Mercury and Annie Lennox) and her singing over the interludes of 'Dead Man Walking'. The latter song also features Zachary Alford on drums, heard here reprising similarly feverish breakbeat rhythms at the same hectic tempo.

Bowie's layered vocal performance in the B sections is covered in effects and formant processing, digitally heightened in pitch to make the voice sound smaller. In the past this trick was achieved with the varispeed functions on a tape machine – it was how the high parts in 'The Laughing Gnome' were made. Throughout the catalogue Bowie uses this effect often to suggest mental illness, unnatural voices and/or dark forces compelling destructive action. In the final act of 'The Bewlay Brothers' (1971), similar small voices are used to evoke something child-demonic and sinister, an effect that was reprised on *1. Outside*'s 'A Small Plot of Land'. For 'Scream Like a Baby' (1980), Visconti manually sped up and slowed down the tape while Bowie recorded his vocal, creating the sensation of the unnatural twisting of reality during the bridge when the troubled character of the song throws himself into a furnace (Visconti Studio 2020). The use of the production signature here suggests a nightmarish aura around the narrator's voice. The final chorus (concluding A section) applies a backwards reverb effect that imparts a darker, demonic edge. The effect leads with the reflection, as if the sound is being drawn in from the ether before it is uttered. It's a premonition, unstoppable, already happening before it's even happened. Bright keyboard tones (Bowie's Korg Trinity) dominate the texture with an icy, lurid fairground quality. The sound lures more spectres from *Scary Monsters*, the brittle, startled keyboard sounds from 'Scream Like a Baby' and 'Because You're Young'.

The three words from Bowie's list are 'crusade', 'tyrant' and 'domination'. The lyric opens with an image of someone scheming a stealth attack; a plan to disguise in women's clothing, then meet somewhere specific with a knife at the ready. Perhaps the widely publicized story involving Taliban soldiers who had been caught wearing burkas in order to disguise themselves was an inspiration (Associated Press 2011). Aside from the faint echo of the red shoes from 'Let's Dance', the song sets up the scene for something nasty. The 'knife' reveal in the lyric occurs just as the metre hastens to 3/4 – as if the phrase is becoming eager and impatient at the mention of the word. As the song progresses the threatening language gets stronger, more monstrous and violent, escalating from the excited knife plot to near-ecstatic promises of genocidal annihilation. The vocal concludes triumphantly, slowing down just before the finish line because it can, it has already won the race. But the song doesn't end there; the victorious final chord crossfades briefly into something strange and oceanic – a lurching, groaning, sunken mass.

In the album sequence this track sits between men with guns. Following on from the massacre of 'Valentine's Day', this track's allusions to American 'fantasticalisation' summon imagery of wars in the Middle East which sowed the seeds for the emergence of Al-Qaeda and ISIS, the dumb and unstoppable American war machine that introduced the covert tactics of terrorism to our modern world. 'If you can see me, I can see you' is a sniper's promise. To take your shot in a gunfight you have to break cover. The following track, 'I'd Rather Be High', continues with similar imagery of guns being trained on men in the sand.

The narrator of the piece is the archetypal tyrant, convinced of their centrality to the universe, taking pleasure in the violent domination of everything they see before them. Becoming increasingly intoxicated with the notion of their own power, the only thing they fear is the idea of karma (the 'fear of rear windows and swinging doors'). However, the musical composition denies the existence of even-handedness and equality, instead establishing unfair advantages and allowing the breaking of rules without consequence. The larger footprint strides easily while smaller ones are forced to run; the musical theme steals time and removes pulses to achieve its ends, destabilizing symmetry and equilibrium. The production evokes the daunting density and tumult of Bowie's mid-1990s era outputs *1. Outside* and *Earthling*, its clever interlocking design lending the chaotic, uneven atmosphere a twisted sense of logic. Like *1. Outside*, the construction is a dark mirror reflecting back at us our most monstrous nature. If offered the chance to dominate or persecute without consequence, would we take it? The archetypal tyrant is selfish and empowered in the pursuit of their own agenda, no matter the cost. 'If you can see me, I can see you' is Bowie's call to enhanced self-perception, its final moments contemplating the murkiest depths of a sombre reflection. In confrontation with the darkest of shadows, will we be able to recognize ourselves?

'You Feel So Lonely You Could Die' (*The Next Day* track 13)

Tempo: dotted quarter note = 80 bpm.
Tonalities: E♭ in the verse, B♭ in the chorus.
Song form: ABCABC (intro, then verse/bridge/chorus x2, lyrics don't repeat).

There aren't many Bowie songs in 6/8 metre.[5] The most famous of these appear on 1972's *The Rise and Fall of Ziggy Stardust and the Spiders from Mars*, a landmark record of the glam era: album opener 'Five Years' and the final track 'Rock 'n' Roll Suicide' are both in 6/8. 'You Feel So Lonely You Could Die' references both of

---

[5] Six counts, grouped into two strong pulses with three divisions; a lilting, swaying variation on the standard downbeat-backbeat drum pattern used in rock 'n' roll.

these, not only in the metre/rhythm, instrumentation and style, but also with direct quotation.

When 'Rock 'n' Roll Suicide' reaches its emphatic key change 'you're not alone!' moment, Mick Ronson's distorted guitar, doubled with sax section and strings, traces a chromatic movement between two major chords a minor third apart (B♭ and D♭, see Figure 4.4). It became one of Bowie's signature motifs and a glam rock trope, the cathartic sound that signalled the euphoric end of a Ziggy and the Spiders set. It was referenced in the musical *Hedwig and the Angry Inch*'s finale song 'Midnight Radio' and also in Morrissey's thinly veiled Ziggy homage 'I Know it's Gonna Happen Someday' (*Your Arsenal* 1992), an album that was produced by ex-Spider Mick Ronson. Bowie responded in turn to Morrissey's tribute by recording his own campy cover version of 'I Know it's Gonna Happen Someday' just a year later (*Black Tie White Noise* 1993), but he notably dropped the glam tropes – no 6/8 metre, no Ronson-esque chromatic line. A payback gesture.[6] In 'You Feel So Lonely… ' those glam references are reinstated, the 'Rock 'n' Roll Suicide' motif (Figure 4.5) along with a classic Ziggy-era arrangement: twelve-string guitar, rock band supported by a string quartet (arrangement courtesy of Visconti) and backing vocals that build and swell in all the right places.

Another Ziggy quotation enters at the very end of the track. As the final chords ring out, Zachary Alford strikes up the same 6/8 drum pattern from 'Five Years', as suspended tremolo strings shiver on top of an uncertain chord, fading away against ghostly ambient guitar tones. 'Rock 'n' Roll Suicide' and 'Five Years' encapsulate *The Rise and Fall of Ziggy Stardust and the Spiders from Mars*; the way that 'You Feel So Lonely… ' stages its concluding moments is like a recreation of a fan playing *Ziggy* on repeat. It could also be read as a reversal, a *Fall* followed by the *Rise*. The 'suicide' chord rings out, Woody Woodmansey's drumbeat strikes up with the promise of a few more years yet.

Like other compositions on *The Next Day*, this song uses different keys to territorialize the structure. With the verse in E♭ and the chorus in B♭, the contrasting sections have a plagal relationship;

---

[6] Bowie: 'It occurred to me that he was spoofing one of my earlier songs, and I thought, I'm not going to let him get away with that' (Wild 1993).

FIGURE 4.4 *'Rock 'n' Roll Suicide' guitar motif from the key change at 2:16.*

FIGURE 4.5 *'You Feel So Lonely You Could Die', showing the 'Rock 'n' Roll Suicide' reference in the guitar part that enters the second bridge at 2:53.*

the classic 'amen' cadence, which you can hear resolving after the final word of the song ('die', at 3:50) with a characteristic twelve-string guitar strum (at 4:00). The two keys are step related in the circle of fifths and the transition from the end of the chorus (in Bb) back to the verse (in Eb) resolves neatly inside itself. The four chords accompanying the punctuated delivery of 'die, ie, ie, ie', when played with a capo on the first fret (it would be logical and much easier to play it this way), spell out the progression D-E-A-D.

Bowie's vocal is precise and powerful, the strongest performance on *The Next Day*. As the arrangement builds intensity in the bridge sections (0:50 and 2:35), gospel-style choir voices open up and swell, reminiscent of Nile Rodgers's choral arrangements in Bowie's 1993 Morrissey cover. Bowie's three guiding words – 'traitor', 'urban', 'comeuppance' – inform potential readings of the lyric. The song is sung from the point of view of someone who has seen a shady character double-crossing people and getting up to such vile mischief that the narrator believes they are deserving of the worst ends possible: suicide by hanging, a quick assassination or, the worst fate of all, dying of loneliness. The curse 'I hope you feel so lonely you could die' directly references Elvis Presley's 1958 hit 'Heartbreak Hotel'; its bitter animosity contrasting sharply with Ziggy's cathartic declaration: 'Oh no, love, you're not alone'.

The lyrics are venomous and over the top, bordering on camp in places (especially in the delivery of lines like 'and people don't *like* you' at 3:12). They describe the treachery of a secretive person that the narrator has been observing closely for some time. It could be about a spy, some traitorous historical figure or a story plucked from the news – fan sleuths online unearthed a local NYC story from 2010 about a man who was dropping anti-Semitic notes around Long Island, a report that Bowie plausibly might have seen (Yakas 2010). Ziggy's spectre occupying so much of the musical and inverse-thematic territory makes possible a reading that the mysterious person being observed is Bowie himself – the one who has been working so secretively. In the context of *The Next Day*'s interests in the complex natures of identity and exposing the dark aspects of the self to the light, Ziggy's empathetic observation 'you've been watching yourself but you're too unfair' from 'Rock 'n' Roll Suicide', and the suspension of the song's finality (offering instead a commencement of 'Five Years' and a different perspective) sets up a dialogue between songs, across time and space. Such a dialogue could recontextualize the song from one of cruelty and vindictiveness to one of redemption from the poisonous effects of destructive, negative self-talk.

Morrissey haunts the song and its other possibilities. The two stars had a relationship that began as one-sided fan worship; Bowie was one of Morrissey's teen idols. They met for the first time in August 1990, backstage at a *Sound+Vision Tour* show in Manchester, and from there embarked on a brief and strange friendship. The year after, they appeared, briefly, on stage together at one of Morrissey's Los Angeles shows, crooning a duet of T. Rex's 'Cosmic Dancer' then, just prior to their trading of musical tributes and jibes in 1992/3, Bowie offered him the song 'Goodbye Mr Ed'; he turned it down, saying 'nothing within the song shouts out to me' (Morrissey 2013, 201). Bowie eventually recorded the song with his band Tin Machine in 1991 (on *Tin Machine II*). Morrissey later performed as the support act on the European leg of Bowie's *Outside Tour* in 1995, before quitting after only nine gigs (there were forty-eight in total). From this point their friendship soured into bitchy antagonism. Morrissey mocked Bowie in the ITV documentary *The Importance of Being Morrissey* (2002) and again to the press in 2004.[7] He then hired Visconti to produce his 2006 album *Ringleader of the Tormentors* and wrote the foreword to Visconti's autobiography in 2008, a possible olive branch that made a détente seem possible. But Bowie didn't seem interested in a truce: he resumed the public back and forth of mild hostilities in 2013, rejecting Morrissey's request to use an image of both stars together on the cover of a re-release of his tribute to the Kray twins, 'The Last of the Famous International Playboys' – too late to factor in on the songwriting here, but it suggests there was residual ill feeling on Bowie's side that outlasted the recording of *The Next Day* (the denied image was replaced on the cover by a photo of Morrissey with fellow northern singer Rick Astley). If this song could cast a real curse, one might believe that it had worked; after coming out in support of far-right politics Morrissey has fallen out of public favour since 2013.

There is precedent in the catalogue for the occasional diss track: 'Teenage Wildlife' (1980) was seemingly targeted at Gary Numan and 1993 B-side 'Lucy Can't Dance' was said to be a dig at Madonna. In the context of their musical shots fired, starting in the 1990s, could this song be a return volley in response to Morrissey's sardonic death fantasy 'You Were Good in Your Time' (*Years of Refusal* 2009), a song that many fans speculated was directed at Bowie specifically? If so, then this withering retort is a queen bitch move, the highest of camp. I asked Visconti whether he thought it could be true. He replied 'I don't know ... It's possible.'

The track sits between songs on *The Next Day* that once again consider the casual mutability of truth and the mystery of identity. Before it, another 'you' song ('(You Will) Set the World on Fire'), where an unnamed female artist (a 'black girl and guitar' who we may presume to be folk singer Odetta, from Dylan's mid-1960s Greenwich Village scene) is hyped for fame by a would-be manager

---

[7] Morrissey was disparaging about Bowie on primetime chat show *Friday Night with Jonathan Ross* (broadcast on BBC1, 14 May 2004), saying, 'He's a business, you know. He's not really a person', and 'I could tell you stories, Jonathan, and you'd never listen to "Let's Dance" again.' A month earlier in an interview with *GQ* magazine: ' ... he is not relevant. He was only relevant by accident' (Nelson 2004).

whose intentions seem slightly disingenuous ('manipulate', 'origin', 'text'). After it, the fevered dream of 'Heat', wherein Bowie's narrator finally admits he doesn't know who he really is at all; if he ever said that he did, then he was a liar ('tragic', 'nerve', 'mystification'). In the middle is an exploration of theft and revenge, complicated and enriched by its temporal connections and linear possibilities. 'Rock 'n' Roll Suicide' from the mirror universe turned upside down and back to front. For me, 'You Feel So Lonely You Could Die' is also instructive, informing an attentive method of reading Bowie's last works at various depths: standing alone, amongst the local references of the album, and also steeped inside Bowie's signifying language and the psychological spaces of questing and questioning identities.

And the next and another day

The songwriting of *The Next Day* de/constructs Bowie's meta-persona and encourages new modes of engaging with his artistry. The melodies, harmonies, rhythms, lyrical webs, arrangement choices and production flourishes are deliberately positioned to arouse memory knowledge, pulling threads into tension from across time, space and our creative imagination. *The Next Day* is the summit, the most sophisticated expression of Bowie's late style so far up to this point. It sits comfortably in a trilogy alongside *Heathen* and *Reality*. It also provides an effective bridge to what comes next: more violent confrontations with the darkness within, further de/construction of identity, new possibilities for creative redemption and unification of the self.

On *The Next Day*, death is possible and present in almost every scene. We encounter characters who are experiencing death or dealing it out, close to death but not quite dying, undead celebrities, dancing with ghosts, walking the dead or being willed towards (or away) from karmic suicide. A parade of bullies and poor bastards, a pantomime of Jungian archetypes reflecting our own dark potentials back to us. The school shooter from 'Valentine's Day' evolves into a fully fleshed-out antagonist in *Lazarus*, a murderous shadow man named Valentine whose only solo songs in the show are from *The Next Day* ('Love Is Lost', 'Dirty Boys', 'Valentine's Day'). Themes of emigration, exile and alienation also carry through from *The Next Day* to *Lazarus*; the loveless and the alienated and the loveless alien refugee who must find a way to quieten his bullying mind.

The Next Day also revises and rearticulates Bowie's star metaphors ahead of ★. 'The Stars (Are Out Tonight)' riffs on the idea that common celebrities don't go out at night to party, they come out at night to hunt because they are desperate creatures, preying on the anxieties and longing of 'normal people'. Its accompanying long-form music video (dir. Floria Sigismondi) features Bowie and Tilda Swinton, playing an ordinary couple, who are stalked by a pair of impossibly glamourous celebrities, played by trans model Andreja Pejić and artist Saskia de Brauw. Each performer brings their androgynous credentials to bear in the video, except for Bowie himself, whose identity remains visibly fixed and stereotypically conservative (aside from a brief shot of a tabloid magazine cover with Thomas Jerome Newton's scandalously undisguised alien face printed on it). Versions of Bowie's previously 'iconoclastic acts of gender transgression' are performed vicariously around and upon him by his co-stars, which, according to Lisa Perrott, enacts a symbolic exchange, purging his past personas and surrendering them to be embodied and shared by others (Perrott 2017).

The song lyric pivots on 'star' definitions and wordplay – the ones described in the song are not the same as the ones in the night sky, scattered to the cosmos, at least not yet. These stars are closer to the Earth: the parasitic celebrities of late capitalism. Stars that are alive or otherwise. The legendary sleepless, hedonistic lifestyles of living stars and the endless workload of dead ones – the corpses that continue to grind, accruing income for the benefit of family estates and corporate entities from beyond the grave. It could also apply to those stars that never retire or disappear from revered popular memory. This image of the sleepless star living forever – burning out of mortal life yet burning on as a legacy – is alluded to in the song 'Hey Hey, My My (Into the Black)' by Neil Young and Crazy Horse, invoking the spectre of Elvis Presley in the context of rock 'n' roll immortality: 'It's better to burn out 'cause rust never sleeps'.

Elvis burned out, but he remains immortal ('gone but not forgotten'). Young is also grimly hinting that death might have financial advantages – for Elvis, out of the blue(s) and into the black. The 'burn out' line was famously borrowed by Kurt Cobain in his suicide note, another rock star that lives on in popular memory, one whose currency, depressingly, improved in value after death. From a cosmological perspective, it is also true that stars never sleep. Like rust, they exist as a constant process of transformation and becoming. Barnbrook's design for the ★ package included a representation of a proton–proton chain, the nuclear fusion reaction by which stars stay alive and burning.

Back in 2003, Bowie made a nuclear star analogy in *Reality* lead single 'New Killer Star'. The chorus claims that he's discovered a star ('new killer' being a play on the popular American mispronunciation of 'nuclear' as *nu-cu-lar*), but it's not a weapon, it's something better – he's found the nuclear stars in your eyes. Life comes from the sun, and all matter, including everything in the universe, originates from stars. These giant celestial fusion reactors, relentlessly smashing subatomic particles together. As particles, we are indeed ancient, immortal and transient all at once. *The Next Day Extra*'s 'Atomica' is another sleepless/nuclear star metaphor, with echoes of Ziggy-style hubris: ready to rock until he explodes, given to hedonism and rapturously holding himself 'like a god'. But he's not a god, he's 'just a rock star stabbing away ... just a pop star chopping away'. Just a rock star. Just a pop star. Not yet a Blackstar.

Stars never get to sleep, but they do change as they age. A red giant is a star in the last stages of its stellar evolution, not quite dying. The first stage of this evolution is known as the 'main sequence' – when stars fuse hydrogen to helium to create nuclear fusion. This reaction, after a long time, changes the interior composition of a star. As hydrogen fuel is spent, the core shrinks and compacts due to gravity while the outer layers of the star expand as it begins burning up other elements it finds in the shell surrounding the core. This is what happens when stars age; they evolve beyond the main sequence to become red giants or supergiants. Larger, more luminous and cooler. That is, if they don't fizzle out first.

Scott Walker summons the imagery of a star burning out in his final solo album *Bish Bosch* (2012). The centrepiece of the record is the mini-opera 'SDSS14+13B (Zercon, A Flagpole Sitter)', his longest song. Described by Scott Wilson as an existential 'mock epic ... allegory of Scott Walker's life and work' that also foretells his death (Wilson 2020, 27), the composition is a dense assemblage of rigid silences, horror strings, grinding noises and sprawling lyrical references that range from toilet graffiti and urinal cakes to transhuman zoophilia, the planets, Hollywood mogul Louis B. Mayer, *Bill & Ted's Excellent Adventure* and beyond. The central character is Zercon, the deformed dwarf jester at the court of Attila the Hun, and the piece traces his attempt to escape the cruelty of his existence by ascending through history (symbolized by the imagery of the flagpole sitter). His ascent is tragic, as he eventually becomes the brown dwarf star SDSS1416+13b, freezing and stranded alone in outer space.

Brown dwarfs are main sequence stars of such small mass that they are unable to retain enough heat to keep the fusion going in their cores. Chris O'Leary described *Bish Bosch* as Scott Walker's own 'red giant phase' (O'Leary 2016). The analogy works in terms of conceptualizing a pop or rock star's late-period evolution: their ascension towards a state where their core inwardly consolidates. They are no longer supporting connections with the cultural life that orbits around them, instead outwardly expanding and becoming brighter, burning up all kinds of new fuel from other internal places. To a red giant star, normal rules of engagement no longer apply. The work becomes a cannibalization, a language of its own in dialogue with itself. Everything that the star is and has been becomes fuel that can be used and burned.

Like T. S. Eliot, Pablo Picasso, Scott Walker, Bob Dylan and Leonard Cohen, Bowie worked during his late period to refine his self-situated language. For him it was visual, textual, musical and sonic, confronting existential anxieties through the articulation of (sometimes uncomfortable) universal truths and the continual excavation and reconstitution of identity. It could be said that the dense and sprawling *The Next Day* project bears the hallmarks of work from an artist also reaching his 'red giant phase'. It took him years to carefully assemble and complete. But for Bowie, time would quickly become a luxury he could no longer afford. In cosmic time, red giants can't last very long. Their thin outer layers soon burn out and blow away, leaving a shroud of interstellar gas and dust around an exposed collapsed core. Only the largest red giants can transform into black holes.

PART TWO

Per ardua
ad astra

5

Icarus takes his pratfall

This chapter is about beginnings and endings. Walter Tevis's 1963 science-fiction novel *The Man Who Fell to Earth* begins with the image of the flight of Icarus, the cautionary mythological tale about overambition, miscalculation and hubris. Icarus's miraculous ability to fly is borne of desperation and ingenuity, but a taste of success leads him to ignore his father Daedalus's instructions to not fly too close to the sun. Like Ziggy, he makes it too far. We know what happens next.

Bowie's career is bookended by his desires to create musical theatre (from 1968's sketchy *Ernie Johnson* to *Lazarus* in 2015) and dreams (from 'I Live in Dreams', a recently unearthed recording from 1966, to the *No Plan* EP, featuring the new songs that lived inside Newton's last dream, fifty years later). It is also bookended by images of flight and transformation. In 1968 Bowie developed a mime performance called *Jetsun and the Eagle*, which attempted to tell the story of the Chinese invasion of Tibet, set to the soundtrack of 'Silly Boy Blue' (from his 1967 debut album) and other incidental music created with the help of new music friend Tony Visconti. The piece was based on the legend of Tibetan yogi Jetsun Milarepa, who through battling his demons was able to gain clarity, growth and the ability to transform into a bird (and, eventually, attain Buddhahood). In the performance Bowie could be seen miming the 'flying eagle', a gesture that he would repeat throughout his career[1]

---

[1] The 'flying eagle' mime was performed on stage at Ziggy Stardust shows; during the guitar solos in 'Width of a Circle' Bowie could mime being trapped in a cage, then finding an opening, escaping and taking flight like a bird. The gesture was revived in Toni Basil's choreography for the *Glass Spider Tour* (1987) and performed in the music video for 'Slow Burn' (dir. Koepke 2002).

– eyes focused on the distance, arms outstretched at shoulder
height, leaning forward as if about to jump... At the end of Bowie's
life these images are resurrected once again in the context of the
character Thomas Jerome Newton being in crisis. He has his own
demons to face and he too longs to be free as a bird.

Life's a bit and sometimes you die:
A short history of Bowie
and musical theatre

The staging of *Lazarus* at the New York Theatre Workshop,
beginning in late 2015, was the fulfilment of a lifelong ambition for
Bowie. Even though he was influential in incorporating character-
driven theatricality into his music and performance style, and had
achieved a measure of success and acclaim as a part-time actor,
Bowie's ambitions to bring his musical ideas into the domain of
legitimate theatre were consistently stifled over the years. It's a
long, frustrated tale of elaborate plans being thwarted, put on hold,
forgotten or buried. That story supplies significant context to our
reading of *Lazarus*, not only in understanding how this ambition
was finally fulfilled at the eleventh hour, but also letting us gain
a more complete sense of how Bowie's late work actively reaches
back, draws from and uses his past in an artful way.

   Bowie's interest in music as theatre was present from the very
early days. Struggling as a teenager in the mid-1960s to find his
footing in London's hectic music scene, a few false starts and
early rejections led the young performer to consider widening his
scope. Under the guidance of his father, Haywood Stenton 'John'
Jones, and early manager Ken Pitt, Bowie was encouraged to try
his hand at cabaret and acting. It was even suggested he might
make a good children's TV presenter (Earls 2019). In 1967, after
his music-hall style comedy single 'The Laughing Gnome' flopped
and his debut album failed to impress, Bowie announced a break
from pop music and enrolled in Lindsay Kemp's class at The Dance
Centre in Covent Garden, where he began instruction in mime and
Japanese dramatic theatre-dance forms noh, butō and kabuki. As
part of the company, Bowie wrote and performed original music for

Kemp's 1967 commedia dell'arte piece *Pierrot in Turquoise or The Looking Glass Murders*. He wrote songs for the production, helped give it a name (turquoise apparently being a symbol of 'eternity' in Buddhism). He also played the part of Cloud, the narrator. The title role of Pierrot was played by Kemp, and he donned a specific costume for it that would stick in Bowie's creative imagination for years; at first drawn by George Underwood on the back cover of *Space Oddity*'s album artwork and then later imaginatively re-interpreted by costume designer Natasha Korniloff for the 1980 *Ashes to Ashes* video (dir. David Mallet).

There was also a mysterious project from early 1968 (which surfaced in 1996 in the form of a tape, sheets of lyrics and stage directions as an item at a Christie's auction) where Bowie had sketched out at least ten songs for a *Tommy*-style rock opera about a character called Ernie Johnson who was planning to throw his own suicide party. Though the tape sold at auction, it has never been made available for the public to hear (it was seemingly blocked by Bowie's estate in 2005). All that exists of it in the public record is a brief mention in Ken Pitt's memoir (1983) and a description published in *Record Collector* (Doggett 1995, 92) outlining the overall plot and song content. It's probably for the best that these early drafts remain buried as, based on the information that is out there, it sounds like some of the material's language was 'of its time' and potentially embarrassing if held up against today's sensibilities. Still, it is interesting that Bowie's earliest and latest attempts at musical theatre culminate with the lead character's death on stage. It's also interesting to note that at least one of the *Ernie Johnson* songs makes use of Polari slang (the only song in Bowie's catalogue that shares this distinction is ★'s 'Girl Loves Me').

Later in 1968, Bowie tried to bring together all of his performing interests into a new physical theatre project, Feathers – a trio that included his then-girlfriend Hermione Farthingale (an actress and dancer) and guitarist John 'Hutch' Hutchinson. The group can be seen performing together in *Love You Till Tuesday* (1969), a short film made to promote Bowie on German TV and boost the 1967 debut album. By 1969, Feathers was already over – Farthingale accepted a role in a big-budget movie musical, *Song of Norway* (1970), a job she had to leave the country for, and the pair broke up. Bowie also parted with his manager (Pitt) that year and split with his record label, Deram. He returned his attention to making music, negotiating a one-album deal with Mercury Records and working with Visconti on the folk-inspired *Space Oddity* (1969). The success of a new recorded version of 'Space Oddity' (the only track on the album that Visconti didn't produce, as he considered it a novelty record) is what sets Bowie on the path to rock 'n' roll stardom.

Bowie's formative time working with Kemp and Feathers brought a theatrical articulation to his stagecraft as a pop performer. In 1974, Kemp explained that these techniques were vocal as well as physical: 'I taught him to exaggerate with his body as well as his voice, and the importance of looking as well as sounding beautiful … [he] learned to free his body' (Brown 1974). The naturally shy David Jones also learned how to perform fearlessly in the guises of other characters, and would come to rely on character constructs to cope with fame.[2] He explained his approach to journalists: 'I'm an actor, I play roles, fragments of myself' (Saal 1972). Later on in his career he would make similar claims in order to distance his personally held views from the problematic politics of his dark performance persona, the Thin White Duke, in 1976 saying, 'I'm Pierrot. I'm Everyman. What I'm doing is theatre, and only theatre. What you see on stage isn't sinister. It's pure clown. I'm using myself as a canvas and trying to paint the truth of our time' (Rook 1976).

The Ziggy Stardust phenomenon had experimental musical theatre in its bones. Some of the songs that appeared on *The Rise and Fall of Ziggy Stardust and the Spiders from Mars* (1972) were materials originally devised for a 1971 Bowie side project called Arnold Corns – a band that was put together to back a completely fabricated frontman (then-19-year-old fashion designer Freddie Burretti, a.k.a. 'Rudi Valentino', who later became Bowie's tailor). The project ran aground but the material found new life once Bowie assumed the lead role as 'Ziggy' and further developed the backstory – partly inspired by the mental breakdown of 1950s pop star Vince Taylor, the cult musician Legendary Stardust Cowboy and what he heard, saw and absorbed (and how people reacted to his androgynous appearance) during a promotional trip to America

---

[2] Farthingale: 'David loved mime … he'd had his first experience of what it's like to be immersed in a character, in full costume and make-up. For somebody quite anxious and fragile – shy, if you like – a character allows you to be braver. That device was something David used for a long time, until he was brave enough to drop it and be himself' (Earls 2019).

in 1971. The look and feel of the early Ziggy Stardust shows took inspiration from surreal, dystopian and decadent theatrical experiences: Andy Warhol's play *Pork* (1971, staged at London's Roundhouse), Stanley Kubrick's film adaptation of the Anthony Burgess novel *A Clockwork Orange* (1971) and Alice Cooper's *Love It to Death* tour at the Rainbow Theatre in Finsbury Park that same year. A year later, in 1972, Ziggy's show at the same venue would up the theatrical ante considerably with stage design and choreography supplied by Lindsay Kemp, a troupe of dancing mimes, costumes by Korniloff and a huge multilevel scaffold set connected by a system of ladders. The show opened with a short clip of Buñuel and Dalí's *Un Chien Andalou* (1929), something he repeated for the 1976 *Isolar Tour*, choosing to show the full twenty-one-minute film in lieu of having a support act. At the Rainbow Theatre, Bowie's next-level rock theatrics would prompt Charles Shaar Murray to exclaim that the show 'made Alice [Cooper] look like a third-form dramatic society' (Shaar Murray 1972).

The Ziggy shows also incorporated elements of Japanese theatre; Kansai Yamamoto's elaborate costumes blended science-fiction fantasy and traditional noh drama. On stage, Ziggy worked with kabuki techniques learned under Kemp – exaggerated physical gestures, every element highly stylized. Ziggy wore *onnagata* (male actors playing women's roles) make-up, inspired by kabuki actor Bandō Tamasaburō V, and this was further developed into the iconic 'astral sphere' (a gold circle painted on his forehead) and the red and blue *Aladdin Sane* lightning bolt by makeup artist Pierre Laroche (who would go on to adapt the legendary looks from *The Rocky Horror Show* stage play for the film version in 1975). It is said that Bowie (as Ziggy) was the first Western artist to perform the *hayagawari* ('quick change') kabuki technique on stage (BBC 2016a).

We can get the sense that Bowie was thinking about making a further move towards more traditional musical theatre even while he was still on tour with the Spiders in late 1972. An early version of '1984' was demoed during the *Aladdin Sane* sessions at Olympic Studios (January 1973), intended for a mooted production based on Orwell's dystopian sci-fi novel *Nineteen Eighty-Four* (1949). In July 1973, the month of his surprise public retirement of the Ziggy Stardust persona on stage at the Hammersmith Odeon, Bowie was interviewed at the Château d'Hérouville studio in France by

Martin Hayman, who is shown a work-in-progress mix of a new 'musical in one act called *Tragic Moments*' (a lost Bowie track that was later bootlegged under the titles 'Zion' and 'A Lad in Vain') (Hayman 1973).

A few months later, Bowie was working on the *Nineteen Eighty-Four* musical with playwright Anthony Ingrassia (who had adapted and directed *Pork* in 1971). Some of this early material was previewed in a televised performance known as *The 1980 Floor Show* and then, after Orwell's widow denied them the rights to the story, the music was repurposed for the comparably dystopian concept album *Diamond Dogs* (1974). In a recorded conversation with William Burroughs for *Rolling Stone* in December 1973, Bowie spoke about his plans to develop a science-fiction musical based on an elaboration of Ziggy Stardust lore, where the benevolent starmen from the album are revealed as ruthless and indifferent alien nomads that ride the cosmos, travelling between black holes. The description is highly detailed: he's already chosen the songs and given characters names and costume designs.

> I must have the total image of a stage show. It has to be total with me. I'm just not content writing songs, I want to make it three-dimensional.
>
> – Bowie (Copetas 1974)

While nothing comes of the Ziggy musical, some of the visual concepts developed for *Nineteen Eighty-Four* were repurposed for the *Diamond Dogs Tour* in 1974. Designer Jules Fisher and set builder Mark Ravitz were brought in to create the set for Hunger City, following Bowie's vision of a multilevel moving set with a design inspired by German expressionist film (Fritz Lang's *Metropolis* (1927) and Robert Wiene's *The Cabinet of Dr. Caligari* (1920)). The tour was as close to full-blown musical theatre as a rock show had ever been, with props and costume changes, a troupe of dancers, a cherry picker crane that extended the performance possibilities of the elaborate set design. A young Michael Kamen was brought in as musical director. While the tour made its way through America, the energy and will to sustain a production on such a scale began to lose steam; Bowie's drug use was escalating, his interests being diverted by Black American music styles (this transitional period was captured by Alan Yentob for his 1975 BBC documentary *Cracked Actor*). Another thing happened that might have put Bowie off the idea of mounting elaborate and expensive theatre projects: MainMan (Bowie's management company at the time) had decided to mount a show on Broadway for the first time, Tony Ingrassia's *Fame*, a comedy based on the life of Marilyn Monroe. It bombed so badly that it closed after only one night, leaving the company $250,000 out of pocket. Another significant connection was made at some point in 1974: Bowie met 22-year-old Robert Fox (then the assistant to theatre impresario Michael White) at a party, where they bonded over shared interests in all things theatrical.

Yentob's documentary aired in the UK in January 1975 and was seen by director Nicolas Roeg and producer Si Litvinoff. They decided that the frail and otherworldly looking rock star would be perfect for the lead role in their film adaptation of Walter Tevis's *The Man Who Fell to Earth*. A month later and Bowie had agreed to star in the project. He moved to Los Angeles to prepare for the shoot and talked to the press about stepping away from rock and roll for good: 'Now I'm going to be a film director. I've always been a screenwriter. My songs have just been practice for scripts' (Brown 1975). He told Cameron Crowe for *Rolling Stone*: 'I'm all through with rock and roll. Finished. I've rocked my roll. It was great fun while it lasted but I won't do it again' (Crowe 1976a).

While *The Man Who Fell to Earth* is categorically not a musical, Bowie would end up engaging with the project as both an actor and musician/composer – though the original soundtrack that he developed in collaboration with arranger and cellist Paul Buckmaster was never completed, according to *Young Americans/Station to Station* co-producer Harry Maslin, due to Bowie's exhaustion (Hopkins 1985). They managed approximately nine cues out of the reported sixty that were required for the film (ibid.). Some of this material was reworked and incorporated into the instrumental side of 1977's *Low* (the backing track of 'Subterraneans' was recorded at LA's Cherokee Studios in December 1975 during those Buckmaster sessions).

At a specific point in the story in both the book and the film, Newton produces strange ethereal recordings that he hopes might be broadcast and so reach his wife and children back on his home planet, Anthea; the conflation of Bowie, Ziggy and the Newton character as alien message-bearing recording artists almost creates a meta level of theatre that winks at the audience who knows enough to see it. While the score to the film was eventually provided by John Phillips (of The Mamas and the Papas), the music that Bowie made would ultimately be broadcast, if not from another planet, then from Berlin – unfamiliar sonic landscapes, unfamiliar dialects, Thomas Jerome Newton in profile on *Low*'s front sleeve.

The next tour (*Isolar*, in 1976) was a bold experiment in straight-up rock 'n' roll, as he explained to Cameron Crowe in *Playboy* that same year. 'I'm actually anxious to try something I've never done in the past – work with a small band, perform with no set whatsoever and use no production gimmickry … I want to see if I can cut it' (Crowe 1976b). It turned out he could, and from this point Bowie separated his music-making, touring and acting into parallel activities (the 'Berlin Trilogy' of albums feature less character-driven songwriting; he accepts acting roles that are more removed from his established star personas with 1978 flop *Just a Gigolo* and a star turn as John Merrick in *The Elephant Man* in 1980 on Broadway). Excluding his brief appearance singing 'Station to Station' in 1981 German film *Christiane F.*, it's not until the BBC's made-for-TV production of Bertolt Brecht's *Baal* in 1982 that Bowie engages once again with musical theatre (though notably not performing original material).[3]

Labyrinth, the 1986 musical fantasy film, was something of a passion project for director Jim Henson and the last film he would direct before his death. It was his idea that the main antagonist, Jareth the Goblin King, would both act and sing in the film, and he courted Bowie's involvement from as early as 1983. Bowie ended up contributing five original songs to the soundtrack and was featured vocalist on four of these. While the film was initially a commercial failure, Bowie's performance was praised by critics and the film has since been rehabilitated to cult classic status thanks, in part, to Bowie's charismatic and unsettlingly sexual performance. *Labyrinth*'s fantasy world had many elements that suited the Bowie brand: surrealist imagery, dreamworld logic and ambiguous sexuality. In press interviews to promote his then-upcoming *Glass*

---

[3] Words by Bertolt Brecht/translated by John Willett; music by Dominic Muldowney and Kurt Weill.

Spider Tour, Bowie spoke again about his early aspirations to create a new kind of music-as-theatre experience:

> [What I always wanted to achieve] was something to do with amalgamating theatre and rock in a way that I hadn't seen before. I'd just only seen daft things like *Hair* and it wasn't quite what I envisaged ... I guess Ziggy was like sort of trying the water out in a first attempt. And even now, I haven't got to where I've always thought it would be, but possibly with the tour coming up I might be putting together something which gets really near to what I first saw...
>
> – Bowie (MTV 1987)

> I'm going to do a stage thing this year, which I'm incredibly excited about, 'cause I'm gonna take a chance again.
>
> – Bowie (Loder 1987)

The worldwide *Glass Spider Tour* (1987) would turn out to be the longest, largest, most expensive tour of Bowie's career up to that point. It was conceived as a return to music theatrics and a fulfilment of his early aspirations of merging surrealistic imagery with rock 'n' roll performance. Drawing parallels to the *Diamond Dogs Tour*, it included fully scripted scenes, projections and moving set pieces. Toni Basil returned to choreograph the Canadian contemporary dance troupe La La La Human Steps. Despite being profitable and well attended, the tour was poorly received by the UK press, who criticized it as being pretentious and over the top. Like *Labyrinth*, these days (especially since his death) the *Glass Spider Tour* has been critically rehabilitated and recognized for its groundbreaking innovations and artistic vision.[4] The harsh criticisms Bowie received at the time led him to reconsider his music career. At the end of the tour, the company famously (and possibly apocryphally) set fire to the gigantic spider stage set in a field somewhere in New Zealand.

---

[4] In 2010, the *Glass Spider Tour* was named 'Top Concert Tour Design of All Time' by the Live Design Achievement Awards (Sandberg 2010); Andy Greene for *Rolling Stone* proclaimed it 'nowhere near as terrible as the legend suggests' in 2013; and Jason Heller, for *The Atlantic*, said it was 'spectacular, beautiful, charmingly pretentious, and weirdly magical' (2017).

1. Outside (1995) was something of a mixed-media piece – a sprawling concept album that incorporated a cut-up detective story, a graphic novel, voice-acted vignettes, new paintings and reconstructions of outsider/performance art pieces. The project was intended to be even bigger – Bowie spoke of it as the first in a trilogy, expanded as a CD-ROM package and developed (in collaboration with Brian Eno and theatre director Robert Wilson) into an operatic production for the 1999 Salzburg Festival. The opera fell through, reportedly due to a clash with festival director Gérard Mortier over the costs of the proposed set design. Bowie would next suggest the possibility of recruiting Tony Oursler for a theatrical version of *1. Outside* (Yahoo! 2000), but again plans of staging anything come to nothing.

> I really wanted to write musicals more than anything else ... At the time I thought that was probably what I was going to end up doing. Some kind of new approach to the rock musical, that was at the back of my mind.
>
> – Bowie (Du Noyer 2002)

Decades later we know Bowie once again took steps towards realizing his elusive dream of creating musical theatre. While not explicitly documented, we can piece together the clues from sporadic accounts that have emerged during Bowie's quiet years after the heart attack in 2004. It is significant that Bowie's friendship with Robert Fox (by this time a successful theatre and film producer) was rekindled at some point in the late 1990s, around the time that Bowie and Iman had permanently settled in NYC.

In 2005, Bowie acquired the theatrical rights to Tevis's book (Trynka 2016), the same year that Roeg's film was made widely available once again with the Criterion Collection DVD release, complete with a 1992 commentary track featuring Bowie, Roeg and Buck Henry. Around the same time Bowie gifted a copy of the book to Fox, adding a personalized inscription 'Robert, I'm not a human being at all. Thomas Jerome Newton. Shhh... David Bowie.' According to Fox's version of events, it wasn't until mid-2013 when he first learned of the plan to create a sequel to *The Man Who Fell to Earth*, and yet at least two playwrights have spoken publicly about being nominally attached to early iterations of what would become the *Lazarus* project.

In Steven Kurutz's piece for *The New York Times* about Bowie's status as a New Yorker (2016), playwright John Guare (*The House of Blue Leaves*, *Six Degrees of Separation*) is quoted as saying Fox had gotten in touch on Bowie's behalf 'about ten years ago ... to discuss a theatre project' (Kurutz 2016). The story goes that Bowie was in a 'dark place' following his recovery from heart surgery in June 2004 and that Fox was (according to Guare) 'trying to coax him back to a creative life'. Apparently, the pair met a number of times to discuss potential themes, but ultimately it came to nothing.

Author Michael Cunningham also had a professional connection with Robert Fox, who co-produced the Oscar-winning film adaptation of his Pulitzer Prize-winning novel *The Hours*. In 2017 he penned a detailed account for *GQ* recalling how he and Bowie had collaborated for a time on an abandoned musical, again 'about 10 years ago':

> After we'd exchanged a smattering of small talk, I asked him if he had anything specific in mind about the musical he'd like us to work on. He admitted that he was intrigued by the idea of an alien marooned on Earth. He'd never been entirely satisfied with the alien he'd played in the 1976 film *The Man Who Fell to Earth*. He acknowledged that he'd like at least one of the major characters to be an alien.
>
> – Cunningham (2017)

Cunningham's story suggests that the collaboration he was directly involved in wasn't explicitly a sequel to *The Man Who Fell to Earth*, though there seems to be some thematic crossover. In his telling, the project was to incorporate mariachi music and a plot point revolving around a cache of lost Bob Dylan songs. No mention from the author as to whether he was aware that Bowie had the rights to develop Tevis's story. Cunningham claims that they were nearly halfway through their first draft 'when David's heart trouble recurred ... Our musical was put on hold. We never revived it' (2017).

It is not until 2013, once *The Next Day* project was out in the open and enjoying its critical success, that Fox claims Bowie brought up the notion of staging a musical that was explicitly a sequel based on material from the book, with the already-chosen title *Lazarus*. In a hotel room in London, Bowie asked his friend for his assistance in pulling a team together quickly.

> Interviewer: The turnaround [for *Lazarus*] in theatre terms was incredibly swift, wasn't it – was that because you knew that there was a ticking clock on it?
> Robert Fox: Originally there was no ticking clock ... but I knew that *Lazarus* was something very important to him, and I knew that Enda is a quick writer and that he and David would spark off each other, which they did. And then when we got Ivo van Hove involved, and he's very amazingly clever and quick at putting things together, the whole thing remarkably came together very quickly. Then David got ill again and he said 'you've got to get it on' and so we did.
> – Q&A with Robert Fox and Michael C. Hall at the BFI (Johnson 2016a)

Fox had encouraged these theatrical aspirations in the years following the 2004 heart surgery and leveraged his connections to put Bowie in touch with potentially suitable collaborators. In 2013, at their meeting in London, he recognizes the personal importance and urgency of the project Bowie is wanting to create. He pulls together a team who can work fast and hastens its completion in time for Bowie to attend its premiere. A gift to his friend: to finally fulfil a lifetime's ambition.

Lazarus?

The show *Lazarus* has no characters known by that name and the word isn't mentioned in the script. It doesn't reference the two well-known biblical Lazarus stories either. So what else could the title refer to?

From Michael Cunningham's account of their ill-fated collaboration, Bowie 'had been thinking about popular artists who are not considered great artists, particularly the poet Emma Lazarus, who wrote *The New Colossus* ... What, said David, are we to make of a poet taught in few universities, included in few anthologies, but whose work, nevertheless, is more familiar to more people than that of the most exalted and immortal writers?' (Cunningham 2017).

Emma Lazarus (1849–87) was a Sephardi poet and activist, involved in raising awareness of the plight of Russian Jewish refugees. She is remembered by history for this one poem, which helped to popularize the idea of the Statue of Liberty as a symbol of America's openness – a mighty 'Mother of Exiles' and welcoming omen for immigrants and refugees, the statue's torch lighting the way towards safe harbour in America. The new colossus promises to welcome anyone, the 'huddled masses yearning to breathe free, the wretched refuse of your teeming shore, the homeless, tempest-tost' to safety and opportunity in the new land of freedom.

In the source book and film, Thomas Jerome Newton lands in America and finds wealth and opportunity, but also addiction and deep isolation. He ends up failing in his desperate mission to save his family and home planet. The character's tragic arc and treatment at the hands of others can be read as an allegory of the immigrant experience; his othering, betrayal, exploitation and isolation commenting on the treatment of outsiders and individuals marked by cultural/racial/physical difference in America. Of course, the ill treatment of outsiders is not solely an American issue. In the wake of global poverty, persecution and conflict, the world is witnessing the highest levels of displacement and forced statelessness on record since the start of the new millennium (United Nations 2021). From the Texas 'border wall' and ICE's imprisonment of asylum seekers in cages to the Afghan and Syrian refugee crises to Brexit and the rise of nationalist sentiments across all continents, the symbol of the alien weakened, exploited and cut-off from home is as powerful and resonant as ever.

In his preface to the *Lazarus* script (published in book form in 2016), Enda Walsh refers to Newton as 'this most travelled of immigrants'. Emma Lazarus's *The New Colossus* is reproduced in full at the end as a postscript. Like Newton, Bowie would end up feeling like an outsider in the same city. In 2003 he said that living in New York was 'a bit like being on a holiday in a place I've always wanted to go to, that doesn't come to an end. So "home" is not quite right, is it? I always feel a stranger here. I am an outsider. I really am still a Brit, there's no avoiding it' (Du Noyer 2003).

Six weeks after the terror attacks on 11 September 2001, fellow Brit Sir Paul McCartney along with a number of prominent musicians organized The Concert for New York City, a charity benefit to honour the victims, first responders and families affected by the attacks. Bowie performed at the event at Madison Square Garden, memorably starting his set with a stripped-back version of Simon & Garfunkel's 'America', sitting alone cross-legged and small on the stage floor, accompanying himself on a Suzuki Omnichord. The performance hits a bittersweet note somewhere between patriotic optimism and fragile lamentation. The *Financial Times* would further observe 'though it sounds strange to hear a tune called "America" sung in a south London accent, the song was ideally suited for an occasion, and indeed nation, caught between despair and dreams of a better future' (Einav 2018).

> In the early days, the Ellie [sic] character was called Ellie Lazarus; that was changed, but the central concept remained: *Lazarus* is of course the overall title for the situation the person is in – that transitional thing of being in purgatory and now not, a man trying to find clarity and rest.
>
> – Walsh (Trynka 2017)

The name Lazarus is associated with two stories from the New Testament. One is Jesus' parable of the 'Rich Man and Lazarus' [Luke 16:19-31]. In it, Lazarus is a desperate beggar who is spurned help by a rich man; both men die, and the tables are turned in the afterlife as the rich man is sent to hell, where he is denied relief, and Lazarus goes to paradise. The other story is of the resurrection of a dead man also named Lazarus who was a close friend of Jesus, who after four days lying dead in his tomb is revived [John 11:1-44]. These stories present ways of understanding and overcoming death; either by trusting that you will be rewarded after death (in the afterlife) for your purity of heart, and commensurate to the amount of unjust suffering you endured in life, or by the direct miraculous intervention of God themselves. Like other accounts of resurrection and the raising of the dead in holy texts, for Christians the story of Lazarus's revival (and/or eternal reward) represents a hope that death is not the end of a life. Lazarus is a bit-part player in the saviour's narrative; his resurrection is the miracle that amplifies Jesus' public notoriety, starting the chain of events that leads to his arrest and crucifixion.

Beyond religious allegorical contexts, Lazarus has become a word synonymous with resurrections, unlikely comebacks or even the artificial extension of earthly life. Sylvia Plath's poem *Lady*

Lazarus (1965) uses extended metaphors of death and resurrection to explore suicidal thoughts and considers the public spectacle that the author's personal suffering had become. While the resurrected Lazarus of the Bible was presumably pleased to be brought back, Plath's poem suggests that her resurrections are an annoyance: she would rather stay dead. The speaker frames her suffering as a form of performance and declares that 'dying is an art, like everything else'. Her deaths and resurrections are theatre, the audience must pay a ticket price to gawp at her pain: 'There is a charge/for the eyeing of my scars'.

Plath's poem subverts the usual perspective and presents death as a kindness, resurrection as a curse. Lazarus's gift of immortality is actually a misery. This concept is alluded to in Bowie and Walsh's version of *Lazarus* – one of the particulars of their Thomas Jerome Newton from the outset of the piece is that *he cannot die*. This is a new character trait for the alien that is not present in the previous texts; the film version portrayed a Newton that aged imperceptibly slowly (if at all) compared to the humans around him, though it is not clear if that is due to his maintaining the same cosmetic human disguise over a long period of time. In the book, by the time Bryce tracks Newton down to the bar in Manhattan in the last act, the Anthean is almost unrecognizable to him, now stooped and frail, blind and assisted by a nurse and cane.

In the opening few minutes of *Lazarus*, Newton expresses extreme annoyance at his inability to die: 'I'm a dying man who can't die actually ... not being able to die is a joke. A fucking terrible joke. Apologies for the f-word.' The audience is allowed to assume at first that his problem of being immortal, or at least extremely long-lived, is somehow due to his alien physiology, with other characters routinely making comments about his extraordinary youthful looks. After a while it becomes clearer to see that Newton is the one standing in the way of his own death. In situating the main character's redemptive arc within a psychological/unconscious space, *Lazarus* parallels specific approaches that were used to great effect by the British dramatist Dennis Potter in *The Singing Detective* (BBC 1986) and his final work(s) *Karaoke* and *Cold Lazarus* (BBC and Channel 4 1996).

Potter's teleplays are distinctive for their use of non-naturalistic, non-linear devices, flashbacks and delirious visions that confuse fantasy and reality. He was also known for steeping aspects of his personal life into his characters and settings. *The Singing Detective*'s protagonist was a writer who is hospitalized with chronic acute psoriatic arthropathy – Potter himself suffered from this disease and, like his lead character Philip E. Marlow (played by Michael Gambon), Potter also had to resort to writing with a pen tied to his clenched fist. Childhood flashbacks are set in the Forest of Dean, where Potter grew up, and on and on, fiction and biographical details dovetail. *The Singing Detective* sends its protagonist on a journey through medicated dreams, unresolved trauma, psychotherapy and confrontations with uncomfortable personal truths, arriving at eventual healing and wholeness. It is implied that treatment and recovery from his debilitating skin condition has been blocked by his unconscious self, which is also in grave need of healing.

The Next Day's final track, 'Heat', has thematic connections to the second episode of *The Singing Detective*, also called 'Heat', wherein the main character hallucinates scenes with his deceased father and misremembers repressed traumatic events from his childhood. According to Enda Walsh, *The Singing Detective* was a shared fascination that he and Bowie bonded over and it became a key reference in their early development of *Lazarus*, alongside Bob Fosse's semi-autobiographical musical *All That Jazz* (1979) (Hunter-Tilney 2016). The music video for the song 'Lazarus', Bowie's last, appears to reference the visual aesthetic of *The Singing Detective*'s hospital ward set.

The last two television dramas written by Potter were completed in the decline of terminal cancer, produced and broadcast posthumously nearly two years after he died. *Karaoke* and *Cold Lazarus* share a central character, Daniel Feeld (played by Albert Finney), and are connected by themes of death, resurrection and redemption. Predictably, Feeld (the character) shows many of the traits that Potter was known to possess, not only aspects of his personality and memories but also his profession and predicament: Feeld is a television writer racing against time to complete two screenplays before his terminal condition catches up with him.

As he faces the end of his natural life at the conclusion of *Karaoke*, he decides to allow his corpse to be frozen and preserved in a cryogenic facility in the hope that one day, once a cure for his illness has been found, he might be revived. *Cold Lazarus* is set 374 years in the future, where Feeld's frozen head has been installed in a science lab to be mined for authentic memories and emotions. Trapped in this future dystopia and forced to repeatedly replay the contents of his mind, it becomes evident that Feeld is aware of his situation and is begging to be put out of his misery. At the climax of the story, which also involves the machinations of various oligarchs and revolutionaries, the frozen head is mercifully destroyed along with the facility it was kept in. Feeld himself is granted a moment of transcendence as his memories play out one last time, now reversing back through his life, memories borrowed from Potter's own life, his triumphs and traumas folding in upon a clear white light.

In pulling off this remarkable feat, Potter managed to stage a resurrection of sorts, two years after his first death. A Lazarus-style comeback that allowed him to continue to work and speak from beyond the grave, stage an imagining of his ideal second death and fictively perform the closure of his public life.

Goodbye Mr. Ed

Walter Tevis's novel *The Man Who Fell to Earth* uses imagery of Icarus's fall as a metaphor of Newton's downward spiral and an overarching structural device. The opening section is 'Icarus Descending, 1985', the final one is 'Icarus Drowning, 1990'.[5] Nicolas Roeg's film adaptation similarly opens with vivid imagery inspired by Pieter Bruegel's 1560 painting *Landscape with the Fall of Icarus* – in which a man plummets to Earth from the sky, but no-one seems to notice or care amid the mundane details of everyday life. Bruegel's painting depicts a common rural scene, farmers getting on with their work completely oblivious to the Greek mythological figure barely visible, flailing in the sea in the right corner; a small detail easily missed. The painting itself is mentioned in the Tevis book in various places; Bryce often contemplates the image and, at one point, quotes Auden's poem *Musée des Beaux Arts* (1938):

Finishing the coffee, he quoted, in a soft, ritualistic voice, without any particular expression or feeling, the lines from Auden's poem about the painting:

---

[5] The dates in the 2016 edition that I consulted were updated; the original dates published in the first edition: 'Icarus Descending, 1972' and 'Icarus Drowning, 1988' (Tevis [1963] 2016).

' ... *the expensive delicate ship that must have seen*
Something amazing, a boy falling out of the sky,
Had somewhere to get to and sailed calmly on.'
            – The Man Who Fell to Earth, Tevis ([1962] 2016, 21)

A corresponding moment occurs in Roeg's film, which quotes
a different poem, *Landscape with the Fall of Icarus* by W. C.
Williams; the 'unsignificant' sound of the drowning Icarus, 'a splash
quite unnoticed' (Williams 1960). The poetic imagery suggests that
despite whatever impossible events might unfold, life continues on
with a shrug; miracles and tragedies occur every day – what can
you do? What does human aspiration amount to in the end anyway,
but a feeble splash in the ocean? The painting became meaningfully
held in Bowie's consciousness, too. In his 1994 interview with
the French artist Balthus for *Modern Painters*, they got to talking
about Bruegel's painting, with Bowie reflecting on how there is ' ...
this tiny little figure, and everybody [in the painting] is continuing
their lives as if nothing is happening. It's this momentous event. So
poignant that these monumental events will take place in our lives,
but life is totally indifferent to it all' (Bowie 1994, 22).

Someone sees it all
Icarus takes his pratfall
Bruegel on his head
            – 'Goodbye Mr. Ed', *Tin Machine II* (1991)

Saying goodbye to *Mister Ed* (a 1960s TV show about a talking
horse) could be understood as a loss of naiveté, saying goodbye
to an impossibly idealized, 'ignorance is bliss' existence. On the
popular primetime American sitcom, which ran from 1961 to 1966,
the star horse's ridiculous ability to talk was never questioned or
explained beyond a single statement made by the horse itself in the
pilot episode, 'The First Meeting': 'Don't try [to understand], it's
bigger than the both of us!' Life is peculiar, we can shrug and dismiss
what we don't understand. Some things are so big they make no
sense. Bruegel, Auden and Williams make a case for the opposite,
for taking notice of the details, especially the strange and troubling
occurrences in the margins that are difficult to comprehend.
    Bowie's song 'Goodbye Mr Ed' (*Tin Machine II* 1991)
slices together evocative folktale-style images from New York

(Andy Warhol's *Skulls* (1976) hanging in a Queens shopping mall; the ghosts of early Dutch settlers jumping to their deaths from the AT&T building), and within these lines Bowie writes in a reference to the lonely Anthean, now trapped in Manhattan after his 'pratfall'. Unlike Bruegel's painting where nobody notices these remarkable things, Bowie assures the listener that 'someone sees it all'. In *Lazarus* we learn that Valentine is the one who 'sees it all', but we, the audience, are invited to bear witness also. In the opening number, 'Lazarus', Newton compels us to look at him and we can't turn away (for nearly two hours, there is no interval). Bowie and Walsh have turned Bruegel on his head: ignore the scenery, focus only on the drowning man in the far corner, now drowning in gin in his penthouse apartment. The falling man. The choking man. The fading man. Look up there, he's in danger.

6

Lazarus

The Man Who Fell to Earth

To enjoy and make sense of *Lazarus*, the musical, you don't necessarily need to have read Walter Tevis's 1963 novel *The Man Who Fell to Earth* or have seen the 1976 film adaptation directed by Nicolas Roeg (starring David Bowie, screenplay by Paul Mayersberg), but it does help. It also helps to have an awareness of how Bowie's identity became entangled with that of a fictional extraterrestrial called Thomas Jerome Newton.

In Tevis's book, Newton is introduced as a humanoid alien from a drought-stricken nearby planet called Anthea. Its climate and implied distance from Earth (close enough to pick up satellite transmissions) suggest it is Mars by another name. We learn that Newton was selected by his people for this solo mission because of his physical strength to withstand both the journey and the heightened gravitational forces on Earth. The Anthean situation is desperate; the planet has run out of water, while its inhabitants have dwindling supplies of fuel and hardly any food. A remnant population of fewer than 300 individuals, the Anthean species faces extinction. To prepare for his mission, Newton studies human language and customs from Earth media that he can access via satellite. He is given a 'human disguise' – cosmetic eye lenses, fingernails and nipples, to hide his alien physiology, and takes with him a collection of patents for superior technology, which he can sell and build businesses with.

After surviving the trip to Earth and crash-landing in Kentucky, Newton quickly gets to work creating the fortune he needs to build a spaceship that will bring the Anthean refugees to Earth. It is not until he is seriously injured in a hotel lift incident that he must rely on the care and kindness of others. He is taken in by a lonely woman named Betty Jo, who introduces him to Earth customs like church and alcohol – the latter leading to problems as he begins to experience strange new emotions and finds his sense of clarity and purpose diminishing. He employs Nathan Bryce, a quietly suspicious academic who in time discovers the alien's true nature. Eventually, Newton ends up in the hands of government agencies that subject him to a battery of cruel tests. One of these results in Newton being accidentally blinded.

In the aftermath, the blind, alcoholic Newton, now trapped on Earth, records a message that he hopes will be broadcast and reach his people on Anthea. Bryce happens on the recording years later and tracks Newton down to a New York bar, where the defeated alien tells Bryce that he was unable to complete his mission because of his blindness and the delay brought about by his captivity (the necessary window of planetary alignment had closed). He can't save his people, nor reach his family, and he can't save himself, having now fallen prey to addiction, materialism and loneliness. Their final interaction portrays Newton in an emotionally and mentally damaged state, behaving erratically and trembling 'like an anguished bird' (Tevis [1963] 2016, 185).

Tevis's story is as much about the human condition as it is about a fictional alien. It depicts a downwards spiral of addiction, loneliness and estrangement. By putting the reader behind the eyes of a non-human entity, we are privileged to consider humanity from an outsider's point of view; Newton's internal monologue, in turn, illustrates his ambivalence, passivity and increasing emotional fragility, gradually tipping over from hope to resignation, and eventually to despair.

Roeg's 1976 film adaptation (set not in Kentucky but New Mexico, where filming took place) removes Newton's internal monologue and tells much of the story through juxtapositions of symbolic imagery and non-linear plotlines in lieu of straight dialogue. The British director's signature visual style, as seen in *Performance* (1970) and *Don't Look Now* (1973), refracts Newton's earthly experience into a sensory overload: noisy, colourful, chaotic, confusing and sometimes bafflingly mundane. Intense experiences are presented synchronously across character timelines that intercut violence and sex, performance and love, emotion, isolation and overwhelming stress. The viewer is left with questions: Does everything happen exactly in the sequence it is shown? Are some moments dreamt? If so, which of the characters is the dreamer? Roeg's impressionistic approach allows for wider themes of human hostility to difference, corporate corruption, passivity and paranoia to be rendered in ways that blur the boundaries between dream worlds, memories, different realities, timelines and points of view.

The character of Newton is slightly altered between the novel and the film. In the book, even though he was selected for the mission for his strength, on Earth he is delicate, with hollow bones that are prone to crushing by the mildest impact (e.g. by the g-forces of an accelerating car or moving lift). He doesn't engage in any sexual activity with Betty Jo, though she does make a pass at him – his obliviousness to which bruises her already battered self-esteem. In the film, Betty Jo's name is changed to Mary-Lou, and she and Newton have a physical relationship, a narrative decision that allows Roeg and Mayersberg to demonstrate inter-species difference and the characters' inability to meaningfully connect or communicate. In the film, Newton is primarily a victim of abuse, betrayals and corporate meddling; in the book it is clear that, while government forces are to blame for some of his misery, it is also due to his own apathy and a developing weakness for alcohol. Bryce and Betty Jo are also unhappy alcoholics in Tevis's book, and it is Newton's arrival in their worlds that excites them out of the doldrums and gives them a sense of purpose.

Common to both versions is the feeling that every character the alien encounters is alienated in some way. In Mayersberg's script, the book's human characters are further developed and given more complex personalities. Nate Bryce (Rip Torn) is shown not as the lonely academic of the book but as more of a selfish opportunist, edgy and brusque, preying on his young female students. Betty Jo, now Mary-Lou (Candy Clark), is still a naïve country girl who likes Jesus and gin, but is now more obviously needy and flawed, capable of being corrupting, controlling and enabling; she warns Newton that the water he sips so carefully isn't clean – better to drink gin instead. She devises ways to make Newton dependent on her and is emotionally triggered by his remoteness and failure to communicate. She transforms her look to fit into Newton's world and attract him: noticing his preference for Japanese-inspired design, she starts wearing a kimono and black wig. Her performance as the kind of woman she thinks Newton wants is mirrored by his imitation of humanity, a performance informed by what he has learnt from watching TV. Stopping their mutual performances and revealing their authentic selves has horrific implications. In a climactic scene when Newton tries to leave Mary-Lou so that he can continue with his mission, she rips her wig off and throws it at him, shouting in anger 'you alien!' In the next scene, responding to her gesture, Newton removes his human disguise and reveals his true self, and at its sight (and touch) she runs away screaming.

The film also depicts Newton's mind starting to break down as he attempts to quieten the chaotic information coming at him from his wall of televisions: 'Get out of [my] mind, all of you ... stay where you belong!' The splintering of his psyche into a multitude of different voices contrasts with the reality that Newton is totally isolated and alone in every way. As psychotherapist Don Butler notes, he has no helpers in his quest: 'No archetypal Wise Old Man or Magician ... he is allowed no Yoda or Obi Wan' (Butler 2016). Newton is homeless, friendless, substance-addicted and trapped in a performance of something he doesn't really understand.

Bowie's performance as the alien hinges on a subtle portrayal of disconnect, discomfort and distress; a catalogue of mannerisms to show a studied awareness of what human life and interaction should look like – affectations studied from TV – but missing a vital core knowledge of being. It is a performance of a performance. Bowie's casting not only capitalized on his by then already established 'alien' brand and otherworldly beauty, it also tapped the performative 'not quite human' aura that was present in his interactions with the media around that time, notably seen in the awkward television interviews with Russell Harty (1973 and 1975) and Dick Cavett (1974). Roeg later said the reason Bowie was so successful playing the role was because he was essentially playing himself: 'We really didn't need to talk about the role at all; he was the part the moment he stepped on to the set ... So much of that performance is simply Bowie being himself – and that's what's so brilliant about it!' (Fear 2011, 34).

After filming, Bowie had a hard time shaking Newton from his system. His next two albums, *Station to Station* (1976) and *Low* (1977), explore themes of emotional detachment, psychic isolation and personal distress, while the cover art for both are photographs taken from the film set. These too are the records most associated with Bowie's personal battles with drug addiction and poor mental health in the 1970s. The timing of the film's shoot in mid-1975, leading up to the production of 1976's *Station to Station*, coincided with the peak of Bowie's drug and alcohol addiction and subsequent descent into cocaine psychosis and occult-fuelled paranoia. While living in LA, he would spend his time indoors out of his mind on high-grade pharmaceutical cocaine, decorating the walls of his rented Bel Air house with occult symbols and suffering terrifying waking visions of the devil.

Photographer Steve Schapiro documented this period, capturing Bowie on set and off – memorably with a marathon overnight shoot involving a number of different costume changes (Schapiro 2016). One of these costumes was deceptively simple: dark slacks, socks and matching cropped shirt, all crudely painted with parallel diagonal white stripes. Bowie posed with his notebooks and next to scribbles on the wall and floor of the mystical Kabbalistic Tree of Life diagram; he also performed the 'flying eagle' and, in another photo, stood rigidly in the style of the *Kroisos Kouros*:[1] left foot forward, clenched fists held tight and close to the body. Bowie would reference this costume and stance in his final music video, 'Lazarus' (2015).

Lazarus pre-production

Even though the touchpaper was lit at their lunch meeting in London's Savoy hotel in the summer of 2013, both Robert Fox and Bowie had busy schedules for the remainder of the year. Bowie was finishing up in the studio for *The Next Day Extra* and filming the music videos for the remaining singles ('Valentine's Day', 'Love Is Lost'); Fox also had his hands full with the premiere of the Lloyd Webber flop *Stephen Ward*, in addition to developing a revival of

---

[1] The *Kroisos Kouros* is a marble kouros sculpture from Anavyssos in Attica, Athens, dated to c. 540–515 BC. Kouros statues typically portray nude male figures in a symbolic stance. They were used as grave markers for dead heroes. The cover of the album *Tin Machine II* featured four repeated representations of the statue, one for each member of the band.

David Hare's *Skylight* (2014) and a new work by Irish playwright Martin McDonagh (*Hangmen* 2015). He was also commencing work as an executive producer on Peter Morgan's Netflix series *The Crown* (2016–22). Progress on *Lazarus* would begin gaining momentum in early 2014 once Bowie had met with the Irish playwright that would become his collaborator and co-writer, Enda Walsh (*Disco Pigs* 1996, *The Walworth Farce* 2006, *Hunger* 2008, *Once* 2011).

According to Walsh, their first meeting in January had the air of a 'proper interview' (Hunter-Tilney 2016). Bowie handed him a four-page outline for a new story based on *The Man Who Fell to Earth*, sketching out the scenario and three new characters that were tangled up in Newton's story – a woman who thinks she might be Emma Lazarus (the poet), a murderer called Valentine and a Girl that may or may not be a soul trapped in limbo. Bowie's outline contained the basic curve of the plot: with his situation deteriorating, Newton builds a spacecraft out of the debris of his isolation and makes one last attempt to leave Earth.

Building on that outline, Walsh said that the pair 'began to talk about death ... about morphine. How the brain would wrestle with itself or what it would see in the moments before death. [Bowie said:] "Can we structure something about that?"' (Hunter-Tilney 2016). They talked about the psychotherapeutic noir of Dennis Potter's *The Singing Detective* and Bob Fosse's cinematic ode to mortality *All That Jazz* (1979). 'We discussed drugs and the drunken state a lot. How to construct something and place it behind the eyes of someone who is totally out of it. The film does it so brilliantly. We thought, we can do that on stage, too' (ibid.). Bowie gave Walsh a catalogue of sixty-nine songs to choose from and then tasked him with coming up with a first draft. In choosing the songs to be included from Bowie's catalogue, Walsh opted for feeling and 'emotional correctness' over narrative sense, an approach possibly also inspired by *The Singing Detective*'s sometimes jarring use of popular song to suggest different mental states within the protagonist's reverie (McCarthy 2017).

Belgian theatre director Ivo van Hove, known for his Brecht-inspired multimedia approach, initially ignored a message from Robert Fox about the project because he thought it had to be a prank. After seeing the working script in July, he felt compelled to take it on, despite being committed to directing two other projects

(*The Crucible* and *A View from the Bridge*) at the same time. He told *The New York Times* that he felt a personal affinity with the play and its themes, which also recur frequently in his own work – stories about outsiders and lonely people 'who can't make the compromises that society demands' (Soloski 2015a).

Henry Hey, who had recently worked with Bowie on *The Next Day*, was hired as musical director and tasked with adapting Walsh's song choices for the stage show. Bowie worked closely with Hey on these new arrangements, swapping files over email and exploring musical ideas in person at Hey's East Village apartment, often coming over straight after the ★ sessions at the Magic Shop studios a few blocks away[2] (ibid.). Hey spoke to me about their collaborative process:

> We were batting music ideas back and forth … Some of the stuff that he quickly scraped together for the demos inspired what I put into the arrangements – some of it felt great and had a gritty quality that I wanted to keep. The spirit of the collaboration was very much, 'Ok, this is what I'm after', and once things had started off, I was given freedom to run with it.
> – Hey (interview with the author, 2020)

A workshop was scheduled in New York in December to read and play through the material; stand-in actors were hired, all of whom were required to sign NDAs (Perkins 2019). Just prior to the event, Fox, Walsh, van Hove and Hey were informed that Bowie was unwell and receiving treatment for cancer. Over Skype, he apologized for his necessary absence and asked them to 'crack on with it' (Trynka 2016). From this point the production comes together quickly: *Dexter* star Michael C. Hall is recruited in January 2015 just as he is finishing his Broadway run as Hedwig; the show is announced by the New York Theatre Workshop press office in April; a casting call is posted in May, with auditions in June and rehearsals starting in October. Joining Hall as Thomas Jerome Newton are the other leads in the three new character roles from Bowie's original four-page

---

[2] McCaslin: 'He didn't even tell us about *Lazarus* until sometime near the end of the process … The ironic thing is Henry Hey is a friend of mine. We were both working with Bowie at the same time, unbeknownst to each other' (Greene 2016).

outline: Elly (Emma Lazarus), to be played by Cristin Milioti (*Once*, *Palm Springs*), fourteen-year-old Sophia Anne Caruso as Girl and Michael Esper (*American Idiot*, *The Last Ship*) as Valentine.

Details about the production and plot were kept under wraps and associate producer Zelda Perkins, working for Robert Fox, was concerned about how the show could be marketed effectively on such little information: 'We had strict instructions from David that we should not give an outline of the story or music to the press … Even the artwork for the production was mysterious … he emphatically chose the most obscure image that revealed almost nothing' (Perkins 2019). As it happened, the tickets sold out within a few hours of going on sale on 7 October.

Lazarus opened at the off-Broadway New York Theatre Workshop on Monday 7 December 2015. Bowie was in attendance and joined in the curtain call with the cast. Smiling broadly, and clasping hands with van Hove and Milioti, he took his last, long bow from the stage. It was his final public appearance.

Lazarus (dir. Ivo van Hove)

New York Theatre Workshop, 7 December 2015 to 20 January 2016. A London production of the play ran at the temporarily erected King's Cross Theatre from 8 November 2016 to 22 January 2017.

As the audience files into the venue, Thomas Jerome Newton is already on stage, lying motionless as if asleep or dead on the ground. He is half covered by a thin blanket and dressed in nondescript beige clothes that could be pyjamas. Versweyveld's stage, bare except for the unmade bed to the far left, is illuminated by a dim light from an open fridge on the far right, filled with rows of gin bottles. Next to the fridge, on the floor, is a record player with Bowie vinyl stacked against the wall – *Low*, *"Heroes"*, *The Next Day* and more. Two large glass windows on either side of a tall, centrally positioned video screen are dressed in beige curtains; on the other side of the glass, the seven-piece band can be seen. The largely empty set looks like a minimally decorated loft apartment and also kind of like a face, everything skin-coloured neutral, the windows like eyes, the video screen the nose. On to this set other characters will come and go, some who appear to be real and others not, and hallucinatory visions will swirl and overwhelm, but Newton will stay present and confined to this space for the full duration, raging, cowering, clashing for nearly two hours without a break. At the show's conclusion, he assumes exactly the same position in the middle of the floor as when he started.

At the start of the play Newton is visited by an old business associate named Michael, who apologizes for not checking in on him more regularly – a conversation that establishes the updated context of Newton's life: he's shut in, haunted by memories of his family, does not appear to be ageing, is still an alcoholic and still thinks about Mary-Lou. We meet Elly, who appears to be Newton's new personal assistant, though she is only ever seen preparing food or making his bed. Somehow Newton can see or imagine her private life, the awkward conversations and strained intimacy she has with her husband Zach, and her crisis of identity, purpose and self-esteem, which becomes a subplot that Newton observes in the peripheries of his own ordeal.

The screen in the middle of the stage periodically comes to life with bright colours, slow-motion memories, live action out of sync and images of characters that emerge from behind it on to the stage. An apparition of a Japanese woman in full geisha costume emerges for 'It's No Game (Part 1)'. A troupe of teenage girls dressed stylishly in dark colours function as a Greek chorus, witnessing, commenting on and sometimes controlling the action. Their purpose remains a mystery to Newton; they could be covert operatives manipulating him, angels or ghosts, or simply figments of his paranoid imagination.

From this place also emerges the character billed as Girl, a pale blonde early-teen dressed in a pale lace dress, who possesses uncanny knowledge of Newton's true identity and past. At first, she doesn't know where she is or why she has been sent (singing 'This Is Not America' and 'No Plan'), though it is suggested that she might be the soul of a murder victim stuck in limbo.[3] At other times it appears that she is working for the mysterious group of girls.

---

[3] A scene featuring a video projection cameo by Alan Cumming as her murderer was later cut from the London production and is not included in the script.

GIRL. So what do we do exactly?
TEENAGE GIRL 1. It's a lot of showin' up and listenin'.
TEENAGE GIRL 2. They're all a bit messed up and tortured
and stuff – but you figure things out for them and give them
hope. Then you get to leave once the work is finished.
(Bowie and Walsh 2016, 15)

Valentine, an intense and emotionally unstable man dressed in
black, appears in Michael's apartment and kills him (maybe not,
the character later gets up and exits the scene) while Valentine
sings 'Love Is Lost'. According to Hey, the dramatic 'dun dun dun'
motif added to the song's introduction and bridge was a musical
detail Bowie insisted on; a moment that foregrounds Valentine as
the pantomime villain of the piece. Elly's subplot develops as she
becomes drawn to Newton and transforms herself into a vision of
Mary-Lou, wearing a blue wig and matching silk dress ('Changes').
She makes a pass at him, as in the book, but is rejected (during
ensemble piece 'Absolute Beginners'). Later, she admits that she was
acting on a fantasy and was just trying to escape her ordinary life:
' ... [it was] not a real love, I know – but madness only. And yet I
don't want my old life back – 'cause to lose "the her" that is still
here might lose me a possibility of a new life. It's a new life I want'
(Bowie and Walsh 2016, 38). She has a frightening interaction with
Valentine in her desperation to be 'surrounded by love', which
ultimately leads to a reconciliation with her husband, who forgives
her ('Always Crashing in the Same Car').
Valentine is on the trail of Newton like a detective, clutching
a torn photograph and asking various characters how he can get
closer to him, leading to a confrontation in the main apartment
that triggers Newton's fury ('Killing a Little Time'). Meanwhile Girl
devises a plan to build a rocket using items from the apartment so
that Newton can finally leave Earth; this takes form as an outline on
the floor made with strips of masking tape. She stands at the glass
window, reaches towards the sky and sings a bittersweet version of
'Life on Mars?'.
Valentine, now loose in Newton's world, antagonizes a loved-
up couple (Ben and Maemi, 'All the Young Dudes') and kills again
while Newton looks on in horror. He is dramatically revealed as
a force of darkness, large black wings of inky smoke unfurling on

the wall behind him as he dances downstage with his bloody knife, plunging the entire theatre into blackout ('Valentine's Day'). The teenage girls emerge with their own knives and stab at a multitude of black balloons that have filled the space, creating a jarring, startling noise like the sound of machine-gun fire.

In the climax of the show it emerges that for Girl to escape limbo she must be killed properly, and Valentine hands Newton the knife ('When I Met You'). Together they push the knife into Girl's body, and she falls to the floor. Something that appears to be milk (or alien blood, or amniotic fluid) seeps from underneath her body, covering the stage floor. Newton kneels over her limp body and delivers a fractured soliloquy:

> NEWTON.   And I'm not of this world. And not yet marked by this place here. Not pinned down in this apartment – not divided into days and praying for my death – and bullied by this broken mind – and before all of this happened to me – and before the journey down here – to wake in the place I was born. And to be up there – and to feel the simple love of family. To be back there in that home – my sad past... rewritten now. (*Slight pause.*) Because my daughter wakes. (*Slight pause.*) Wake up. (*Slight pause.*) One last time, wake up, wake up. Wake up. (*Slight pause.*) And half-asleep and her arms about her brother – she talks his dream from him and keeps him in that sweet unreal place. (60)

Girl awakes and remembers that her name is Marley. Talking to Newton, she reminisces about Anthea and he speaks to her as if she is his daughter. They play together while singing a subdued minor key arrangement of '"Heroes"'. With the words 'I wish you could swim, like the dolphins' they slide around on their stomachs through the milk-like puddles and laugh. At the end of the song Marley rolls Newton over into his original position on the ground, now within the shape of the masking tape rocket, a coffin surrounding his form. As she exits the stage in darkness, an overhead camera projecting Newton onto the tall screen shows him to finally be at rest as his rocket takes off to the stars.

In the hands of van Hove and designer Versweyveld, *Lazarus* is a violent and grubby show. As the action progresses there are

marks and stains that gather and remain – greasy handprints on
the glass, detritus and markings left on the floor, strewn laundry,
milk and blood, tears and sweat and spit that collects on the
characters' clothes, gets in their hair and stays on their faces. By
the end, Valentine is splattered in gore and Newton is soaking
wet like a newborn. The integration of video projections, which
utilize both the main central screen as well as the whole stage area,
bathe the environment in sudden, strange imagery – at one point
Newton seems to be transported to Berlin; in another scene, as he
tears up the set in fury, the apartment projects the same occurrence
obviously recorded at a different time, playing out of sync with the
real action. The video-projected elements clash and juxtapose in
meaningful ways against the neutral-toned set in a similar way to
Roeg's film, making use of surreal imagery and colour to suggest
altered states and the slide between fantasy, reality and paranoia,
and to imply intense sensations and extreme emotions.

Annie-B Parson's choreography is tactile and brute: characters are
thrown around and onto beds, pinned against walls, held by their
necks, dragged by their limbs; they slump in defeat against fridges
and cower in dark corners. When Zelda Perkins saw the first dress
rehearsal, she recalled how these troubling and 'discombobulating'
details were clearly to 'Bowie's absolute design and delight':

> His eyes were ablaze and he immediately started talking
> excitedly about what we had just witnessed ... Did I like the new
> arrangements of his songs? What did I think of the choreography?
> Wasn't it marvellously tangled and surprising?
>
> – Perkins (2019)

Lazarus is intense and, at times, even difficult to watch. It
deliberately disorients and tests its audience, not only in the
sense that the plot is challenging to follow (especially in a cold,
first viewing) but also in the way that it swiftly pivots between
pantomime humour and brutality, hazy dream logic and moments
of shocking realism, stopping periodically along the way for a song-
and-dance version of a well-known Bowie tune. The presence of
violence and masochism in Bowie's artistry is not unusual, nor is
his abstraction of it via stylized performance; his most theatrical
rock shows, the *Diamond Dogs* and *Glass Spider* tours, included
aggressive choreography that portrayed the artist variously being

tied up with ropes, assaulted by gangs and thrown around like a rag doll. However, the violence in *Lazarus* is directed in such a way that it lacks the camp and obvious artifice of a David Bowie rock show experience; now situated within a fraught, tense narrative, and put in the hands of skilled dramatic actors, the depictions of violence create an atmosphere of terror.

The cruelty that those on stage must endure, particularly the two main female characters, Elly and Girl/Marley, is another troubling aspect of the production. In grappling with the female suffering and sacrifice written into *Lazarus*, we still have the taste of *The Next Day*'s violence in our mouths – not least because the darkest character in the show, Valentine, performs only songs from *The Next Day* as he perpetrates his crimes: 'Love Is Lost', 'Dirty Boys' and 'Valentine's Day'. Valentine's villainy is clearly announced as archetypal within the context of the play, which raises the suggestion that other main characters might also be visionary figments from Newton's fragmented psyche, drawn from the heightened representations of humanity he has studied from films and TV, and the experience of his own traumatic relationships.

'Lazarus'

Song 1 in the musical (2015, 3'39"). Track 2 sung by Michael C. Hall and company, track 20 sung by David Bowie, *Lazarus (Original Cast Recording)* (2016, 6'24"). David Bowie version also included on ★ (track 3, 2016, 6'22") and the *No Plan* EP (track 1, 2016, 6'24").

Tempo: *Lazarus* OST version 63bpm; Bowie version 65bpm.
Tonality: A minor.
Song form: AABA (verses, bridge).

'Lazarus' is the first musical number of the show. It starts just after Michael's visit and his context-establishing conversation with Newton. It follows a basic AABA (ballad) form, only with no repeated material; every A section contains a melodic variation that escalates in pitch and intensity.

Henry Hey's arrangement of 'Lazarus', as it was based on Bowie's original demo, sounds different to the ★ version that

was elaborated on by McCaslin's band.[4] In both the show and
★ versions, the introduction sets a descending saxophone figure
against a rising lead guitar bend, a downcast slump followed by a
lift that straightens back up again. Hey's arrangement leads with
bluesy Wurlitzer keys in front of a solid, loud rhythm section;
Michael C. Hall's vocal is supported at times by the chorus of
Teenage Girls. Bowie's ★ version (which also appears on the *No
Plan* EP and at the end of the *Lazarus (Original Cast Recording)*) is
nearly three minutes longer than the show version, with an extended
30 seconds of intro and an extra 2'10" added to the end with a sax
solo by McCaslin and an outro that reprises the opening textures.
An improvised picked bass solo by Tim Lefebvre shifts in restless
8th notes (inspired by The Cure and British band Fink (Johnson
2016b)). Bowie performs an extra guitar layer that is not present in
the show version, the jagged power chord slide from G to A.[5]

The A sections have a chord progression that oscillates between
i (A minor) and VI (F). Within these repetitions, the melody climbs
up the minor chord, its tonal frame like a barred cage inside which
the vocal pushes against.

A1 (verse 1) is centred around the tonic note (A). A2 begins
higher, in the middle of the A minor chord – on C, feeling more
precarious. The B section (bridge) shifts tonal focus to the relative
major, posturing with its dominant 7th shapes around C7 and D7.
The melody climbs higher again, to the top of the triad with an E.
In Bowie's performance, this rides the edge of his vocal break. In
the recapitulation to A3, the song moves back to the minor i-VI
progression (A minor – F), but now the melody is left stranded in
the top register, maintaining the same intensity. In the musical the

---

[4] Henry Hey told me that, of the four new compositions for *Lazarus*, 'No Plan'
and 'Lazarus' (known originally as 'The Hunger') were completed in late 2014,
their arrangements based only on Bowie's demos; those for 'Killing a Little Time'
and 'When I Met You' incorporate elements from the versions recorded in the ★
sessions in early 2015. This is why the alternate versions of the 2014 tracks sound so
different, and those of the 2015 tracks so alike.
[5] Similar guitar figures also performed by Bowie: 'Plan' (*The Next Day Extra*) and
the alternative 'Blackstar' edit for the opening credits of *The Last Panthers* (dir. Johan
Renck). Pegg (2016) points out that the 'Lazarus' guitar overdubs were performed
on the Fender Stratocaster that Marc Bolan gave to him after the taping of their
appearance together on the *Marc* show on 7 September 1977. Bolan died in a car
accident nine days later.

FIGURE 6.1 *'Lazarus', melodic structure ascending through the tonic triad with each section. Tonic triads shown with smaller note heads.*

song ends here. The ★ version continues with an elaboration of the song's themes: McCaslin's saxophone solo that simmers, gains momentum, takes flight, struggles and then plummets back down to earth. After the crash, the opening section is reprised with elements disappearing in the order they entered.

The lyrics set out the stakes for Newton and what will unfold in *Lazarus*: 'This way or no way/you know I'll be free'. It also foreshadows some of the imagery in the lyrics to the show's last song, '"Heroes"'; where he sings of his past glory in 'Lazarus' ('I was living like a king'), in the finale the words are future-facing, even in the face of death: 'I, I will be king'. The reference to scars and unstealable drama in the first verse could be read as a nod to Sylvia Plath's *Lady Lazarus*, where the concept of personal suffering is presented as theatre. There is a play on the word 'high'. The man 'up there' at risk of falling to earth from a great height could be a suicidal man about to jump, someone who's dropped his phone over the edge by accident, he couldn't call for help if he tried – he's completely on his own. He could be high on drugs, brain whirling, stranded in his altered state, connecting back to Bowie's own substance abuse crisis in 1975, the era when Bowie physically embodied the character of Newton on film. Connecting to (then) present-day Bowie is the song's setting high up in a New York penthouse – his family home, a rooftop apartment in downtown Soho, just four blocks away from the New York Theatre Workshop.

Freedom from this dangerous predicament is embodied by the image of the bluebird, a symbol rich with signification. Bluebirds and swallows represent good luck to sailors and are common tattoos for seamen who clock up 10,000 miles at sea. A harbinger of happiness (the 'bluebird of happiness' as a common idiom), the bluebird is referenced in Harold Arlen and Yip Harburg's song 'Over the Rainbow' from *The Wizard of Oz* (1939), the melody of which Bowie had lightly plagiarized in the chorus of 'Starman' (1972). Before Bowie signed up to play the part of Newton in Roeg's film, it was reported that he might co-star with Elizabeth Taylor in George Cukor's film *The Blue Bird* (1976). It could also refer obliquely to British speed racer Donald Campbell, who broke several water and land speed records in the 1950s and 1960s with his space-age Bluebird cars and boats. Like Newton, Campbell built a special rocket powered vehicle (the Bluebird Mach 1.1) that never made it to launch day; he died in 1967 in an accident while attempting to break his own water speed record. A more banal reference could simply be to Bowie's favoured microphone, the Bluebird SL large-diaphragm condenser mic. According to Visconti, this was the microphone that he used to record all of the vocals on ★, brought in from his home-studio setup.

Bowie's 1968 mime piece *Jetsun and the Eagle* was performed against a backing tape of 'Silly Boy Blue' (*David Bowie* 1967). An early song about the mistakes of a young Buddhist monk that get in the way of his rebirth and ascension, there are lines that resonate with 'Lazarus' and its bluebird imagery: 'You've tried so hard to fly, you'll never leave your body now you've got to wait to die'. It was one of the songs Bowie had planned to revive for the unreleased *Toy* project in 2000 (he also performed it live in 2001 at the Tibet House benefit concert at Carnegie Hall).

Tevis's book closes on the image of the alien like an anguished bird, frail and trapped. As punishment for his failure and weakness, Newton must now forever hide his true self and, like Charles

Bukowski in his poem *Bluebird* (1992), keep his vulnerabilities hidden from view. To grant freedom to Bukowski's hidden bluebird is to be openly vulnerable and brave, to allow the child in you to exist. The through-line of *Lazarus* is that Newton will eventually allow himself to be vulnerable and childlike again, playing with Girl and building the rocket ship out of rubbish, allowing himself to hope in something implausible. He finds a kind of happiness in remembering he is a father and rediscovers 'the simple joys of family' that he was openly longing for in the conversation with Michael during the opening moments of the play.

On stage during 'Lazarus', Newton at one point presses his body against one of the glass windows, his fingers leaving greasy smudges that remain visible for the rest of the play; a reminder that Newton remains a trapped creature in this place. Henry Hey revealed that an early title for this composition was 'The Hunger' (Trynka 2016). This is most likely a reference to the 1983 Tony Scott film that Bowie starred in alongside Susan Sarandon and Catherine Deneuve, adapted from the 1981 Whitley Strieber novel of the same name. In *The Hunger*, Bowie plays John Blaylock, a human-turned-vampire companion to an ancient, more powerful vampire named Miriam (Deneuve). While her blood grants John a kind of immortality, he is fated to eventually rapidly age, his body becoming a desiccated corpse while he yet remains conscious. Miriam can't bear to put her lovers out of their deathless misery, so she stashes them in steel coffins in the attic of her New York apartment. John is kept there alongside all of Miriam's former paramours from throughout time, trapped and moaning in their eternal suffering. Just like John, Newton is in danger of being stuck in an existence that is no better than an eternal living death. What both characters crave is a peaceful end. A way out of their cages.

The official music video for 'Lazarus' uses a shorter edit (4'05") of Bowie's version of the song. It was shot in November 2015 directed by Johan Renck, who also helmed the video for 'Blackstar' (the first single from ★, shot in September and released on 19 November 2015). Lazarus was ★'s second single released ahead of the album, coming out on 17 December 2015, but the video appeared later on 7 January 2016, three days before Bowie died.

In an interview filmed for Francis Whately's BBC documentary *David Bowie: The Last Five Years* (2017), Renck revealed that, while he knew Bowie was unwell, during the filming of 'Lazarus' he was unaware that Bowie had just been informed his condition was terminal: 'I found out later that, the week we were shooting, it was when he was told it was over, they were ending treatments.'

The video begins with a shot of a hand emerging from an ornate wooden wardrobe, then establishes the setting: a drab, hospital room with a tiled wall. The choice to present the video in a square 1:1 aspect ratio achieves an uncomfortable closeness in the crowded central imagery, as well as a frustrating obstruction; we are denied a measure of contextualizing information and lateral detail. Bowie is shown lying in a solitary sick bed. His eyes are bandaged and it is clear from his gestures that he is anxious, gripping the blanket tightly to his chest. The costume Bowie wears is a reprisal of the Button Eyes character from the 'Blackstar' video (covered in more detail in chapter eight). Now reclining in his hospital cot, in this cold, desaturated, medicalized setting, Button Eyes's bandages take on new, disturbing associations: the treatment of wounds, echoes of the staged mutilations and blindings of Austrian performance artist Rudolf Schwarzkogler's *3rd Action* photographs (1965).

Renck is on the record as saying it was his idea to revive the Button Eyes imagery from 'Blackstar' (Pegg 2016, 153), which implies that the association of the terrified, blinded character with that of 'Lazarus' (and, by extension, Newton and Bowie) was not originally part of the plan. And yet the image of Lazarus with bandaged eyes seems to exist already as a minor character from a short story by painter and writer Leonora Carrington.[6] *White Rabbits* was written in 1941 during a period of personal transition after she had just arrived in New York. In this macabre urban fairytale, the protagonist encounters a strange married couple who feed rotten meat to their pet rabbits and appear to have skin made of stardust:

As the woman's torchlight touched his face I saw he had identical glittering skin, like tinsel on a Christmas tree … The woman followed my gaze and chuckled: 'That is my husband. The boys

---

[6] Being interested in surrealist art, Bowie would have been aware of her work, which explores Jungian and dream symbolism and weaves pivotal autobiographical detail into renderings of the fantastical. Carrington was the only British-born woman included in the Surrealist scene from the 1930s and was one of the movement's last surviving members.

used to call him Lazarus.' At the sound of this familiar name, he turned his face towards us and I saw that he wore a bandage over his eyes.

(Carrington [1941] 2018, 8)

There is another character in the 'Lazarus' music video, a monster under the bed. The menacing presence, appearing like an angel of death, is played by dancer Elke Luyten (who choreographed the movements on both 'Lazarus' and 'Blackstar', and appears in the 'Blackstar' video, too). When we see her under the desk, she breaks the fourth wall, performing Bowie's familiar 'shh!' gesture, suggesting not only the obvious narrative – that she is silently sneaking up on her prey – but also alluding to other secrets embedded in the video. She points and gestures with tensed fingers towards the figure, threatening to pull him down below. Seemingly in response, he begins to rise, helplessly levitating from the bed. At the peak melodic point when he sings 'this way or no way', his arms are outstretched as if he is pinned down in the air by an unseen force. The gesture echoes Chris Burdon's crucifixion pose, as seen in *Trans-Fixed* (1974), a photograph of the performance artist nailed to a Volkswagen car (who Bowie references in the lyric to 'Joe the Lion' ("*Heroes*" 1977)), as well as the 'flying eagle'.

In the bridge of the song another Bowie character appears, now without bandages, stood in front of the wardrobe. And he's dressed in familiar garb; a deliberate reference to the Tree of Life and the kouros-inspired Schapiro images from 1975, Bowie's costume is all black, with white stripes painted diagonally across the front of his body. The crude stripes have been incorporated into Bowie's costumes at other points in his career, notably on the *Glass Spider* and *Outside* tours. It has been suggested (in online fan discourse) that the lines could relate to the concept of silver cords – the tethers that can supposedly be observed wrapped around and trailing behind the astral body of a person who is travelling between dimensions (Crookall 1981, 49). An interesting clue emerged when the *David Bowie Is* exhibition arrived at its final stop in Brooklyn: prototype sketches of Button Eyes and a drawing of a male figure dressed in black covered in the characteristic white stripes, stood in the kouros pose, with the scribbled caption 'Somnambulist for Lazarus video'. Underneath, Bowie's signature is dated 2015 and decorated with a tiny rocket motif drawn in a similar style to the masking tape rocket that Newton uses to 'travel home' at the end of the play.

The identification of the mysterious striped Bowie costume as the sleepwalker connects the image to the character of Cesare the somnambulist (played by Conrad Veidt) from the German expressionist silent horror film *The Cabinet of Dr. Caligari* (1920), a favourite of Bowie's and an identifiable visual reference in his work elsewhere (Morley 2016). The wooden wardrobe of 'Lazarus' already looks similar to the cabinet in which Cesare is kept in the 1920 film, from which he emerges to deliver his dire predictions of future events. Cesare's costume is black from head to toe, form-fitting, with dusty white lines crisscrossing the front of his body. The unusually stiff way that Bowie's somnambulist moves also seems to be inspired by Veidt's idiosyncratic physical embodiment of the original character. The presence of a person asleep and dreaming is a motif that connects back to the play, specifically the troubling visions that emerge from our hero's final reckoning with the unconscious. As Newton is visited by his own terrifying shadow in his final dream, the reappearance of Bowie's intrepid astral somnambulist from 1975 could be representative of a dark side of himself that also must be overcome.

Bowie's somnambulist sits down at a wooden writing desk, on which sits the jewel-encrusted skull from the 'Blackstar' video. The scenes at the desk recall similar imagery from *Heathen*'s inner sleeve (Klinko and Indrani 2002), which depict Bowie sitting at a wooden desk, pen in hand, notebook open, seemingly waiting for creativity to strike. Both of these images could have taken their inspiration from historical artistic representations of *St Jerome in his Study* by Renaissance artists Antonello da Messina (completed *c.* 1475), Albrecht Dürer (1514) and Joos Van Cleve (1528), all examples of a style of art prefiguring the genre of memento mori.[7] The artworks depict the saint, a fifth-century priest and scholar known for his early translations of the Bible from the original Greek and Hebrew texts into Latin, working at his desk in absolute concentration. In his study he is surrounded by objects symbolizing transience and death.

---

[7] Memento mori is a Latin phrase meaning 'remember you must die'. A memento mori painting would usually be a portrait with a skull included prominently in the scene.

Back in the video, at his desk Bowie suddenly receives the flash of inspiration that he was waiting for in 2002. He starts to write furiously in his notebook. He can't get the words down quickly enough: his writing runs off the paper, on to the desk and down to the floor. He's running out of time. In the closing moments, Bowie rises from his desk and begins to edge backwards in stiff movements towards the wardrobe. He gets into it and closes the door behind him.

> Somebody on set said, 'You should end the video by disappearing into the closet.' And I saw David sort of think about that for a second. Then a big smile came up on his face. And he said something like, 'Yeah, that will keep them all guessing, won't it?'
> – Renck (Hiatt 2016b)

'Lazarus' is a pin that holds Newton and Bowie together as a single entity, and the video draws attention to the last time their identities converged in 1975. Lyrically steeped in Bowie myth, and explicitly part of the play's fictional narrative world, it is a way for both Newton and Bowie to charge a ticket price for the viewing of their scars. It fulfils Bowie's ambitions not only to create a unique kind of musical theatre but also to finally underscore Newton's story with his own soundtrack. While holding definitive meanings ambiguously out of reach, the music and the story actively invite the audience to conflate this version of Newton with Bowie himself. It dares us to wonder if the piece could work as well without the artist's death to provide both the compelling critical context and final theatrical flourish.

Reviews after the New York Theatre Workshop's press night were mixed, though the majority were generous in spirit. Many expressed their bafflement at the obtuse and at times contradictory plot, and the song choices that didn't neatly relate to the action on stage. 'Unapologetically weird ... almost incomprehensible and oddly intriguing' (Soloski 2015b); 'Great-sounding, great-looking and mind-numbing' (Brantley 2015); 'A work of blistering nihilism, no small sum of inscrutable foolishness... ' (Gerard 2015). Kory Grow gave one of the rare rave reviews for *Rolling Stone*: 'A surrealistic tour de force ... At its core, *Lazarus* is a two-hour meditation on grief and lost hope (with no intermission), but it takes so many wild, fantastical, eye-popping turns that it never drags' (Grow 2015). My friends and I were among the audience in attendance that opening week and we were similarly dumbfounded. Our opinions were split on whether it was a real success. Fans of Bowie shows had purchased their tickets expecting to experience something like a gig; theatre fans had purchased theirs expecting a coherent narrative experience. After-show discussions spilled from the theatre to the street and into the local bars and coffee houses as perplexed and discombobulated fans attempted to process what they had just seen. Something dark and confusing, heartbreaking and hard to take in.

In the aftermath, those involved in the project attempted to help its audience understand that *Lazarus* was not a regular jukebox musical. Michael C. Hall would refer to it in public as a 'piece' that was deliberately complex: '[*Lazarus*] is not that straightforward a piece ... but then again neither is that [referring to Roeg's film]' (Johnson 2016a). Ivo van Hove told *The Guardian* that Bowie himself referred to the piece as 'a play with my music' (Kellaway 2016). Enda Walsh would tell attendees at the 2017 Dublin David Bowie Festival that the 'shitstorm' of ideas in *Lazarus* was by design: '[The story has] been infused with morphine ... it barely hangs together. The idea was to make something that's a bit messier and scrappier' (McCarthy 2017).

In 2016, as the show was being prepared for its London run, Walsh reflected on his experience working on *Lazarus* with Bowie: 'There were times, especially later on, when it became very personal, for both of us. I'll never have that experience with a collaborator again – to be working thematically on something he was going through himself' (Stanford 2016). The project turned out to be a personal 'masked autobiography' for Ivo van Hove also, though he chooses to keep his mask on:

> I do think the show will make even more sense now than it ever has ... I give it all as Bowie gave it all – in a masked way. I have called my productions masked autobiographies. They say something about how I feel, what I am afraid of, what I am hoping for ... this is a very personal production but I cannot give it all away.
>
> – van Hove (Kellaway 2016)

7

The next bardo

'Look in his eyes and see your reflection
Look to the stars and see his eyes'
– 'SHADOW MAN' (BOWIE 1971)

The *Bardo Thodol*, known in the West as *The Tibetan Book of the Dead*, is a guide for Buddhists navigating the transitional states between death and the next rebirth. It's taken from a larger collection of teachings known as the *Profound Dharma of Self-Liberation through the Intention of the Peaceful and Wrathful Ones*, divulged by the Tibetan *tertön* (a teacher, or discoverer) Karma Lingpa (1326–86). These transitional states – bardos – are categories of experiences that a person's consciousness must travel through, divided into three stages: the moment of death (*chikhai bardo*, also the 'painful moment of dying'), the experiencing of reality (*chonyid bardo*, the 'vision of the wrathful deities') and the karmic event of becoming (*sidpa bardo* or 'of seeking rebirth') (Holocek 2013). The purpose of these experiences (and others, for it gets suitably complex) is to assist in the transformation of an individual's consciousness, often via the dramatic display of psychic hallucinatory projections, in order to purge one's excessive karmic content ahead of the next life. How to achieve a good death.

When an English translation appeared in 1927 (by Dr Walter Y. Evans-Wentz, who came up with the English title), the book grew in popularity in the West, eventually becoming a favourite text of post-war countercultural scenes. In their book *The Psychedelic Experience: A Manual Based on the Tibetan Book of the Dead* (1964), Timothy Leary, Ralph Metzner and Richard Alpert (later named Ram Dass) took part in research that tested the therapeutic potential of psychotropic substances (LSD, mescaline, psilocybin) to induce visionary states of altered consciousness. These experiments hinged on the notion that hallucinatory imagery brought up by the unconscious self is revealing of truth and, in recognition of that truth, ego death can occur and liberation of the self is made possible (Leary, Metzner and Alpert 1964). William Burroughs subtitled his novel *The Wild Boys* (1971) as 'A Book of the Dead', while Brion Gysin (inventor of the literary cut-up technique, popularized by Burroughs) adapted the *Bardo Thodol* into his extended *Bardo Hotel* universe, where each room is a transitional post-death state, and his final, quasi-autobiographical film and literary work *Beat Museum/Bardo Hotel* (1982).

Carl Gustav Jung, the Swiss psychoanalyst and writer, also took an interest in the text, providing a psychological commentary aimed specifically at non-religious Western readers, which was included with the third English edition (1965). Chiefly interested in the way the *Bardo Thodol* provided structure and momentum to unconscious experience and contents, Jung came to view the book as a great psychological work. We know the young Bowie was himself interested in Tibetan Buddhism from the mid-late 1960s onwards and was an avid reader of countercultural literature. It shouldn't surprise us to learn that he was also interested in the work of Jung, exploring the Jungian concept of the id/shadow, an unconscious aspect of the personality, in an early song 'Shadow Man' (1971) and dropping his name into the lyrics of 'Drive-In Saturday' (1973).

It was an interest that he shared with his friend, artist Tony Oursler. Both men were fascinated by liminal spaces and the role of the sub/unconscious self in the creative process; dream states and symbolism, alternate and projected identities – one man exploring through song and performance, the other through video, sculpture and light. In a conversation with author Gianni Mercurio (2016), Oursler expanded on his preference for a Jungian approach in his art-making, one that 'looked at the unconscious as a potential creative force to be harnessed ... channelling voices, different characters and dialoguing forces within', adding that 'the publishing of *The Red Book* and Jung's succinct ideas of how to use creativity and the subconscious as an everyday tool are something that brings meaning back to the [art-making] discourse' (Mercurio 2016, 25). As a creative wellspring, the sub/unconscious can be the source of magic; it is the way that new ideas from within us feel like they were born elsewhere, the way our art teaches us about ourselves, reveals something of who we really are. Some of Bowie's favourite art movements – the Dadaists and Surrealists – were wholly preoccupied with exploring such ambiguous, liminal territories. Jung believed that the creative impulse to make art was driven by the subconscious self and that this dialogue between the selves can take a toll on a person's psyche: 'Art is a kind of innate drive that seizes a human being and makes him its instrument ... There are hardly any exceptions to the rule that a person must pay dearly for the divine gift of the creative fire' (Jung 1933, 175).

The Red Book was Jung's own private dream journal-cum-art project, a personal record of his own 'confrontation with the unconscious', a series of disturbing visions that he experienced during a time when he was close to having a psychotic breakdown as Europe stood at the edge of the First World War. It was finally published in 2009 and its handwritten pages, paintings and drawings were shown at the Rubin Museum of Art in New York (October 2009 to February 2010). Naturally, Bowie and Oursler went along, Oursler reflecting later: 'David and I discussed Carl Jung's *[The] Red Book* in relation to [his] alternative view of channelling characters while making art ... to my mind, Bowie's collection of personas offers just such a liberating trajectory, while also providing an alternative to the American cliché of rugged individualism and fixed, "authentic" identity' (Oursler 2016).

Jung offers an alternative way of seeing and conceptualizing the troubling aspects of the psyche to Freud, for whom archetypes, fixations and psychological complexes could often be reducible to repressed trauma of some kind, something to be pathologized and ideally cured. In the Jungian framework, the presence of recurrent imagery emerging from places beyond and below conscious awareness – surfacing in dreams and visionary imagination – contain wisdom and direction for our lives. The characters appearing in dreams are iterations of the self, archetypes rendered and articulated through the imagery and languages of myth, folklore and (these days) popular media. The Jungian approach suggests that personal growth and self-understanding can be found in dialogue with these inner figures by recognizing and embracing them as teachers.

With Jung's embrace of the archetypes as necessary and balancing elements of the integrated self, he validated (and perhaps soothed)

Bowie's experiences with disturbing visionary episodes and removed the stigma from types of mental illness, such as the schizophrenia that his half-brother Terry Burns suffered from, recasting visionary capability as a creative gift, granting access to imagery from under the radar of consciousness. As John O'Connell would note,[1] Terry's plight 'gave Bowie a deep appreciation for writers who found in schizophrenia special rather than shameful qualities' (2019, 115). According to Tanja Stark, understanding Bowie's relationship to Jungian concepts is 'key to unlocking the essential thematic concerns that repeatedly permeate Bowie's creativity – the proliferation of archetypal images, his profound engagement with the unconscious, his complex relationship with the numinous, tension between opposing polarities and the ongoing spectre of a shadow that threatens to overwhelm and displace surface realities' (Stark 2016).

> I suspect that dreams are an integral part of existence, with far more use for us than we've made of them, really. I'm quite Jungian about that.
>
> – Bowie (Roberts 1999)

There are clear indications in the script and staging of *Lazarus* that suggest what the audience is experiencing is a dream sequence. The show begins and ends with Newton lying in the same location on the floor with his eyes closed. After 'It's No Game (Part 1)', and just prior to Girl's first appearance, Newton wonders aloud to himself, paraphrasing Hamlet, 'In this sleep of death – what dreams may come… ' (Bowie and Walsh 2016, 10) Throughout the play he seems to understand that much (if not all) of what he's seeing and experiencing is not real ('you're just another dream, a delusion, a chemical belch in my head', ibid., 13). Despite maintaining a generally open and slippery stance on what the show could be about, the dream context is more or less confirmed by Walsh in the introduction to the script: 'It's a strange, difficult and sometimes sad

---

[1] O'Connell's *Bowie's Books: The Hundred Literary Heroes Who Changed His Life* (2019) explores the list of 'Bowie's top 100 must-read books' (revealed when the V&A's touring exhibition reached Toronto in late 2013), with short essays about each. The comments about Terry's plight relate to an essay about *The Origin of Consciousness in the Breakdown of the Bicameral Mind* by Julian Jaynes (1976). Number 41 on Bowie's list.

dream Newton must live through – but in its conclusion, he wins his peace' (ibid., ix). In a subsequent interview, he told former *Mojo* editor Paul Trynka that the beige apartment set with two glass windows was 'not an apartment; it's a head, a mind' (Trynka 2016). Elsewhere, Walsh's references to morphine and end-of-life battles[2] add disquieting context to our dreamer's predicament.

Opium dreams are historically associated with art and creativity, explored experientially by eminent writers from the Romantic era such as Samuel Taylor Coleridge (*Kubla Khan* 1816), Thomas De Quincey (*Confessions of an English Opium-Eater* 1821) and the composer Hector Berlioz (*Symphonie Fantastique* 1830). For patients taking a high dose of opioids to manage their pain, opioid-induced hallucinations (OIHs) are a common disorienting side effect. This is known to manifest acutely as forms of mental confusion, delirium and hallucinations as patients edge closer to death. We are never given information about Newton's health or why he finds himself on the edge of life and death – he could be lying alone in his apartment, as he appears, or in a hospital bed, like Bowie's representation of 'Lazarus' in his final video.

By presenting a range of symbolic dramatic imagery, suggested to be playing out in a troubled protagonist's mind, *Lazarus* shares structural, psychotherapeutic and thematic qualities with Dennis Potter's BBC drama *The Singing Detective* (1986, already mentioned by Walsh as an inspiration and briefly discussed in previous chapters). The staging of musical numbers in both works serve similar ends; less tethered to a narrative than you would find in a usual 'musical', the music taps into emotive and atmospheric states.

The Singing Detective mixes up genres and exposes its viewer to 'kaleidoscopic subjective perspective(s)' and the 'explication of the roles of the Oedipus complex and Original Sin in the creation of neurosis' (Fuller 2015). The story is being written and rewritten in the protagonist Marlow's head while he lies hospitalized with a psychosomatic condition; his shifting memories and paranoid fantasies bully him, he hallucinates song and dance numbers in sublimation of his moods, anxieties and desires. His healing occurs as his own inner detective solves the unconscious mystery

---

[2] Cited in previous chapter. (Hunter-Tilney 2016)

of his trauma and sickness; the therapeutic process a 'Freudian investigation [that] amounts to an almost religious purification' (ibid.). Like *Lazarus*, *The Singing Detective* was complexly woven from fictions and threads of autobiographical detail, deliberately playing into Potter's reputation and notoriety.

Another hospital/deathbed dream namechecked by Walsh as influential was Bob Fosse's semi-autobiographical fantasy *All That Jazz* (1979). In it, protagonist Joe Gideon (Roy Scheider) is ailing and, by the end, dying; inside his dreams he directs extravagant musical sequences starring his wife, daughter and mistress. After a series of heart attacks and undergoing coronary artery bypass surgery, these dream sequences become more elaborate and fantastical. As doctors try to save him on the operating table, he hallucinates a final show where everyone significant from his past is in attendance and he is able to thank them and say goodbye, the dream providing a moment of closure, forgiveness and healing that he was not able to achieve in his real life.

Dream analysis

Recognizing the unconscious context and archetypal themes present in the play, it seems appropriate at this point to adapt a Jungian methodology to a reading of *Lazarus* as a dream. The analysis will slightly modify the Jungian textual approach used by John Izod in his 2001 book *Mind, Myth and the Screen*, which he used to analyse the archetypal and symbolic content in films and narrative visual media. According to Izod, one of the primary functions of such an analysis is in identifying 'undercurrents of collective feeling' present in a theatrical work that 'audiences accept as shaping myths of our time' (Izod 2001, 7). In this first perspective, the theatrical presentation is analysed as if it is dream imagery that speaks to the larger construction of meaning for the benefit of the wider audience; what shared understandings and beliefs (myths of our time) are impacted and developed by the work. Newton is an already established symbol of isolation, weakness and pity. The character is also entangled with Bowie's other alien/ated personae, his personal struggles with addiction, a moment of spiritual and psychological crisis, and his status as an outsider/immigrant in New

York. In *Lazarus*, these myths are updated, rewritten and enriched with new details. In much the same way that Bowie's *1. Outside* tapped into the energy of a collective cultural image of the serial killer and *Heathen* caught the spirit of a collective memoriam for the death of the twentieth century, *Lazarus* touches upon collective undercurrents of media saturation, crisis exhaustion and mental disorientation that mark the 2010s.

The second perspective for the analysis exists inside the narrative itself, as the audience bearing witness to Newton's dream attempts to deconstruct and understand it and, in so doing, better understand the nature of the conflicts being depicted. A Jungian dream analysis would typically include a process known as 'amplification' – a method of deploying one's active imagination to gather up the ideas and images that are associated with a specific symbol, with the aim of revealing the connections between elements in a psychological complex. Izod outlines an approach (informed by the psychologist James Hillman, a key figure at the Jung Institute in Zurich) where different kinds of symbols can be 'read' in different ways to analyse the connected ideas and imagery in a work of dramatic fiction. First, the identification and gathering of symbolic elements through amplification, followed by construction and elaboration of their connections and creative potentials. The analysis yields meanings in both perspectives – for Newton in a psychoanalytical sense, and for the audience to make sense of the dramatic narrative and consider its relevance in the contexts of Bowie's oeuvre and as a contained theatrical experience.

Tevis's original text, *The Man Who Fell to Earth*, and Roeg's film adaptation have established a vocabulary of visual-narrative devices and symbolic imagery that *Lazarus* plays on. Borrowing from Roeg's style of direction, the play's narrative jumps between time, disconnected locations and inebriated states. Drab scenes are intercut with sudden jolts of colour and sound, non-linear projections of real and imagined memories appear out of sync, and like the film, the play depicts fantasies involving wet and/or shiny bodies in motion.

Throughout the play, the colour blue is a feature of Newton's hallucinations and is referenced in the bluebird imagery of the opening number, 'Lazarus'. Blue is a complimentary opposite (on the colour wheel) to the brown/beige of the set and Newton's pyjamas, and its use in the play can be read as a symbol of yearning.

In his memory projections of Mary-Lou, she wears a gleaming silk blue dress and matching wig and he keeps the former, a treasured keepsake, in a tissue-lined box under his bed. In Catholic illustrations the Virgin Mary is often depicted wearing blue, symbolizing her grace and divine favour, and blue is also associated with royalty, the bloodlines of kings and queens, heroism, justice, the police, Superman's cape, Luke Skywalker's lightsaber. Blue is also associated with sadness and depression, 'the blues', and the physical manifestations of bruising and extreme cold. Electric blue was the colour of Bowie's room in 'Sound and Vision' (1977), a reference to the actual paint on the walls of his Berlin flat and also his state of mental health at the time as he withdrew into a lifestyle of solitude and boredom, waiting for creative inspiration to arrive.

Blue is the colour of oceans and sky, the water and oxygen that make life possible, the vast expanses of which symbolize freedom, limitlessness, optimism and adventure. Newton had originally travelled to Earth in search of water, which for the Antheans represents life and survival. Stark (2015) observes that a quest for water, what she suggests is symbolic of spiritual thirst, is a recurring symbol in Bowie's catalogue, from the panic-stricken children of the mythic 'Glass Spider' (*Never Let Me Down*) to 'Looking for Water' (*Reality*) to the blocked waterfall in 'Heat' (*The Next Day*). The beyond-sky realm (towards the stars) is a remote dimension that is inaccessible to men and women, it is the former home of the gods, the great next frontier for humanity's exploration. During the pivotal ensemble number, 'Absolute Beginners', when Newton for the first time feels hopeful about his future and the plan to build a rocket, the lighting on stage swirls with blue.

GIRL. So what is it you want?
Above them is turning blue.
NEWTON. To be back in the stars
GIRL. Then that's where we'll go
The music surges. (Bowie and Walsh 2016, 38)

The story of Newton's fall to Earth echoes established myths – Icarus and Daedalus, Adam's fall after the original sin, the visitation of Christ on Earth and the kiss of Judas. The associated narratives of hubris, temptation, failure and betrayal continue to resonate here; though *Lazarus* is set in the present with these events part of

Newton's past, he is now dealing with the residual effects of those traumas. The book and film leave Newton's fate in stasis – damaged and rendered impotent by humanity, he cannot complete the 'hero's journey' and return to his realm with the reward he set out to find. This failure to re-emerge from the underworld paints Newton as a symbol of martyrdom and corruption. His entrapment, 'locked into a living death … is a mockery of the immortal gods … his condition reminds us of our own' (Izod 1992, 94).

As in *The Man Who Fell to Earth*, the 'human' characters that Newton interacts with are rendered in sketch form, their backstories are vague, their motivations obscured, and he cannot read their intentions. America is still a strange and unwelcoming place – certainly not 'home' – and Newton is shown to be trapped by its cultural vices: alcoholism, capitalism, individualism and self-pity. As he lies motionless on the stage floor, the first sound we hear is the booming playback of Ricky Nelson's 'Hello Mary Lou' (1961), a song that also features in the film. It wakes him up, bringing narrative threads from the original book and film texts to bear on the current situation; 'Hello Mary Lou/goodbye heart' suggests that his toxic past relationship with her is a continuing source of pain for the character, and it prevents him from his rest.

Michael, who we meet at the start of the play, is a business associate of Newton who seems to be experiencing guilt over the dynamics of the relationship. His awkward encounter with Newton echoes Nathan Bryce's shallow attempts at reconciliation at the end of the book and film. Michael sings 'The Man Who Sold the World', a song that contains imagery of fragmented and split identities, ghosts of past lives passing one another on the stairs. Bryce's blurry, faintly eroticized obsession with Newton is also evoked in the conversation between Michael and Valentine, where the latter brings up the former's presumed homosexuality (Valentine: 'I stood by you when you told your family that you were a gay man.' Michael: 'I'm not – for one thing – I'm fucking straight! Now get the fuck out of my apartment' (16)). Michael, if not a 'real' person, can be read as a projection of Newton's fears of betrayal and distrust of human dealings – even when they seem profitable or based in kindness. Valentine's assumptions about his sexuality, if we read him as Newton's dark avatar (archetypal shadow), point to Newton's misunderstanding of the boundaries and differences between professional, platonic and romantic relationships. In a similar way, the character of Elly projects

Newton's fears relating to dependency, intimacy and human 'love' as a form of entrapment. In his dream he imagines her unhappy home life with her husband Zach, her emotional neediness and desire to find a new life in a new guise and start over. This desperation for reinvention resonates with another moment in the play when, at his lowest point, Newton puts *The Next Day* on the record player and sings 'Where Are We Now?', reminiscing about Bowie's mythical past in Berlin as imagery of the old city is projected against the beige set. Bowie went to Berlin as a kind of celebrity refugee, to recreate his identity (again) after a personal crisis point, which escalated simultaneously as he embodied Newton in Roeg's film. This moment draws attention to Bowie's presence in the play, not only as the composer of the song and the person who once played the Newton role, but specifically to the convergence of two personas reflecting on loss within the single moment.

Elly gradually transforms into his image of Mary-Lou, putting on a blue wig and shiny, glittered clothing, including the dress he kept so carefully under the bed, which perplexes Newton, who seems wary and frightened rather than attracted to her. As in *The Singing Detective*, Elly could be a nurse or a carer and Newton's hallucination is a sublimation of his confused, tangled up desires and fears – the thing he yearns for in his loneliness, but is also very afraid of. In the book and film, being cared for by Betty Jo/Mary-Lou after his serious injury in the elevator is what eventually leads to Newton's entrapment on Earth, his ensuing addiction and the failure of his mission. It is plausible that the presence of a caregiver at the end of his life could trigger a confusion of feelings and post-traumatic stress.

The murderous Valentine is the shadow figure of the piece, dressed in black and flashing red colours – amidst the beige and blue, Valentine's stage lights and backdrop projections are fiery red and orange; he also becomes smeared in blood over the course of the play. He is everything that Newton's conscious ego does not identify itself as: wildly emotive, decisive and vengeful. In Roeg's film the only glimpse we have of Newton's latent violent power fantasies is the gunplay he subjects Mary-Lou to when she visits him in the penthouse where he is being held captive. Valentine is triggered to violence by the presence of love and intimacy: when Michael expresses his regret and longing reflecting on his last interaction with Newton, Valentine appears and does his dirty work. When engaged couple Ben and Maemi share their love story Valentine sees red and alarm sounds ring out, leading to the gruesome murder of Ben in front of his own stag party. And when Elly begins to fall in love with Newton, Valentine appears by her side and whispers in her ear, eventually nearly strangling her in the doorway of an open fridge. Valentine's bitterness at his isolated and loveless existence has given him the twisted psychology of a mass shooter (the point of view portrayed in the lyrics to the song 'Valentine's Day'), an incel-terrorist soured by loneliness who becomes incensed when he is ignored and sees others enjoying what he believes he can never have. Throughout all the texts Newton is portrayed as someone who fundamentally misinterprets relationships, who learned about 'love' and the vocabulary of human intimacies from watching television. In the play, as he imagines Ben and Maemi interacting as a couple, the scene lurches towards the pornographic: gratuitous, animalistic and over the top.

The confrontation between Newton and Valentine is preceded by a version of 'Dirty Boys', setting up imagery of rival gangs preparing to fight in the street, the anticipation of a violent showdown. Their eventual encounter is not a violent one, but an awkward conversation (Valentine: 'I've come here to help you, sir... ') that triggers Newton to expressing his own murderous fury and bitterness ('Killing a Little Time'). Raging against the idea of love, he calls it a 'phony pain', and sings that he loves only 'the sound of an empty room' and 'the end of love'. There are references here again to water, only now in the form of 'criminal/furious rain' that are aggravating his rage, the longed-for thing that is now whipping upon him in an unexpected and unwanted form. Rain symbolizes unhappiness and foreboding as well as cleansing and renewal; storms and tempests can be symbolic of great trials and challenging circumstances. In *The Red Book*, Jung interprets the rain in his own difficult visions as 'the great stream of tears ... the tearful flood of released tension ... the mourning of the dead in me, which precedes the burial and rebirth' (Jung 2009, 164). 'Killing a Little Time' also contains lyrical references to medical procedures and what could be interpreted as a hospital ward environment: hearts that stop beating, open wounds, screams in the night, bleeding in a bed, falling, choking, fading, 'broken lines' that call to mind the visual readings of vitals on a patient's monitor. The music is chaotic and dark, troubled with destabilizing rhythms, turbulent drum rolls,

discordant horns, churning riffs, the vocal delivery seething with
bitter anger and self-pity. The lyric 'I've got a handful of songs to
sing/to sting your soul, to fuck you over' could be read as a meta-
reference to the intensity and tough mortal themes of *Lazarus* and
the new meanings the work might stimulate after Bowie's passing.
The lyrics that sing through spite and anger resonate with the myth
of Jetsun Milarepa, who wrote poetry and songs as a means of
overcoming his own internal resistance to growth. The lyrical hook
'just killing a little time' could be a mocking reference to the act
of being idle and stuck, unable to die, or it could be a riposte on
'Time' itself (*Aladdin Sane* 1973). After Newton's encounter with
his shadow, Valentine lucidly sets out the pathway to redemption –
to rewrite the trauma and escape.

> VALENTINE. There are so many things that make the world
> such an ugly place to live in and I've seen them – and I guess
> you have too. It can be truly horrible, right? And beautiful
> things – like friendship and being in love – can turn sour –
> and that sourness can turn a person blue. I've always thought
> there has to be something more beautiful than what we've
> been given down here. It's possible to rewrite this bad world
> and escape it. So if I can give you anything at all, Mr Newton –
> it will be the support and help you need towards finding
> a more peaceful place. I know I can do that. I know I can.
> (44)

The Man Who Fell to Earth source texts both expose the
presence of potentially sinister observers: FBI agents; a lone figure
who witnesses Newton's lifeboat crash to Earth; powers that
exert covert control over his life for purposes that remain unclear.
In the play, this paranoid element is represented by the group
of ethereal teenage girls, who at first seem to be an organized
band of spirits that drive his hallucinations, sometimes in cruel
directions. Eventually, it becomes apparent that their aim is to
orchestrate the necessary confrontations in Newton's mind that
will allow him to experience a kind of purification and create the
healing and closure he needs. At the climax of the play, when he
is given the knife and is tasked with killing Girl, the leader of the
group (Teenage Girl 1) sings an urgent, overlapping duet, 'When I
Met You'. Newton has his revelatory moment of clarity (the lyrics

mirror a passage of *The Red Book*: 'What am I? What is my I? I always presuppose my I. Now it stands before me – I before my I' (2009, 461)). Now in dialogue with his self, the other voice tells him the sources of his trauma, echoing the lost heart identified in Ricky Nelson's song at the start of the play ('Hello Mary Lou/ goodbye heart'): 'She stole your heart you don't understand … she tore you down'. Newton argues with the voice about whether he deserves forgiveness for failing, before both voices join, integrated and in consensus: before this encounter he was numbed ('the walking dead'), confused ('kicked in the head') and distrustful of everything; now stood before his 'I', 'God's truth' has been revealed.

> *(Newton.)* It was such a crime
> *(TG1.)* She tore you down
> *(Newton.)* It was such a time
> *(TG1.)* When I – when I
> *(Newton.)* I was torn inside
> *(TG1.)* When I
> *(Newton and TG1.)* When I met you
> When I met you
> I was too insane
> Could not trust a thing
> I was off my head
> I was filled with truth
> It was not God's truth
> Before I met you. (59)

The plan to 'rewrite the bad world' follows Newton facing up to the teaching moments that each of the other three main characters set up for him – the trials of the bardo. For Elly, his resistance of the thing he yearns for, which he now realizes was only a toxic, mutually damaging love, allows him to heal the wound of his addiction. For Valentine, their encounter initiates Newton's awakening from passivity, triggering a release of his repressed emotions, allowing him to recognize the full extent of the damage caused to his psyche by his isolation on Earth. For Girl, who represents his kind and kin, Newton's healing and the conclusion of his mission to Earth is achieved by her symbolic death. As a spectral image of his lost daughter in limbo, her identity is indistinct and nameless; after the brutal act that severs Newton's attachment, Girl becomes Marley and, with Newton no longer clinging to the guilt of failing his family and species, her entity is allowed to exist outside of Newton and his dream.

In Jung's dreams from *The Red Book*, his anima figure and lost 'soul' were represented by a female counterpart. Elsewhere in Jung's writings, when in dreams he finds himself journeying through the underworld, his anima/soul appears as a young girl or nymph (Jung 1951, 184). Symbolizing the repressed, unconscious feminine complexes in a man's psyche, Jung suggested that if the encounter with the shadow is the 'apprentice-piece' in a person's development, then coming to terms with the anima/animus is the 'master-piece' (Jung 1981). A female God figure that walks into his life out of his dreams. From *The Red Book*:

> I wandered for many years, so long that I forgot that I possessed a soul. Where were you all this time? ... My dreams have represented you as a child and as a maiden. I am ignorant of your mystery. Forgive me if I speak as in a dream, like a drunkard – are you God?
>
> (Jung 2009, 131)

The uncomfortable androcentrism in Jung's writing about gendered archetypes exposes an ingrained conservatism about male and female social roles. Many of these are also reflected in the world's myths and throughout history – heroes and maidens, mothers and whores, wise men and old hags. Jung's reasoning is inductive, drawing generally from the collective, male-centric predisposition of its time. Most symbolic systems that flow from the collective consciousness are patriarchal for this reason; what is unexpected is seeing them embedded and elucidated in Bowie's work, where one might expect to find push back against gendered conservatism. Jung defined the feminine archetypes in terms of receptivity and service, and here we see an innocent girl, representative of the hero's soul, being sacrificed so that the male protagonist can achieve his objective. We could chalk this up to Newton and his subjective perspective being informed by watching too much TV – the archetypes appearing in his dream merely replicating the worldview and situation of the sick alien to whom they are 'revealed'.

And yet, the vulnerable and suffering waif (the archetypal anima) figure is a recurring image in Bowie's song catalogue – lost, young female characters, often with pale hair and blue-grey eyes ('Life on Mars?', 'What in the World', 'Scary Monsters (and Super Creeps)'). The character of Girl/Marley fits neatly alongside these, particularly with Sophia Anne Caruso cast in the role at fourteen; she is all pale-blond teen elfin innocence.[3] Girl's sacrifice and signification as something 'pure' and innocent, has echoes of the butchering of the fourteen-year-old Baby Grace Blue from 1. *Outside*, the horrific crime vividly described in the album's enclosed short story titled *The Diary of Nathan Adler, or the Ritual Art-Murder of Baby Grace Blue: A Non-linear Gothic Drama Hyper-Cycle*. Like *Lazarus*, there are clues in the presentation and performance of 1. *Outside* that suggest the overarching murder mystery is staged in a psychological space, a play performed by archetypes that are really fragments of the same identity (Fremaux and Usher 2015, 70). The construction of a psychological crime scene being played out theatrically by stock/archetypal characters also connects back to Kemp's 1967 commedia dell'arte piece *Pierrot in Turquoise or The Looking Glass Murders*. In 1. *Outside* Bowie narrates all the parts and appears in Photoshopped drag as each of the characters; Bowie is murdered by himself, his own mutilated corpse turned into an art piece, and then he investigates his own murder by process of non-linear cut-up. Bowie's anima, the inner other opposite of the 'Bowie' persona, is a necessary victim; vulnerable, confused, her innocence is sacrificed in the pursuit of art.[4] The violence is necessary to Bowie's creative process, the rock 'n' roll suicide killing of 'aspects of his self – personas and archetypes – in the service of his art' (Furby 2018, 169). Girl's murder is dramatized as a moment of horrific and heroic kindness and faith; her death and his letting go of attachment to the hope that she represents allows Newton to pass through the

---

[3] In *Lazarus*, Caruso also happens to bear a slight resemblance to dancer Louise Lecavalier, member of the La La La Human Steps troupe, featured in the music video for 'Fame '90' (dir. Gus Van Sant), and the teenaged animated rag doll in the 'Strangers When We Meet' video from 1995 (dir. Samuel Bayer).
[4] Another symbolic figure from 1. *Outside*, the minotaur, appears (as a horned shadow) in the music video for 'Valentine's Day' (2013), suggesting similar consistency for the Bowie persona's other archetypal identities maintained over time.

trial, sliding through the spilled amniotic milk, wet and giggling towards his newborn existence.

In acknowledging the purposeful blurring and entangling of Newton and Bowie as characters within the shared settings, mythologies and terminal circumstances in the *Lazarus* narrative, it's important to understand that they are not meant to be read as one and the same – as Trynka notes, the characters have differences: 'Bowie did not share Newton's self-pity, nor did the alien have access to the singer's incessant jokiness' (2016). That said, it is difficult to fully ignore the biographical alignment of Newton and Bowie's shared love of family and the redemptive narrative of new hope and second chances that late-in-life fatherhood brought to David Jones. When promoting *A Reality Tour* back in 2003, he told the *Scottish Sunday Mail*:

> I desperately want to live forever ... I just want to be there for Alexandria. She's so exciting and so lovely so I want to be around when she grows up. I think, 'When am I gonna let go of her? When she's 20?' Nah I wanna see her get married. 'When she's 30?' Nah I wanna see what she's like as a mother. I don't want to let her go ... For Joe [Duncan], it was just bad luck he had a dad who had to be out on the road for his own career ambitions. It's a shame. In a way, I've never forgiven myself for that.
> – Bowie (Sloan 2003)

The song '"Heroes"' is canonical in popular music culture, one of the most well-known of Bowie's career. Chris O'Leary dubbed it a 'consensus masterpiece' (2011) and David Buckley called it 'perhaps pop's definitive statement of the potential triumph of the human spirit over adversity' (Buckley 2015, 63). The lyric puts forward the romantic notion that a pair of ordinary lovers, survivors existing in a grim and dangerous place, could experience momentary elation and transcendence by dreaming of a different life for themselves – recasting their story as one of royalty and specialness. Triumph and heroism.

The monomyth, or 'hero's journey', archetype is a common narrative template for stories, coined by literature professor and author Joseph Campbell in 1949. In it, a character sets out on an adventure or a dangerous quest to retrieve something important, faces conflict and eventually ultimately triumphs over adversity, returning with a boon – a trophy, new knowledge – while being usually changed or positively transformed by the process. Izod notes that in the story of *The Man Who Fell to Earth*, Newton is conspicuous as a hero figure that doesn't return: his quest remains incomplete. His failure offers audiences a mirror: 'Newton reflects at us our inadequacies to the calls of heroism' (Izod 1992, 95).

In *Lazarus*, Newton's heroic ending is finally written and the quest is completed. Newton accomplishes his life-enhancing return by achieving union with the self, even if it is only momentary (just for one day). In triumphing over his bullying mind, he achieves what Jungian psychology refers to as *individuation*, a transformative process of self-actualization brought about by the integration of the disparate elements of the personality into an assimilated well-functioning whole. The moment of Newton's death is also the moment of his departure back to the stars – his rocket launch is more like a karmic gust of the *Sidpa Bardo* wind, lifting the dead man up and out of his cage on Earth and on to the next place.

Lazarus's musical director Henry Hey created a radical rearrangement of '"Heroes"', having faced resistance from Bowie about its inclusion. He explained:

> We had a meeting at David's office to go over the songs and we got to '"Heroes"', which was in the script. And David said, 'Now, I'm afraid we can't do that, it's too overexposed.' Because everybody knows '"Heroes"' as this anthem, you know? To do it in a traditional manner would have meant, 'Oh, here we are with a jukebox musical, and we're paying off at the end'. And David abhorred that idea. I could see Enda's and Ivo's faces – they were unhappy [about losing the song]. I said, 'I have an idea, let me try something.' I knew what it needed: to be cathartic and mark the end of a journey, rather than be a glorious finale. I went home and mocked up a demo. I emailed it to David and he said, 'Well, you've won me over.'
>
> – Hey (interview with the author, 2020)

It starts with subdued piano, the melancholy feeling intensified by a switch from the usual major tonality to G minor, and weary-sounding horns. The characters, Newton and Marley, sing to each other with affection, replacing the words "cause we're lovers' with "cause we're free now'. And with that admission the song begins to ascend. Gentle drums enter like a pulse of warm blood and the tonality shifts to the relative B♭ major, the bass standing on the 3rd and 5th notes of the triads, creating a fragile harmonic stability; nothing feels sturdy or certain, but it is also weightless and easy, the music doesn't touch the ground. The last verse provides another key change, lifting Michael C. Hall's voice into his tenor register, triumphant, open and tender in C major. The use of harmony inversions throughout was a subtle psychological device to delay finality, according to Hey: 'I didn't want the bass line to ever fall on the root, it would feel too grounded; the only time that you hear the root note of the chord is at the end, which is supposed to be the finale.'

The lines in '"Heroes"' about swimming like dolphins are references to Alberto Denti di Pirajno's *A Grave for a Dolphin* (1956), included on Bowie's list of 100 books that changed his life. A text that was hugely significant to him, it not only inspired the lyric in question, but also a tattoo on the back of his calf that he drew himself, depicting a horned, naked figure riding on the back of a dolphin. The ink also included the Serenity Prayer (adopted widely by AA's twelve-step programmes) in Japanese *katakana* script and the name 'Iman'. In the foreword to his wife's autobiographical book, *I Am Iman* (2001), he explained the tattoo represented a 'confirmation of the love I feel for my wife and my knowledge of the power of life itself'.

A good death

Knowing David, however briefly, taught me about how certain works of art – not to mention certain principles of physics, certain laws of nature, certain methods of healing – start out sounding implausible.

– Cunningham (2017)

Death and impermanence are found in every facet of Tibetan Buddhist teaching. In preparing mindfully for a good death, one has an opportunity to shape destiny; death presents unique possibilities for individuals to triumph over cycles of suffering and push potential spiritual advancement towards something better. Both Bowie and

Visconti were interested in Tibetan Buddhism at various points in their lives and, as a philosophy, Visconti still subscribes to it:

> Buddhism is still meaningful to me as a philosophy full of symbols that can help us understand our mental states. It also has a well-documented after-death experience. If we believe that these lamas [teachers] did pass through it and they have conscious memory of it … I mean, you can speak with a real live reincarnated lama, they don't even need to quote *The Book of the Dead*, they'll just talk about it and what it's like. Specifically, choosing your rebirth and searching for your parents.
> – Visconti (interview with the author, 2020)

We journey with Newton through the bardo states between death and rebirth, the hallucinatory swirl of psychic projections – thoughts, emotions, attachments. A stream of pure consciousness, existence emancipated from time. The bardo states are the 'not quite yet' of 'No Plan', the place where a person exists in their essence of nowness: ' … all the things that are my life – my moods, my beliefs, my desires, me alone, nothing to regret'.

The realization of impending death (life's transience) is portrayed as a transformative healing force in the story of Jetsun Milarepa, a murderer and black-magician-turned-poet who followed the tantric path to enlightenment and ascended to Buddhahood within a single lifetime. Bowie made specific reference to 'nowness' (impermanence) before a performance of 'Seven' for VH1's *Storytellers* TV series (1999): 'I remember in the Seventies [the countercultural activist] Abbie Hoffman saying to me, "Tomorrow isn't promised," reminding me that if we move one grain of sand the earth is no longer exactly the same … Which brings us to this song of nowness.' The song 'Seven' is pinned around an idea of existential knowing; when given only seven days to live, the proximity and certainty of death throws down a challenge for living in the fullest sense, otherwise what's the point? Every one of those days not spent living is another way to die.

For Dennis Potter in 1994, the profound experience of transience was only revealed to him once his future was taken away by his terminal diagnosis (which he said fell on Valentine's Day). In his final interview, with Melvyn Bragg, filmed three months before his death at fifty-nine from liver cancer on 7 June 1994, he took swigs from a flask of liquid morphine and described how the knowledge of his approaching death had heightened his awareness of beauty in the world:

> I grieve for my family and friends who know me closest, obviously, and they're going through it in a sense more than I am. But I discover also what you always know to be true, but you never know it till you know it ... The only thing you know for sure is the present tense, and that nowness becomes so vivid that, almost in a perverse sort of way, I'm almost serene. You know, I can celebrate life.
>
> Below my window in Ross[-on-Wye, in Herefordshire] ... the blossom is out in full now, there in the west early. It's a plum tree, it looks like apple blossom but it's white, and looking at it, instead of saying, 'Oh that's nice blossom' ... last week looking at it through the window when I'm writing, I see it is the whitest, frothiest, blossomest blossom that there ever could be, and I can see it ... But the nowness of everything is absolutely wondrous, and if people could see that, you know. There's no way of telling you; you have to experience it, but the glory of it, if you like, the comfort of it, the reassurance ... not that I'm interested in reassuring people – bugger that. The fact is, if you see the present tense, boy do you see it! And boy can you celebrate it.
>
> – Potter (Poole 1994)

For Potter, the decoupling of experience from the linear push towards the future, being cut adrift from attachments to now only exist in the present tense, has liberating, healing potential – glory, comfort, reassurance. Nirvana, or some kind of heaven, free from the grip of time – forever and ever/just for one day. These ideas echo within pages of Jung's *The Red Book*: 'Therefore I behold death, since it teaches me how to live' (2009, 267).

Bowie's version of 'No Plan', a true hymn to nowness, was released posthumously on the *No Plan* EP on what would have been his seventieth birthday, almost a year after his death, in addition to being included on the *Lazarus (Original Cast Recording)* (2016). Outside of the show's context the song takes on a different feeling – when sung by Girl inside Newton's dream, who yet doesn't know who or where she is, it feels uneasy. Here it has a gentler arrangement, cushioned by pillowy synths, airy flute and saxophone, and dreamy guitar. Bowie's uplifted vocal performance brims with warmth, gratitude and bittersweet consolation. In stark contrast to the existential thought experiment of 'Seven', 'No Plan' is soaked through with a similar knowing that Potter described to Bragg in his last interview; a knowing that you always knew, but that you never know until you know.[5]

An accompanying music video for 'No Plan', directed by Tom Hingston, intended as a 'gift for the fans' (Hingston 2017), shows a shabby shopfront of 'Newton Electrical', located on Foxgrove Road, Beckenham – where Bowie rented a flat in 1969, the year he released *Space Oddity*. A wall of TVs in the shop window suddenly flicker on with static and interference, as if controlled by a ghost. Lyrics from the song appear on the screens intercut with imagery from New York streets: a bluebird in flight, balloons rising, a rocket leaving Earth's atmosphere. A crowd of mesmerized onlookers gathers outside the store. The effect is one of a reassuring message being relayed from the afterlife and, while we know this video was not devised by Bowie, its existence speaks to the continuing entanglements of Newton, Major Tom and other Bowie myths in popular consciousness.

Enda Walsh would later tell Paul Trynka that he suspected Bowie particularly enjoyed the repetitive, ceremonial nature of theatre performance: 'I imagine he could've made a film [but] … the strange repetitious nature of it, having to live it all the time. I'm sure, yes … He wanted to see that' (Trynka 2016). *Lazarus* has been resurrected many times since Bowie died and will continue to perform to packed houses all over the world. At the time of writing, the official website lists shows currently in production from São Paulo to Oslo, Melbourne to Hamburg. While some of the newer productions have strayed somewhat from the original van Hove/Versweyveld/D'Huys look, they all continue to ceremoniously grant Newton his 'good death' – one that is not felt as a theft, but framed as a goal.[6]

---

[5] In other words: 'the moment you know you know, you know' ('Where Are We Now?').

[6] It also lives on as a filmed performance that was premiered globally as a live stream for three days (8–10 January 2021) in commemoration of Bowie's seventy-fourth birthday on 8 January and the fifth anniversary of his death on 10 January. The filmed performance was from the London production at the King's Cross Theatre in 2017.

Potter had staged his public dying in *Karaoke* and *Cold Lazarus* by binding up his personal myths and creative legacies with a pair of connected, final pieces; works that pivot on and draw power from the death of their author. Bowie pulled off a similar manoeuvre in the final months of his life and, in giving us access to his dying through the visceral, shared experience of live theatre, he and Walsh created a space for fans to share in their own grief and healing.

To close it in that way he closed it, was beautiful. A lot of people would say that's a really good death.
                                                    – Walsh (McCarthy 2017)

PART THREE

8

Black holes, black music, black arts, black hearts and button eyes

★ begins with its first single, 'Blackstar', released on 19 November 2015. Originally more than eleven minutes long, it was pragmatically cut to 9′57″ to conform to the iTunes policy of singles not exceeding ten minutes. 'Blackstar' is gothic and arcane, one of Bowie's most memorable and darkly beautiful compositions. Its perfumed textures and dense atmospherics feel reminiscent of the shadowy sound worlds of *1. Outside* and *Heathen*, albums that share similarly mortal, paranoid, parareligious themes. The lyric is allusive and loaded with potent imagery that could tease interpretative pathways towards cosmology, alchemy, TV shows, sun deities, science fiction, hermeticism and more. The accompanying music video, devised by Bowie and directed by Johan Renck (*Chernobyl*), is pure dark sci-fi, loaded with numinous symbolism. It presents the artist alternately as a trembling blind man (the bandaged Button Eyes), a religious leader and a grinning trickster, and it strongly hints at Major Tom's fate – a skeleton in a spacesuit, his bejewelled skull used as a relic in a strange ritual. Taken together, 'Blackstar' is an epic presentation and, for anyone wishing to attempt a reading, a juicy prospect.

'Blackstar' (★ track 1)

Tempos: A1 = 130 bpm, B = 98 bpm, A2 = 98 bpm.
Tonalities: B phrygian dominant in the 'A' sections; F# major in the 'B' section.
Song form: ABA ternary.

The music is structurally, stylistically and sonically adventurous, moving between two contrasting sections that are differentiated by key, tempo, arrangement and performance style. The pieces are arranged in ternary ABA form, similar to Bowie's other long-form tracks that incorporate dramatic shifts in energy and tone within the single piece – 'Sweet Thing/Candidate/Sweet Thing (Reprise)' (1974) and 'Station to Station' (1976). The first section is built on a harmonic progression that subtly shifts between B and C major, calling to mind the exoticism of Middle Eastern scale modes and reminiscent of Radiohead's hypnotic *Kid A* opener 'Everything in Its Right Place' (2000). Bowie uses a phrygian dominant mode in these sections;[1] in this instance it reliably summons something dark and strange, as it does in 'Neuköln' (1977) and also in the verses of 'No Control' and 'I'm Deranged' (1995); the tonality has the darkness of minor in the changes but the openness of major in the resolution. Shadows and moonlight. Bowie's melody delivers the lyric in a style suggestive of prayer: serene and repetitive, focusing on single notes in the style of sacred benediction (or magical incantation), made even more numinous by a pitch-manipulation effect that copies the vocal a perfect 5th higher, suggesting the rigid parallel movement of Gregorian chant. The end of the phrase (Figure 8.1) remains uncomfortably unresolved, terminating on A (artificially harmonized with E) in a haze of frozen reverb and delay, while the band resolves to B major. The composition repeatedly underlines 'your eyes' with these troublesome notes – a splinter in the phrase, something doesn't fit.[2]

Underneath these musical elements, the arrangement is a brooding textural expanse made up of McCaslin's low flute tones, Jason Lindner's keyboards (a stable of Wurlitzers, Prophets, Moogs), Ben Monder's guitar, sounding like a celestial harp, and

---

[1] Phrygian mode is like a standard natural minor scale, only with a flattened 2nd degree; phrygian dominant mode (also known as phrygian major, Freygish or Spanish phrygian) has an additional raised 3rd, making the root chord major. The characteristic phrygian modal effect is associated with flamenco music and folk melodies like 'Hava Nagila' (Israeli) and 'Misirlou' (Turkish).

[2] A trend in Bowie's melody writing, where the phrase lands on a dissonant note and teasingly denies a resolution, like in the line 'Cos you can never really tell when somebody wants something you want too', from 'Stay' (*Station to Station*) or 'My father ran the prison', from 'Heat' (*The Next Day*).

FIGURE 8.1 *'Blackstar', irresolution of 'your eyes'.*

Tim Lefebvre's floating bass, synth strings and vivid atmospheric effects: gurgling bleeps, sweeps and spatial trails. Mark Guiliana's impatient drumming moves between a contained, stuttering beat (Figure 8.2 A1(a)) and a more driven, propulsive groove (Figure 8.2 A1(b), reminiscent again of 1. *Outside*'s 'No Control'), with the rhythmic shift feeling like a barrier being pushed through, tilting the energy from hesitation to anticipation and then back again. McCaslin's saxophone appears at first in nimble, swirling tendrils, leading to a brief solo that climbs up from its knees and hits the roof at the top of the octave. The solo summons a subtle shift in the mix at 2:16, which opens up a brighter clarity above 10 kHz that can be heard in the hi-hats, bringing the whole scene into sharper focus. As the section progresses, Bowie's voice picks up strange spatial effects that spark and bounce off specific lyrics – heady clouds of reverb and refracting echo tails that lay on thick and dissipate just as quickly. At approx. 3:55 a spectral 'A Day in the Life'-style segue stitches this section to the next, leading the way with McCaslin's barking sax, fixatedly poking at the unresolved sonority that has haunted the entire section. The drums disappear, collapsing under murky atmospherics, and Bowie's voices trace an outline similar to the section's main theme, still uncomfortably lacking resolution, with an unnaturally eerie charge due to the sound being partially reversed. The musical transition dramatizes this moment like the arrival of a spiritual apparition after fevered supplication.

The second (B) section of the song transposes the action to the dominant F# major, brightening the scene with smooth gospel-style changes emerging from the fug like rays of sunlight, floating

FIGURE 8.2 *'Blackstar', drum rhythms in each section. From section B onwards, rhythmic urgency is stripped out.*

effortlessly down F# – C#/E# – E – G# minor/D# – B minor/D – F#/C#. The progression is familiar to the ear of anyone versed in 1960s-era pop and soul[3] and it comes as a musical relief, dissolving the tension built up from the first section. Bowie's voice is higher, his delivery sweeter, even as the lyrics become strangely troubling: big promises and puffed-up self-aggrandizement, leading to assertions of personal power as the 'blackstar'. The music gathers up some R&B swagger when Bowie sings 'I can't answer why', riffing between C7 and C# with a low soul-band sax section and sharp rhythm guitar backbeat smacking with spring reverb.

The lead voice is joined in call and response with the harmonized prayer voice from the previous section. These repetitive background declarations of 'I'm a blackstar' have an uncanny edge – where in the past Bowie's varispeed pitch experiments on the voice can imply the breakdown of sanity or a shifted reality, here the deformed, signal-processed voice sounds dazed and assimilated.

---

[3] The progression, I – V6 – ♭VII – ii4/3 – iv6/3 – I6/4, is similar to 'Someday at Christmas' by Stevie Wonder (1967), but also shares this quality with 'Baby Love' by The Supremes (1964), 'You Make Me Feel (Like a Natural Woman)' by Carole King and Gerry Goffin, sung by Aretha Franklin (1967), and 'Mary France' by Jean-Jacques Perrey (1968).

A compliant, brainwashed voice. A short chromatic slide from C# to C then B, and the music pivots effortlessly to the phrygian dominant territory of the start for the reprise of the A section (at 7:23). This reprise feels familiar, but for these differences: the leading voice is now altered, tamed and exhausted; and the music has a slightly slower tempo, pinned down by a minimal zombie drumbeat (Figure 8.2 A2), the syncopated bass helplessly locked in. No more energy, no more anticipation. Whatever was prayed for in the first section, and answered in the second, has observably (at least musically and sonically) altered the third. As the music ambles to its conclusion the machine starts to fall apart, the shambolic discipline of the bass and drums slacken to a rough stop; flutes and sax, guitar and keyboard instruments quietly and erratically jabber as they disperse.

From the accounts of the band and production team,[4] we know that 'Blackstar' was one of the last songs to be tracked with the band during the third round of Magic Shop sessions in March 2015, but it was the first that Bowie laid his final vocal takes on, a job that took two days to complete (unusual for him; final vocals were often done in only one or two takes). Similarly, this was the track that engineer Tom Elmhirst mixed first. Its extended length proved to be a challenge, taking him two days to get a handle on the composition's unique structural tensions: 'You can't give it all away too early. You have to allow the natural dynamics to come through. When it drops into that middle section, the solo voice, there is a sense of relief' (Zollo 2017). Assistant engineer Erin Tonkon likened the structural approach of 'Blackstar' to that of a film, with subtle production choices helping to provide continuity and cohesion: 'There are three sections in the song and we looked at it sonically as a film. The thread that ran through it all was David's backing vocals with reverbs and delays.' The application of spatial effects in the production of Bowie's vocal leads the cinematic storytelling throughout the song. Never applied as a blanket treatment, but used in a painterly way to highlight specific phrases, the effects illuminate and refract specific words ('eyes' (1:21), 'all' (2:59), 'fall' (5:04), 'loud' (5:13)); the effects also separate the

---

[4] Chronological information from Pegg (2016) and O'Leary (2019), in addition to interviews that I conducted with key collaborators and members of the studio team.

characters attached to Bowie's differentiated vocal performances, giving them a unique and recognizable patina – for instance, the heavenly leading voice at 4:41 sitting within pillowy light delays, rubbing up against the differently textured background vocals at 4:55, then shifting to more sinister lyrical territory with a brittle, edgier sound at 5:23.

The cryptic lyrics afford the curious listener several avenues of interpretation. Certainly, after the event of Bowie's death, the temptation to try and decode the song (and its video) to unearth symbolic meanings was irresistible to many. When Bowie claims to be 'the blackstar', what might he be referring to? Is it another name for a cancerous lesion, a black hole, a reference to Saturnian astrology, a Jungian or alchemical shadow, a temporal plot device from a *Star Trek* episode, or did it refer to a big day of gangland assassination in *Peaky Blinders*? And what of this mysterious 'villa of Ormen'? The draft lyric sheet for 'Blackstar' that was added to the touring V&A show when it arrived at the Brooklyn Museum shows the original draft referred to a 'villa of Allmen' before being changed at some point in the process. Perhaps a reference to collective humanity, or deliberately singling out 'all men' in opposition to 'only women' from the same verse, a separation that is reflected in the video where the ritual participants are all female, and the sacrificed individuals are all male. Scholar Alec Charles suggests the near homophonous 'all men'/'or-men' could be read 'as a site of androgyny, of *women-or-men*' (Charles 2021, 240). This new tidbit of information arrived long after fans and commentators had mined the word 'Ormen', 'serpent' in Norwegian, for every speck of meaning, from tales of Viking long ships and grisly punishments to serpent myths from creation and the Ouroboros (Rogers 2016). In a track that seems so loaded with symbols, on an album with a title that is itself made up of symbols, it's easy to get carried away trying to crack the code.[5] Yet the primary images contained in the composition – eyes, stars, supplication, transformation – might afford listeners a way in and an opportunity to find footing in the song's mysterious world.

---

[5] Visconti: 'You know, it's funny, he's got a Bluebird microphone and a Blackstar amplifier... '

Black holes

It was Aleister Crowley (or the entity Aiwass, which he claimed was speaking through him) who said, 'every man and every woman is a star' (1904), echoed sixty-six years later when Joni Mitchell affirmed to her generation 'we are stardust' ('Woodstock' 1970), and a decade after that when Carl Sagan agreed that we are all made of 'star stuff' (1980), the materials of our bones, blood and DNA originating from the interiors of collapsing stars. Black holes, like the rest of us, are born from stars, too. In the complex storyline constructed (presumably after the fact) around *The Rise and Fall of Ziggy Stardust and the Spiders from Mars*, Ziggy became a rock star himself in the process of delivering a message of hope from alien 'Star Men' to doomed humanity only to be destroyed on stage, torn apart by the hands of his fans. This narrative grew more complex the following year when Bowie had developed the story further towards a possible theatre piece[6] – the 'Star Men' are actually an alien race called the 'Infinites', 'black hole jumpers, those who traverse the paths of dead stars' (Copetas 1974). The twist: Ziggy was the dead star they wanted and fame caused his star to 'explode' – dying on stage actualizes his transformation to a black hole, hastening the Infinites' material appearance on Earth. The star-as-metaphor for human potential and hubris, corrupting and incorruptible, desirable and dangerous is one that Bowie returns to repeatedly in his work. But there are stars and then there are stars. The new star that he discovered in your eyes, for instance, or the sleepless celebrity vampires, watching you from behind tinted windows of stretch limousines. The itemized list of different stars in the 'Blackstar' lyric draws conscious attention to the star-lore that already exists in Bowie's catalogue. It also sets up the idea that this Blackstar character is (at least claiming to be) more powerful and evolved than any other star you could think to mention.

There is a subtle difference between black holes and black stars. A black hole is a star that has collapsed under its own weight to the point that not even light can escape the force of its own gravity. A black star refers to a gravitational object that's very

---

[6] In late 1973, describing the plot of the Ziggy musical to William Burroughs. (Copetas 1974).

similar to a black hole, but still contains matter; a collapsed star that may be transitioning towards singularity – not possessing an observable event horizon or threshold point of no return, not yet the big 'nothing' as there is still detectible light that can escape the object. And there are mysteries within it – theoretically – such as quantum energy, quarks and particles; creative potentials. Theorists predict that towards the centre of a black star there are strange new laws governing space and time (Barceló et al. 2009). Thinking pragmatically, the fact that a black star is a *thing* and not a mysterious gaping *nothing* makes it easier to represent as an image.

> Burroughs: Where did this Ziggy idea come from, and this five-year idea? Of course, exhaustion of natural resources will not develop the end of the world. It will result in the collapse of civilization. And it will cut down the population by about three-quarters.
> Bowie: Exactly. This does not cause the end of the world for Ziggy. The end comes when the Infinites arrive. They really are a black hole, but I've made them people because it would be very hard to explain a black hole onstage.
> Burroughs: Yes, a black hole onstage would be an incredible expense. And it would be a continuing performance, first eating up Shaftesbury Avenue. (Copetas 1974)

Another enduring theme in Bowie's songwriting is space travel, which is often associated with ideas of lone adventure, isolation, decline, mental illness and transformation. Major Tom, the fictional astronaut from Bowie's first hit (1969's 'Space Oddity'), came to exemplify these connected themes, with his hero quest (to find an answer to a question? To find himself?) encapsulating Bowie's oeuvre from 1969 to 2016, the entirety of his journey as a 'star' on Earth. After being launched on a mission into space, Major Tom becomes disconnected from earthly communications and surrenders navigation to his spaceship, says his farewells to his wife and, from this point, presumably continues onwards on an open-ended adventure. A decade later in 'Ashes to Ashes' (1980) we learn that Major Tom has developed troubling addictions and has hit his all-time lowest point while traversing galactic voids. Though he's not referenced explicitly in a lyric again (not counting Neil Tennant's additional lines in the remixed version of 'Hallo Spaceboy' (1995)), Major Tom is a suggested presence in the music video for 'Slow

Burn' (2002) and again as the dead astronaut/skull relic in the video for 'Blackstar', with his corpse seen reclining in a picturesque otherworldly landscape, later floating headless towards an eclipse.

Of course, 'Space Oddity' took some inspiration from Stanley Kubrick's film *2001: A Space Odyssey* (1968), which explores themes of humanity's relationship with technology and the universe, following its protagonist Dr David 'Dave' Bowman (Keir Dullea) as he and his team investigate mysterious alien monoliths that have appeared throughout the solar system. At the climax of the film, Bowman's pod is pulled into a black hole that acts as a portal and shows him travelling through a surreal vortex of colour, streaking flashing lights and strange planetary landscapes. Before he vanishes through the portal, Mission Control hears his final words: 'The thing's hollow. It goes on forever, and ... oh my God! ... It's full of stars!' The infamous Star Gate sequence is intercut with scenes of stars exploding (going supernova) and close-up shots of Bowman's eyes, suggesting that the multidimensional travel is affecting him inwardly as well as outwardly. Ultimately, Bowman is irrevocably changed by this experience, reborn into the form of a new celestial being, the foetal Star Child, naked and wrapped in utero light-energy, eyes wide open.

Interestingly, the handwritten 'Blackstar' lyric drafts (added to the *David Bowie Is* exhibition in 2018) show some of the rejected lyrics from the B section of the song declaring what he isn't ('not a no-show, fallback, black mark') and what he is ('a sun star, bladestar'). Keeping with the sci-fi theme, it's perhaps a trivial coincidence that Bowie's sixty-ninth and last birthday (8 January 2016) was also the inception date (birthday) of anti-hero and Nexus 6 replicant Roy Batty (Rutger Hauer) from *Blade Runner* (1982). In a tantalizing 'what might have been' scenario, Bowie was the first choice of director Denis Villeneuve to star as the antagonist Niander Wallace in the sequel, *Blade Runner 2049* (Adetula 2017). We know that Bowie was a fan of the original film, as the tribute wreath he sent to the funeral of his half-brother Terry quoted Batty's 'tears in rain' monologue[7] (Gilmore 2012). This shared birth/release/inception

---

[7] On the note accompanying the funeral wreath, Bowie borrows from Batty's famous final soliloquy, writing: 'You've seen more things than we can imagine, but all of these moments will be lost, like tears washed away by the rain. God bless you – David' (1985). A very similar line – 'vanish like tears in the rain' – appears in the lyric of 'Girls', the B-side of 1987 single 'Time Will Crawl'.

could be nothing more than happy synchronism, but it opens a channel of pleasing resonance: the ★ project arriving on Bowie's birthday (so close to his death day), while on some parallel fictional plane Batty is 'born', starting his short journey to fight for the extension of his lifespan, ultimately destined to fail but not before confronting his creator.

Black music

It was Terry who turned his brother on to jazz at a young age (playing him Mingus, Coltrane and Dolphy), as well as instigating Bowie's lifelong interests in Tibetan Buddhism, science fiction, Beat Generation literature, soul music and R&B. It was these shared enthusiasms for jazz and R&B that led Bowie to pick the alto saxophone as his instrument and you can hear how these foundational music inspirations seeped into Bowie's songwriting: from jazz, he took modal effects, lopsided time signatures, elastic form and structure, and a will to extend the boundaries of pop and rock music and create space for improvisation and experimentation; from R&B came catchy hooks and danceable rhythms, keyboards and horn sections adding swagger to everything from *"Heroes"* to *Tin Machine* to *Earthling*. He added Mike Garson's avant-garde jazz-inspired style to the high glam sound of the Spiders, most dramatically heard in the genre-smashing free-improv centrepiece piano solo in 'Aladdin Sane (1913–38–7?)' (*Aladdin Sane*). From the Ziggy era onwards, Bowie would also begin (tentatively and sporadically) integrating his own sax playing into his projects – from the layered section work on 'Soul Love' (*Ziggy Stardust*) and the soul-inspired solo from 'Sorrow' (*Pin Ups*) to the avant-jazz 'Subterraneans' (1977, *Low*, originally composed for the aborted *The Man Who Fell to Earth* soundtrack). He was one of the first white artists to record at Sigma Sound Studios in Philadelphia (the birthplace of Philly soul, also associated with Gamble and Huff's influential PIR label, a vital precursor to disco) and would eventually innovate new rock fusions that combined American (soul, funk, disco) elements with European music styles (glam, motorik, early electronica) with his powerhouse rhythm section (all musicians of colour – Carlos Alomar, George Murray and Dennis Davis) in the late 1970s.

In 1975, Bowie was only the second white artist (after Elton John) to appear on the landmark American dance music show *Soul Train*, exposing his sound to new non-rock audiences and propelling soul-inspired tracks 'Fame' (*Young Americans*) and 'Golden Years' (*Station to Station*) to the top of the charts. With the help of disco pioneer Nile Rodgers, he would finally break through to mainstream megastardom with the funk-inspired *Let's Dance* and, that same year, publicly called out MTV for not programming Black music videos. He said to MTV VJ Mark Goodman: 'It occurred to me, having watched MTV over the last few months, that it's a solid enterprise, really. It's got a lot going for it. I am just floored by the fact that there's so few black artists featured on it. Why is that?' (MTV 1983). Like most white music stars, Bowie took heavy inspiration from Black music cultures that paid huge commercial dividends, though one gets the sense that he never did so in the spirit of concealment or outright theft. Bowie was in a love affair with Black American music from the very start.

Both ★ and the 2014 single version of 'Sue (Or in a Season of Crime)' stand in the catalogue as the fullest expressions of Bowie's love of jazz. Ron Hart would comment that these late choices to work with 'jazz musicians pushing the genre itself deeper and deeper into the twenty-first century is perhaps his greatest gift back to the genre – *Blackstar* is surely positioned to rekindle the relationship between jazz and rock in the same way Kendrick Lamar's *To Pimp a Butterfly* reunited the craft with hip-hop' (Hart 2016). Assistant engineer Erin Tonkon remembers that Lamar's 2015 album was listened to 'all the way through from start to finish with David in the studio', along with D'Angelo's *Black Messiah* (2014): 'He was just blown away and so inspired by that music.' Tony Visconti would add, 'We loved the fact that Kendrick was so open-minded and he didn't do a straight-up hip-hop record. He threw everything on there, and that's exactly what we wanted to do. The goal, in many ways, was to avoid rock and roll' (Greene 2015).

Following his death, ★ stormed the charts and Bowie became the number one artist in the world; within two weeks there would be twelve of his albums in the UK top forty – a feat that no other artist had accomplished aside from Elvis Presley, following his death in 1977 (Pegg 2016, 477). Like all young musicians of the 1950s, Bowie grew up under the ubiquitous shadow of the King, cribbing plenty of his stage moves and make-up tips. In the 1970s, the pair shared a record label, RCA, and there were rumours of would-be collaborations between the star label-mates. Bowie's 1975 hit 'Golden Years' was apparently offered to Presley, who declined (Buckley [2005] 2012, 237). The iconic *Aladdin Sane* lightning bolt make-up was inspired by Presley's TCB (Taking Care of Business) logo (and also by the logo on an old rice cooker in album photographer Brian Duffy's studio).

In a 1997 interview with *Q* magazine Bowie spoke about their coincidental birthdays and how he once thought it might have some manner of cosmic provenance: 'I couldn't believe it, he was a major hero of mine. And I was probably stupid enough to believe that having the same birthday as him actually meant something' (Cavanagh 1997). Bowie could have been playing with these connections by referencing one of Presley's obscure cuts: 'Black Star' (1960). Originally intended to be the title track for a film of the same name, the song was retitled 'Flaming Star' and re-recorded when the film project was renamed. Written by Sid Wayne and Sherman Edwards, the song is sung from the perspective of a character who wishes he could bargain with death for more time – the star that the protagonist can sense over his shoulder is death itself.

And when a man sees his black star
He knows his time, his time has come

– 'Black Star' (1960)

Presley's ambiguous relationship with Black culture was also something that Bowie thought about in the context of his own work. Ian Penman reflected on this when he interviewed Bowie in 1995 for *Esquire*:

We were talking about his great watershed album *Young Americans* and he said something very sane and economical about it: 'Yeah, it was like: how do you give the white man soul without pretending to be a black man?' The very thing he was so often criticized for – being the Great Pretender – was, in fact and in essence, the one thing he wasn't. But the query he put to himself – how do you give the white man soul? – vibrated at other frequencies. This was also the time of cocaine, Crowley, Caucasian messiah complexes.

(Penman 1995, 64)

Black arts, black hearts

Occultism and surrealism both use symbols to engage different levels of consciousness, to penetrate the mysteries and facilitate creativity through the disruption, expansion or destruction of the confines of rational thinking. While it can take various subversive shapes, based on different texts and traditions, in the forms that found new popularity in the 1960s it mirrored surrealism's engagement with the sub/unconscious, with its 'faith in the power of dream and trance images, and in the stream of words uncensored by the intellect' (Koenig 1996).

Bowie's songwriting engaged creatively with these esoteric concepts at various points in his career; at the level of intellectual curiosity on *The Man Who Sold the World*, *Hunky Dory* and, later, in *Station to Station*, where, fully immersed in occult activities and on the brink of full-blown cocaine psychosis, Bowie was reportedly painting sigils on the walls of his Los Angeles home, concocting hexes, chanting spells and generally losing his grip on reality. There is also a curious tension between art, identity and authenticity emerging during this period; Bowie is engaging warmly with Black music culture, while at the same time embodying the shadow figure of the Thin White Duke, his icy Aryan aura seemingly at odds with the funk and soul-inspired music he was producing at the time. It is the Duke that sings about 'flashing no colour' and 'making sure white stains' – longing to be connected with love yet feeling nothing at all, settling for a cold embrace with the dark side of his Europeanness (Leorne 2015). In 'Blackstar' there is a curious line about 'seeing right', with eagles, daydreams and diamonds in his eyes, which has an unsettling whiff of right-wing American 'freedom' rhetoric and Nazi imagery. Whoever this self-proclaimed blackstar is, he's making big promises and not providing clear answers – he can't answer why, you just have to trust him. He's going to take you home and confine you there without shoes or a passport. Your life is not worth that much anyway – 'you're a flash in the pan/I'm the great I Am'. In this part of the song the lyrics suggest that the heavenly, crooning voice is confidently seducing others into a dark and dangerous belief system.

Imagery associated with notorious English magician and poet Aleister Crowley appears from time to time in Bowie's work. Crowley can be linked to the Kabbalist symbolism in 'Station to Station', the scribbles on the walls in the famous Schapiro portraits from 1975 and specific ritual poses in Bowie's imagery and performances. For example, the overhanded-floor-touch move, performed in many music videos ('Fashion', 'Ashes to Ashes' (both 1980), 'Dancing in the Street' (1985), et al.) was a signification of the 'magical movement from Kether to Malkuth' ('Station to Station' 1976) on the Kabbalistic 'Tree of Life' – pulling heaven down to Earth.[8] This symbolic act mirrored Bowie's personal philosophy as an artist: 'I'm actually very nineteenth century – a born Romantic. Unlike Brian [Eno], who's terminally end-of-20th century ... Brian is someone who will take things from low art and elevate them to high art. Whereas I do precisely the opposite: I'll take things from high art and demean them down to the street level... ' (Penman 1995, 61)

The lyrical repetition of the line 'at the centre of it all', as a few commentators (including Pegg, 2016, 41) have pointed out, has a familiarity with Crowley's Star Sapphire ritual (Crowley 1938): 'Let him return to the Centre, and so to the Centre of All (making the Rosy Cross as he may know how)', which echoes another lyric from 'Slow Burn' (2002): 'And here are we at the centre of it all/slow burn'. The purpose and specific nature of this ritual are shrouded within obfuscating language in the original text, though the 'Rosy Cross' likely refers to ritual sex magick.[9] The lyric is given its eerie charge by the dark atmosphere of the music and Bowie's invocational delivery, but it is unlikely that the casual listener would register any higher meanings beyond this. The remaining occult references contained in 'Blackstar' are made via imagery – the five-pointed star icon, featured in the album artwork by designer Jonathan Barnbrook, and the subversion of religious imagery (holy

---

[8] The 'Tree of Life' is a diagram used in some mystical traditions (Jewish and Hermetic Kabbalah, also adapted within Crowley's system of Thelema), consisting of ten interconnected spheres or nodes (called sephiroth) representing aspects of reality (God's creation) organized into a structural hierarchy with pathways of movement between. The movement that goes from Kether (crown/godhead, the primordial energy of creation) to Malkuth (Earth/the physical realm) describes a journey from the highest to the lowest of the sephiroth (White 2019).

[9] 'The fundamental symbols of the Rosicrucians were the rose and the cross; the rose female and the cross male ... exemplifying the reproductive processes' (Hall [1928] 2011, 152).

books being held aloft, quaking ritual movements, scarecrows in
crucifix pose) contained in the music video.

The enigmatic black star symbol has been read as a reference to
the Ancient Egyptian alchemical symbol of the Black Sun (or Sol
Niger), the raw material of creation not yet transformed – a symbol
that Jung attached to the idea of light and shadow coexisting in
consciousness, the synthesis of opposites in alchemy and psychology
(Jung 1970, 117). The Black Sun is also a name given to a Nazi
symbol (*schwarze sonne* in German) commonly seen in propaganda
imagery associated with neo-fascists, far-right extremists and white
nationalists. In speaking with *Rolling Stone*, McCaslin claimed
that Bowie had told him the song 'was about ISIS' (Islamic State)[10]
(Greene 2015), leading Spencer Kornhaber in *The Atlantic* to
speculate on how a song about stardom and inflated ego could be
connected to the idea of Islamic extremism, ' … and about how
indulging one's ego can, paradoxically, inspire others to forget
their own. You can see how radical clerics and suicide bombers fit
the dynamic here' (2016). The pentagrammic black star icon that
appeared on the album artwork was devised by Barnbrook and,
by his account, did not take inspiration from the occult, but rather
once again from Russian constructivism, Kazimir Malevich's *Black
Square* painting.

Unveiled in St Petersburg/Petrograd in 1915 while the First
World War raged, with one Russian revolution in recovery
and another brewing, *Black Square* is precisely what its title
suggests it is: a painted black square on a white linen canvas,
measuring roughly 80cm in each axis. It was purposefully hung
in a traditionally venerated position in the gallery that, when
translated to a traditional Russian home, would be reserved for
orthodox saints and icons: a site of spiritual significance. Among
the many interpretations of the work, it has been said to reflect
'an impotence and redundancy in its detachment from the forces
of life' (Troncale 2020) or convey 'sheer, surging, untrammelled
possibility' (Schjeldahl 2011); 'the most frightening painting known
to man' (Tolstaya 2015); an image that depicts 'nothing and nobody'

---

[10] In the only public comment Bowie made about the album, this was officially denied;
in response to McCaslin's comments a spokesperson told *The Mirror*, 'Blackstar is
not about the Middle East situation' (McGeorge 2015).

(Sarabyanov 1990, 279). The image became Malevich's signature motif, an icon representing his identity and enduring legacy; he signed his subsequent paintings with it and a black square also marks his grave. The ★ visual concept was designed from the start to be shareable and recognizable in big or small formats – the fact that the five-pointed star icon was already available as a Dingbat font meant the album's artwork could be transmitted in a multitude of different forms and easily incorporated into any text. In the end, Barnbrook designed five different versions of the star cover,[11] which were subsequently integrated into the inner sleeve/booklet design. Each star suggests different meanings – with eight, twelve, sixteen and twenty points, they look like religious stars, sun symbols, comic book-style explosions and, finally, an official seal like one would find on a certificate or diploma. I asked Barnbrook if Bowie came to him with the black star visual concept already in hand: 'You asked me if David came forward with the ideas, and he never did … especially with *The Next Day* and ★ his approach was really "How do you respond to this? I'm not gonna explain the songs or anything… ".'

The different black stars, each one unique and symmetrically perfect, bear some resemblance to the mandalas that Jung obsessively drew and painted in response to his dreaming, driven as he was towards the centre of things: 'The centre is the goal, and everything is directed toward that centre' (2009, 80). A foundational concept in Jung's writing is not only the identification of the 'I' at the centre, but a population of 'I's that make up the total self: 'Inasmuch as the I is only the centre of my field of consciousness, it is not identical with the totality of my psyche, being merely a complex among other complexes … In this sense the self would be an (ideal) greatness which embraces and concludes the I' (ibid., 59).

Button eyes

The 'Blackstar' video, filmed in September 2015, begins with close-ups of an astronaut's suit, opening up to reveal it reclining against

---

[11] Barnbook: 'There are five different black stars and I tried to get Sony to do five different covers … the idea was to have different kinds of stars and to show the different aspects of the meaning of a word.'

rocks in a blue landscape on a remote planet, the scene is dimly lit by a solar eclipse. The suit is old and battered, held together in places with electrical tape; a yellow smiley-faced patch can be seen on the front, a reference to GERTY, the artificial intelligence from the science fiction film *Moon* (2009), written and directed by Bowie's son, Duncan Jones. A young woman with a tail and monobrow[12] approaches the corpse, gently detaches the dead astronaut's jewel-encrusted skull, then delivers it to a nearby town where a group of women have assembled, and a ritual is about to commence. The town seems to be lit from the centre by a candle that has accumulated a large amount of melted wax, giving the interior scenes a warm glow. We first see Bowie as a panicked blind man with bandaged eyes (Button Eyes) who sings the incantational passages from the A section of the song while figures behind him convulse and shake, as if possessed. By the second verse, Button Eyes has calmed down somewhat, making slower movements and half-smiling as he sings. By the transition to the B section of the song, in the same costume but now without the blindfold, he is seemingly possessed of a different character – Bowie stands resolute with eyes fixed on the distance, holy book held aloft, the symbol of the blackstar on the cover.

Shifting character again, Bowie delivers the contrasting middle section of the song from a church-like attic, under shafts of warm blurry light. Now the opposite of panicked, his performance is confident and mocking, embodying the archetypal trickster. Nearby, three living scarecrows, male, blindfolded with button eyes, are positioned in a grassy field, suggesting the scene of Jesus' crucifixion. The figures writhe and grind, as the ritual with the women, who are also shaking like the three figures we see behind Button Eyes in the attic, takes place. Eventually a surreal-looking monster, a black mass of dreadlocked fur and no face, is summoned. It rushes to attack the scarecrows with its large hook, while a heavy storm breaks over the town and Button Eyes struggles and falters. The clip ends with a brief flash of Barnbrook's black star icon.

---

[12] Barnbrook: [during their early talks about the artwork] 'He was very interested in the fluidity of gender, and people who are non-binary, and he had shown me these drawings of women with tails, which later appeared in the "Blackstar" video.'

The collaboration with director Johan Renck on the video for 'Blackstar' had a starting point in late July 2015, while the track itself was undergoing finishing touches. It was Renck who initially reached out to the Bowie camp, requesting permission to use his music for the opening theme for Canal+ and Sky Atlantic's six-episode crime drama *The Last Panthers*. Bowie responded with an early, alternate version of the final verse of 'Blackstar', with new keyboard and guitar parts added. Now acquainted as collaborators with shared interests in surrealism and the psychomagical dream realism of directors such as Alejandro Jodorowsky and Andrei Tarkovsky (Pegg 2016, 43), Bowie worked closely with Renck to produce his final two videos ('Blackstar' 2015, 'Lazarus' 2016).

The influence of German expressionism is also apparent here in the composition and staging of the exterior scenes – the stylized alien landscape with its curled edges and two-dimensional painterly quality, is framed by the eclipse in such a way that suggests the overall shape of an eye. The ancient town lit from the centre, with its symmetrical buildings in perspective, call to mind iconic imagery from the silent films of Robert Wiene and Fritz Lang. It's possible that the use of colour in the narrative was similarly inspired by the differently tinted and toned nitrate prints from Wiene's *The Cabinet of Dr. Caligari* (1920), as the 'Blackstar' video makes use of blue, ochre, amber and green washes to suggest ex/interiority and location.

The choreography in 'Blackstar' was devised by Elke Luyten (who also worked on 'Lazarus') and her collaborator Kira Alker. Luyten also appears in the video – first as one of the three shaking acolytes behind Button Eyes, and later as the volunteer in the ritual who accepts the skull. The eerie convulsing movement was said to stem from a suggestion made by Bowie, connected to the always-moving background animations he noticed in a Popeye cartoon (Lynch 2015), but the movements could also be connected to a similar shaking 'bunny hop' (Perrott 2019) gesture seen in the video for 'Fashion' (1980). In the context of 'Blackstar', it brings an unmistakable ecstatic-religious connotation that suggests Quaker/Shaker worship and voodoo ritual. The approach to movement seems to cross-pollinate with the 'Lazarus' video (filmed two months later), a strangely stiffened dancing style common in both, alongside the reappearance of Button Eyes and the adorned skull on the writer's desk.

There is a focus on sight; blindfolds, buttons for eyes, close-ups of eyes sending communicative signals, and at times the audience's view mimics failing senses – partially blurred vision, flaring light and strange shifts in position, as though the viewer has one or the other eye momentarily closed. The eyes at the centre of it all hold some significance and the missing and/or mutilated eye is a potent symbol of surrealist art (Eager 1961). Bowie's famously mismatched eyes, the result of a childhood injury, eventually became an iconic symbol of his unusual beauty, individuality and artistic vision; with one pupil permanently dilated, it meant Bowie saw the world slightly differently. A gift, and an impairment. He often used the symbol of the bandaged, blind or masked man: feeling towards the future in the 'Time Will Crawl' video (1987); the sectioned man with sensory-style eye bandages in 'Jump They Say' (1993, a reference to the 1962 experimental film *La Jetée*); blindfolded and wrapped up with dead fish as Ramona A. Stone (embodying another photo in Schwarzkogler's *3rd Action* series) from *1. Outside*; the clouded eyes of *Heathen* and the accompanying desecrated artworks with their eyes scratched out in homage to death-obsessed photographer Joel-Peter Witkin. Pegg points out that Bowie had also performed as a 'blind pilgrim' on stage during the *Glass Spider Tour*'s 'Loving the Alien' sequence and in late-period live performances of 'Heathen (The Rays)' (2016, 44). In 1976, in the alias of the Thin White Duke, Bowie opened his live performances with a cloth mask covering his eyes (after the traditional precursor showing of Dalí and Buñuel's eyeball-slicing short *Un Chien Andalou*). Here, the buttons sewn into his bandages seem to be mocking his blindness – a symbolic image that Perrott interprets as a representation of loss of agency (2019). Buttons as eyes is a visual metaphor that Neil Gaiman deploys in his dark fantasy *Coraline* (2002), signifying the acceptance of captivity and compliance with the world one finds oneself in. The buttons also echo the Greco-Roman myth of Charon, the ferryman who accepts payment in pennies on the eyes of the dead, holding their eyes shut, before taking the deceased to Hades.

When the *David Bowie Is* archive made its final stop in Brooklyn in 2018 it included new ★ artefacts: sketches and storyboards under the heading 'disunited states of mind' – prototype drawings of the Button Eyes character, one with eyes completely covered, another with the bandage mask slipping off, revealing real eyes underneath.

One of these 'states of mind' cannot see what's coming. The image strikes to the heart of our anxieties about death and what comes next, providing a fittingly poetic image of how it feels to not be able to see beyond your own end. There is no knowledge without perception. The big 'nothing' of death is a riddle, for how can we know that there is nothing if we are stripped of all perception and can't see or sense it? Cognition requires an object to observe and vice versa (Bauman 1992). Death ends existence, and so completes it, but the dead person lacks the ability to appreciate the totality of their 'life as a whole' (Heidegger [1927] 2019, 72). Being diagnosed with life-threatening cancer is a cruel knowledge to receive. A paradoxical trade-off where one is forced to surrender knowledge of the future in exchange for the kind of unnatural knowledge no-one would want to possess – when you might expect to die and how much (or little) time there is left. It's funny how a terminal deadline gets stuck on your eyes.

9

Chaos and chemistry

At its core, the musical style of ★ is a fusion of experimental rock and electronica, played with élan by improvising jazz musicians. It's a noticeable move away from the straight-ahead rock aesthetic that characterized the two preceding albums, *The Next Day* and *Reality*. The contrast in sound between ★ and Bowie's solidly established late style felt like an old-school style shift – those jolting, palate-cleansing changes he was known for making, for instance between *Hunky Dory* and *Ziggy*, *Never Let Me Down* and *Tin Machine*, *Earthling* and *Hours*.... Sometimes, hints and clues embedded on the last record can point in the direction of the next. *The Next Day*'s finale 'Heat' (2013), with its Scott Walker dry-ice atmosphere and solemn yet tender modal colour, could arguably serve as a link, at least from the end of the album to the opening moments of 'Blackstar'. However, more than the continuation of haunted atmospherics, ★'s new territory is distinguished by a tangible sense of barely tamed chaos, especially in the first half; textural intensity, a feeling of losing control, where the music itself seems on the edge of danger (like the darker waters previously navigated on *1. Outside* (e.g. 'A Small Plot of Land', 1995) and *Earthling* (e.g. 'Battle for Britain (The Letter)', 1997)). The clues that Bowie was headed in that direction track back to the dark disorder of *The Next Day*'s 'If You Can See Me' and were indicated with even more clarity in the collaboration with Maria Schneider and her jazz orchestra for the 2014 single version of 'Sue (Or in a Season of Crime)' and its surprising B-side, a home-demo version of ★'s "Tis a Pity She Was a Whore'.

Schneider and Bowie met and began working together in May 2014, after he and Visconti went to see her and her band play at

Birdland, a jazz club in midtown Manhattan. 'Sue' was developed
in a collaborative spirit, with Schneider's input on the structure
and thematic treatment earning her a co-writing credit. Paul
Bateman and Bob Bhamra, a production duo that had made drum
'n' bass tracks under the name Plastic Soul, are also given a share
of the songwriting credit – 'Sue' interpolated the bassline of their
composition 'Brand New Heavy' (1997), using it as its foundational
rhythmic motif and seemingly drawing further inspiration from its
jungle breakbeat energy. No doubt a musical reference that Bowie,
not Schneider, brought to the table, since we know he was an avid
follower of emerging dance music producers during the mid-to-late
1990s (Power 2020). Collaborative ideas were sketched out and
workshopped live with the orchestra's rhythm section, arrangements
were tweaked and the whole lot was recorded in July at New York's
Avatar Studios (these days once again known by its original name,
Power Station). The session was engineered by Kevin Killen[1] with
Visconti co-producing. Schneider's ensemble for 'Sue' included
future ★ musicians Mark Guiliana and Ben Monder on drums and
guitar, respectively, and Donny McCaslin on alto saxophone, one
of the two primary soloists handpicked by Bowie (the other being
Ryan Keberle on trombone).

     The song's churning film-noir-esque arrangement passes over
its seven-minute-plus running time like a threatening weather
system; skittish drum patterns and syncopated bass (Jay Anderson)
are smoothed over by long sweeps of big band horns that surge
past the ear, bending in pitch like an engine Doppler effect, with
contrabass clarinet (Scott Robinson) adding resonant sharpness to
the low end, an edge of violence. Pressure builds through lydian
modal shifts between G and A/G, increasing to crisis points that
crash on E minor. The texture is always shape-shifting, coming and
going, rising and falling, ridden by Bowie's central vocal which is
sometimes elongated and stretched across the sonic expanse, at
other times focusing on a single note in a rhythmic, almost liturgical,
recitativo. Schneider directed the primary soloists, McCaslin and
Keberle, to eschew traditional solo breaks in favour of a more

---

[1] Kevin Killen, esteemed producer and sound engineer, enters the story here,
engineering the sessions for this version of 'Sue', then the ★ sessions at Magic Shop
in early 2015. He also engineered the *Lazarus (Original Cast Recording)* in 2016
(produced by Henry Hey, and also tracked at Avatar).

constant 'improvisational decoration and commentary' around Bowie's vocal (O'Leary 2019, 617). This meant that the players were reactively performing against Bowie for the duration of the song, filling the gaps with improvised gestures. In the end Visconti and Bowie used McCaslin's take throughout (mixed slightly to the right), with Keberle's solo featuring in the quieter transitional section that occurs in the fourth minute of the track (mixed slightly to the left, 4:09–5:07). It's busy and volatile, a raw and elemental danger reined in under Schneider's steady hand. 'Sue (Or in a Season of Crime)' ended up winning in the category of Best Arrangement for Schneider at the 58th Annual Grammy Awards (2016).

The B-side to this early version of 'Sue', which was released as a single in November 2014, is Bowie's home demo of "Tis a Pity She Was a Whore'. In the history of Bowie's sometimes-half-formed B-side offerings (for example the *Omikron*[2] soundtrack offcuts '1917' and 'No One Calls' that showed up on the *Hours...* singles in 1999), never has a production so unpolished-sounding (by commercial standards) seen the light of day on an official release. Produced at home using his Zoom multi-track recorder, and playing all of the instruments himself, the track opens with sampled explosions and gunshots that repeat in a stiff rhythm, ushering in a driving drum loop reminiscent of the one from 'You've Been Around' (*Black Tie White Noise* 1993). Pointillistic staccato figures on piano and saxophone begin with tentative accents that accelerate as their pitches ascend – the effect of these patterns grating and evolving inside their misaligned orbit is similar to that of Steve Reich's early minimalist phasing experiments.[3] The vocal performance is unusual in its distorted sound and rather genial delivery, contrasting with the affronted lyric and the general thrust and drama of the outer musical arrangement. Visconti explained that the fuzzed-out vocal

---

[2] *Omikron: The Nomad Soul* was an adventure computer game developed by Quantic Dream and published by Eidos Interactive in 1999. Bowie and guitarist Reeves Gabrels wrote and produced the original soundtrack, and Bowie appeared as the character Boz in-game.

[3] Reich deployed phase-shifting in his early work, exploiting the phenomenon when tape loops of differing lengths move towards and away from synchronization in interesting ways (*It's Gonna Rain* 1965). Reich later applied similar processes to live performance, notably in 1972's *Clapping Music*, which was itself sampled and looped in James Murphy's 'Love Is Lost (Hello Steve Reich Mix by James Murphy for the DFA)' remix.

effect was a happy accident: 'He just slammed distortion on his voice unwittingly'. The resulting composition is a strange, thrilling, messy jumble of unlikely colours and ideas.[4]

The track is named after John Ford's notorious play *'Tis Pity She's a Whore* (1633), historically controversial for its romantic portrayal of incest, though Bowie's lyric doesn't appear to connect with the play's themes in any obvious way. The digital press release for the single (posted online by the official channels on 10 November 2014) offered another angle: 'The song ["'Tis a Pity"] acknowledges the shocking rawness of the First World War,' however aside from the line 'that was patrol/this is the war' and the sounds of bombs and guns, there is little other information that we can spin narrative sense from. The image of a shell-shocked soldier becoming the unwitting victim of petty crime might have been inspired by the TV show *Peaky Blinders*, which was airing at the time and reportedly Bowie was something of a superfan.[5] Pegg (2016, 285) interprets the lyric to be more aligned with poet Robert Southey's literature on the slave trade. The lyrics on the page are impressionistic enough to slip into any narrative construction where a man has been duped and left feeling shaken and emasculated by the actions of a woman. After the male violence and fantasies of domination that characterize sections of *The Next Day* (not to mention the use of the term 'whores' in the opening and closing songs on the album), and the suffering and sacrifice of Girl in *Lazarus*, the female characters that inhabit the lyrics on ★ are notable for their power and agency – from controlling the 'Blackstar' ritual and fleecing gullible old fools in 'Girl Loves Me' to the efficiently executed mugging of "'Tis a Pity' and the way 'Sue' decides to leave her controlling lover with a note.

While the function of the reference to Ford's play in the song's title is unclear, some connections might be plausibly drawn between the play's themes (of obsession, betrayal, a fateful note

---

[4] Visconti is a fan of this version, he told me: 'It's amazing, it rivals the recorded version that we produced on ★!'

[5] According to writer Steven Knight, Bowie's team had gotten in touch to say that he was a 'big, big fan' of the show, and Bowie had sent a photo of himself wearing a *Peaky Blinders*-style cap with razorblades in it to lead actor Cillian Murphy in 2015; Knight was also sent an advance copy of ★: 'It seems that his people were keen to establish that we could use it before he died' (BBC 2016b).

and a gruesome murder) to the narrative traces contained in 'Sue'. With the two compositions paired together as sides A and B of a single release, the resonances of their proximate themes feel more pronounced than on the album proper, where they are separated in sequence by 'Lazarus'. Unreliable and ambiguous in the order of events it sets out, listeners are free to wonder if 'Sue' is simply a cut-up confession from her killer, or the confused, one-sided fantasy of somebody who was merely obsessed with her from afar. Is Sue of sound mind and body? The repeated use of her name, reminding her of where and who she is, telling her the results of her X-ray... seem vaguely infantilizing. On the other hand, the name being caressed repeatedly over that long lydian angle calls to mind the romantic obsession of *West Side Story*'s 'Maria'. 'Sue' constructs a blurred image of caregiving, obsession and control, and by the end of the song it is unclear whether the crime has taken place at all. Our erratic narrator describes pushing her body down beneath some weeds, but afterwards finds Sue's note, which informs him that she has left him for another man. It's up to the listener to decide if Sue managed to get away or not.

Another helpful clue was included with the press release, hinting at an alternate way of approaching "Tis a Pity': 'If Vorticists wrote Rock Music it might have sounded like this'. The Vorticists were a short-lived, London-based variation of the cubist art movement, founded by poet Ezra Pound and artist Wyndham Lewis in 1914. Their philosophies and aesthetics were articulated in a manifesto that pushed back against British decadence, 'plunge(ing) to the heart of the Present' to 'produce a New Living Abstraction ... WE ONLY WANT THE WORLD TO LIVE, and to feel its crude energy flowing through us' (Lewis 1914). The group combined reality-shattering cubist fragmentation with hard-edged industrialized imagery that prefigured brutalism. The movement tuned in to a potent symbolic image of the times – the *vortex* – which Pound defined as 'that point in the cyclone where energy cuts into space and imparts form to it ... the pattern of angles and geometric lines which is formed by our vortex in the existing chaos' (Vengerova 1915). The radical group formed just as the First World War began, in that same early-twentieth-century psychological turbulence that drove Jung to his *Red Book*. The movement would be over by the war's end. After the horrors, British art culture rejected futurism and the avant-garde in favour of traditionalism and a return to order.

As a meditation on chaos, "Tis a Pity' makes sense, with its mess of ideas thrown together into the swirl: violence, confusion, crisis, Britishness, cowardice, fragments of reality and brutality spinning and phasing in a vortex of lyrical and historical imagery, music and sound. The narrators of both 'Sue' and "Tis a Pity' feel kin to the tyrants and tragic-cases of The Next Day, only now the stories have an element of comeuppance written in. The fresh musical approaches evident in both, the controlled squall of 'Sue' and the rough and tumble of "Tis a Pity', foreshadow the sonic and musical tensions of ★. It's significant that Bowie chose to revisit both pieces on ★, with new arrangements that further intensify sensations of chaos. Bowie had wanted to continue working with Maria Schneider on his album project, but she was too busy with her own then-forthcoming Grammy Award–winning album The Thompson Fields (2017). However, she would be the crucial vector that connected him with his final legendary sideman, Donny McCaslin, and his band (Tim Lefebvre, Mark Guiliana, Ben Monder and Jason Lindner). McCaslin's approach to collaborative working impacted the shape, colour and energy of ★. Not only offering Bowie an opportunity to explore a fresh musical aesthetic, McCaslin and his group made special efforts to stay prepared, rehearsed, ready and responsive, which actively facilitated states of expressive flow, creating space for intuitive creativity in the studio. By passing his compositions over to a group of improvising musicians, Bowie was given access to a creative zone that allowed him to engage with and communicate chaos in his songwriting, through the creation of intensities, forces and sensations.

Initially, Schneider nudged Bowie towards McCaslin and his group by recommending his 2012 album Casting for Gravity – an adventurous blend of jazz and electronica that drew inspiration from the wild fusion jams of Weather Report, Herbie Hancock's Head Hunters (1973) and the intricate electronica of Richard D. James (Aphex Twin). That busy summer (2014), in addition to recording and mixing the Schneider collaboration, Bowie and Visconti went to the Magic Shop (with musicians Zach Alford and Jack Spann) to cut some demos for Lazarus and develop new material that would become the seeds of the ★ project – the 'four or five' new demos that eventually reached the hands of McCaslin over the intervening months ahead of the first ★ sessions in January 2015. The directive from Bowie was to remain in the present, to not look backwards:

We were initially going to start recording ★ in the fall, and then it got postponed. I had these songs, I was checking them out and I thought 'Okay, let me check out his catalogue, so I can put this into context with everything that came before' … I had an email exchange with him about it, and the spirit of that exchange was 'Hey, I'm starting to check out some of your other stuff', and he wrote back, 'You know, I'm into some different stuff now' … And that kind of affirmed my gut … to keep ploughing ahead with processing the music that he was sending through my own musical language.

– McCaslin (Mohammad 2020, episode part 1, 20:25)

A working pattern that emerged between them involved a batch of demos being sent to McCaslin ahead of the scheduled recording days, which occurred across weeklong stretches in January, February and March 2015. In the gaps between these sessions, Bowie would send new material over – the first sessions covered the *Lazarus/No Plan* EP material and the existing songs from 2014 (including other songs that never came out, according to McCaslin); newer material that made it on to ★ (tracks like 'Girl Loves Me' and 'Dollar Days' in the second week of sessions, 'Blackstar' and 'I Can't Give Everything Away' in the third) would arrive during the process, suggesting that Bowie was still writing through the tracking stages of the production, inspired and spurred on by the collaboration. 'Dollar Days' would surface spontaneously in the studio, without being demoed ahead of time. McCaslin sketched out arrangements, the band studied the music and rehearsed; they would arrive and set up ahead of time and work through any technical issues so that when the time came to hit record, McCaslin and his band were ready to go right out of the gate. With downtime kept to a minimum, the tracking stage of ★'s production came together remarkably quickly compared to the protracted processes of *The Next Day*. 'Mr McCaslin is a one-take man,' recalled Visconti:

We didn't have a lot to sift through [in the edit]; what you're hearing on the record is mainly take one. The band would have a run-through with David, then come out and we'd listen to it. And that was it! Then they would look at us like 'Ok, what's the next song?' An hour! An hour to do one song.

– Visconti (interview with the author, 2020)

This meant that Bowie and Visconti had time with the players to explore additional arrangement ideas, like overdubbing McCaslin's playing into layered ensemble sections: 'There are some tracks where he did four or five saxes, a whole sax section.' Such stunning efficiency is a trait of working jazz musicians, as McCaslin would later reflect: 'In the jazz world, budget is almost always an issue. So you're making a record in one or two days, maybe three. In this situation it's like "Oh, we've got a week!" Now I've got another four days ... that is unheard of in my experience.' Having the luxury of time allowed him to engage with the music in a deeper way than usual: 'That ability to really focus, to imagine how this would sound on these different woodwinds I play, and there's time to do it ... I think part of how [having more time to record] affected me was getting to the kind of depth, emotionally, that I'm striving for' (ibid., part 2, 15:06).

McCaslin speaks about his experiences working on ★ almost exclusively in terms of intensity and sensation, recalling most vividly the shared moments of creative magic that he experienced with Bowie and the group. Shared sensitivity to sensation and creative chemistry amongst ensemble musicians doesn't just happen overnight and Bowie was fortunate to find in McCaslin's band a group that had played together on stages and in studios for years; they could readily tap into that wellspring. What was surprising, however, was how adept Bowie was at jumping into the mix:

[With the band] it is a conversation, a lot of improvising, a lot of changing the direction of the music on somebody's suggestion ... This feeling like we can just take on different roles at any moment. What was really beautiful was how David absolutely participated in that dynamic. He just stepped right in. And that upped the ante for all of us ... it felt magical. I would finish the day in the studio and be going home thinking 'Man, that was a great day. I hope that tomorrow is like that ... ' And for the most part every day was. We felt that connection happening in the room.

– McCaslin (ibid., part 1, 31:52)

Part of the 'conversation' of shared group creativity involves being silent sometimes, creating space for others to fill. Jason Lindner described how McCaslin, as bandleader, created room for the rhythm section to 'make a mess of things, to open it up and get really free, go to other dimensions' (Sequential 2016). Visconti observed a similar quality in Bowie, and how he worked with musicians in the studio over the years: 'David inspires people to be creative with his material and he makes space for them. Once they see they have his permission, and they see that he really means it, amazing things can happen.' Space and trust to allow for amazing moments such as those capacious and impossible-sounding performances from Mike Garson ('Aladdin Sane' 1973), Robert Fripp ('Teenage Wildlife' 1980), Reeves Gabrels ('Looking for Satellites' 1997) and so many others.

Working with improvising musicians with an already finely tuned chemistry meant that the instrumental backing for ★ could be tracked live, capturing a special energy. This was Bowie's preferred way of working, the 'greasy' process that Gerry Leonard had once described (Leonard 2013) being the special quality created by musicians working together in real time, playing off each other in the same environment. 'Liveness' can be a rare and precious quality in our contemporary age of digital multitrack recording, with its capacity for piecemeal and remote musical construction, and increasingly sophisticated editing tools promoting more refined and atomized aesthetics in mainstream music culture. Before the arrival of digital audio workstations, before pitches and rhythms and timings could be surgically corrected and errors airbrushed out, and further back to when recording to tape only allowed for a limited number of discreet tracks, and reels only held so many minutes of material… acoustic musicians simply had to be really good. And if they weren't technically amazing, they needed to at least have some exciting chemistry about them – energy, attitude, drama.

Around the time of the ★ sessions there was a collective feeling that popular music's taste of liveness was returning. The tyranny of tempo grids, quantization and pitch correction was entirely absent in D'Angelo's *Black Messiah* (2014); the band performances on tracks such as 'Ain't That Easy' and '1000 Deaths' were so loose, so relaxed, so *felt*, they threatened to fall apart at any moment. Kendrick Lamar's *To Pimp a Butterfly* (2015) was groundbreaking in its embrace of live jazz performances, glorious and messy on tracks like 'For Free?' and 'u'. Lamar's record showcased, among many other players, musicians signed to independent LA music label Brainfeeder – Thundercat, Flying Lotus (who founded the label) and Kamasi Washington. Brainfeeder spawned a scene responsible for promoting acts that fused jazz and improvisatory elements with mainstream pop styles. This is music that stands out for its liveness and joyful virtuosity – ensemble energies, drifting emotional currents, face-melting solos, chaos and catharsis.

There are even more ways to summon and guide chaos energy beyond the notes, performances and accumulations of kinetic charge – there is the materiality of the recorded sounds themselves. A world of signal processing and sound effects that can underline and saturate sound, make it curve in the air, break the laws of physics, bend space and time. ★ is loaded with such sonic wizardry, blurring the light between sound events. From the band's pedal collections, amps and half-rack units, Eventide H9 and Harmonizer gear to Visconti's closet of custom effects and Tom Elmhirst's banks of reverbs and vintage delays. For the sessions where James Murphy was there (the second of the three weeks, in February 2015), sounds were processed through his vintage EMS Synthi AKS – the suitcase synthesizer famously used by Bowie, Eno and Visconti on the 'Berlin trilogy' of albums (*Low*, *"Heroes"* and *Lodger*) and later included as an artefact in the V&A exhibit. Harking back to that era, Visconti summarized his creative philosophy to me in simple terms: 'My whole style of production is about mangling sounds; you start out with a pure sound and I'll make sure it's well-mangled, transforming it into something brand new.'

These two compositions, "Tis a Pity' and 'Sue', share similarities in their lyrical perspectives – both are sung by men who are left feeling stunned and slighted by their circumstances. And yet the musical compositions achieve more than mere portrayals of these narratives, as the songs are animated with chaotic forces. In her book *Chaos, Territory, Art: Deleuze and the Framing of the Earth*, Elizabeth Grosz theorizes that the meaning of art springs from 'the intensities and sensations it inspires', not just from the artwork's original intention or the quality of its constituent elements, but in the way that it 'become(s) expressive, to not just satisfy but also to intensify – to resonate and become more than itself', merging with, 'eternalis(ing) or monumentalis(ing), sensation' ([2008] 2020, 4). Art that stands apart from its creator, 'preserved in itself ... *a bloc of sensations*' (Deleuze and Guattari 1994, 164). In the musical analysis of these pieces, we can consider evidence of the summoning of intensities and sensations, the calling forth of something new, flung out from the vortex. Liveness, or a new living abstraction. Forces against flotsam, the feeling of life's crude energy flowing through us.

"Tis a Pity She Was a Whore' (★ track 2)

Tempo: quarter note ≈ 132 bpm.
Tonality: F major.
Song form: A/B alternating (instrumental sections and solos/ sung verses).

The album version of "Tis a Pity' retains the core elements of the demo: a stubborn driving beat, the whirlwind of ascending, quickening, phasing, jutting notes on saxophones and piano, close-knit harmonies that shift minimally, and a central melody that feels relatively stable, almost disconnected from the swirling chaos surrounding it. Instead of opening with guns and explosions we have the sound of Bowie inhaling sharply through his nose, exhaling through his mouth – a sound that can be heard throughout the opening moments leading up to the start of the vocal. The sound brings Bowie's performing body into sharp focus, as we feel his excitement and trepidation.

The chord progression is unusual in that it moves through inverted harmonies, where the bass note is not the root of the chord. The only time the song stabilizes in a grounded way, with its root note in the bass, is on the final F7 chord that finishes off the song. The rest of the time the bassline balances its weight on precarious scaffolding; the effect is one of destabilization – the music's feet never touch the ground until the final moment, it remains suspended within the space of the spiralling vortex. Lefebvre's distorted bass pulses in sync with the kick drum, bouncing around the triads with the force of a rubber ball. The teetering harmonies are supported during the verses by doo-wop-style backing vocals 'oohing' and 'ahhing' across edging chord changes; Bowie and Tonkon's voices layer up in rich stacked harmonies, sometimes joined and bolstered by keyboard pads. The voice leading in these background harmonies is economical and smooth, often shifting a single note to transition to the next chord, creating streaking flat lines in the texture, juxtaposing against the swirling, poking, arcing, bouncing, driving force of everything else.

Pointillistic staccato from two saxophones and a piano surrounds the listener on all sides, ascending at different rates, tensions ever tightening; McCaslin's alto saxophone with different performances separated far left and right, and a twangy upright piano that moves about in the stereo space. They disappear for the most part when Bowie sings, returning with lurching centrifugal g-force intensity in the three instrumental breaks that follow each of the song's three verses (1:23–2:08, 2:36–3:20, 4:03–end). The saxophones left and right rip through furious solo passages of intense blowing while the piano notes intensify into violent, hammering octaves. McCaslin recalls that he was invited back to Human studios for a day to perform some overdubs, including a new additional solo for this track:

> They wanted me to do another sax solo … I was really happy to have another chance to play on it. I'm in a booth, David opens the door and puts this old mic on the floor in the hallway … then there's a story that he recounts with Tony about 'Oh, remember how we did this in such and such session?' … and I was just thinking, 'Man this is beautiful. This is like rock and roll history'.
> – McCaslin (Mohammad 2020, part 2, 34:05)

The 'mic on the floor' trick can be heard on the solo that is panned to the right side, a familiar Bowie sax sound (boxy, honky, resonant) most recognizable when McCaslin hits the second break at 2:37. In the final break you can hear Bowie excitedly whooping, a section of the live scratch vocal preserved from the tracking sessions. It was a moment that surprised McCaslin: 'I remember clearly, David lets out this "whoo!" … We [the band] were just like in a frenzy, and the energy was so palpable for all of us. His demonstrative little yell there really captured that moment we were all feeling.'

Bowie's vocal performance on the album is stronger and more robust than the home demo version, and this time it's not distorted. The approach and execution of the high F notes throughout are made using his 'head voice', sometimes delivering the note at end of phrases ('war', 'whore') with an arytenoid rattle.[6] The vocal melody is occasionally traced, echoed and underlined by a bright

---

[6] When a vocalist's arytenoid cartilages/vocal cords interact and touch in the larynx while singing.

synth line that triggers memories (for me, at least) of the synths from 'Underground' on the *Labyrinth* soundtrack (1986). The drumming pushes the song relentlessly forward with an elevated heart rate, harmonic distortion giving the kick drum and ringing snare a pulverizing, almost industrial strength. Pitched electronic percussion bubbles in from the outside edges now and then, 808 tom fills and the odd white noise hit from Guiliana's Roland SPD sample pad. The intense sensations in the composition are achieved by the aggregation of forces: the spinning of elements on the stereo axis (around the listener's head), the ratcheting melodic tension of saxophones and piano on their stubborn vertical ascent, bass ricocheting against drums that eagerly push forwards through the temporal, the harmony suspended and barely balancing, a huddle of human voices floating in the centre of the tornado. The song doesn't really resolve as much as it feels like the end of a wild ride; after the whooping climax of the final instrumental break, the backing vocals wiggle amongst themselves and the harmony shifts from Bb7/Ab to an F7/A – the sassy dominant 7th quality of these chords conveying a cheekiness, like the music is poking its tongue out at us. The rollercoaster reaches a stop, we're left flush-faced, dizzy and euphoric.

'Sue (Or in a Season of Crime)'(★ track 4)

Tempo: 170/85 bpm depending how you choose to count it.
Tonality: G major/G lydian.
Song form: ABA, loose ternary.

The harmonies at the core of 'Sue' are deceptively simple, oscillating between two chords: G major and its relative, E minor. However, the ways in which Bowie's arching, elongated melody sits against those harmonies generates drama, irresolute tensions and forward impetus. 'Sue' is the last of Bowie's great lydian melodies – a mode that he has employed on and off throughout the catalogue and, like phrygian (used in the A section of 'Blackstar'), it's relatively rare to find in pop music (compared to, say, dorian or mixolydian modes). The lydian scale is major with a sharpened 4th degree – Bowie uses it in compositions such as 'Warszawa' (*Low*), 'Sons of the Silent Age' (*"Heroes"*), 'Repetition' (*Lodger*), 'Untitled No. 1' (*The Buddha of Suburbia*), 'Leon Takes Us Outside', 'The Hearts Filthy Lesson' (both *1. Outside*) and 'Heat' (*The Next Day*). The mode affords us an eerie melodic angle, the tritone – throwing C# on top of the G chord, the uncannily lifted note on '*I* got the job' and '*for* your grave'. The same tritone also drives the primary bass and guitar riff – the *diabolus in musica* interval that was once outlawed in the Renaissance period, its ambiguous and unsettled character deemed wholly inappropriate for music that should only express the grace and majesty of God (Kogan 2017). Naturally (inevitably?) this 'devil's interval' became associated with heavy metal music, a trend attributed to pioneering band Black Sabbath and the opening hook of their debut single 'Black Sabbath' (1970). In 'Sue' we are treated to some heavy tritone riffage from Monder, Lefebvre and Guiliana that draws on that unsettling *diabolus* power.

This riff orients the track towards rock, away from the jazz-band stylings of the Schneider arrangement, and Guiliana's playing leans in to a more aggressive, harder-edged breakbeat style. McCaslin was keen to find a hook that would differentiate the ★ arrangement of 'Sue' from the previous one, which he felt held a 'definitive' status. To do this, he found moments in the song form where he could push the playing intensity further.

> We tried a couple different things with the song form … and it just wasn't locking in. I went back to Maria's version and mapped out a version from the score, a condensed version with clarinets and flutes on some of the key lines … Then we got to a certain point in the form and it just went kind of free … Remembering it now, I'm getting goosebumps. We're playing around and then they got to that thing where David modulates [sings high E♭ on 'Sue, goodbye' at 2:55] … and those guys just bend. It was total mayhem. I was just freaking out.
> – McCaslin (Mohammad 2020, part 3, 3:45)

Lefebvre would describe that same moment in an interview he did alongside Monder for *Premier Guitar* magazine as being given 'eight bars to just rage' (Von Bader 2016). The raging bars at 3:06–3:17 are the moment when the hectic texture gathers its energy and focuses itself like a colossal laser. From this point the music terrorizes with surges of complex virtuoso drumming and intense guitar atmospherics overdubbed by Monder, using his Lexicon LXP-1 reverb half-rack with the mix dialled to 100 per cent which, he said, 'makes this giant wash of sound and makes whatever note you play sound *really* good' (ibid.). Bowie's stretched-out vocal rides the storm, recalling the drama of similar moments where he holds constant on long notes that sail over the top of quick-paced chaos: ('I need you flying' in 'Saviour Machine' (*The Man Who Sold the World*), 'Poor dunce' in 'A Small Plot of Land' (*1. Outside*)). In these moments, 'Sue' has the hectic energies and intense more-is-more textures of *Earthling*, and the genesis of that sound, *The Outside Tour* in 1995.

> I LOVE it when it rocks, I love it when it has balls! I love it when it has big, hairy massive balls on it! ... I am definitely not a minimalist. Layer it on! The thicker the better!
> – Bowie (Wells 1995)

Chaos is killing me

Throughout his career Bowie had invited chaos and chance into his creative practice, readily embracing experimentation and risk. Burroughs and Gysin's cut-up approach remained an integral part of his process, morphing into a Mac-based automatic cut-up writing program, the Verbasizer ('What you end up with is a real kaleidoscope of meanings and topic and nouns and verbs all sort of slamming into each other' (Apted 1997)). Eno and Schmidt's *Oblique Strategies* cards and Eno's essay *Roles and Game-Playing* – the experimental improvisation game he devised for the *1. Outside* sessions (Eno [1996] 2020, 395) – were activities designed to free creativity from the limits of logic and familiarity. Safety is undesirable, *risk* is where it's at.[7] Chaos is where creativity happens, and it is the reality of our existence.

---

[7] Bowie: 'If you feel safe in the area you're working in, you're not working in the right area. Always go a little further into the water than you feel you're capable of being in. Go a little bit out of your depth. And when you don't feel that your feet are quite touching the bottom, you're just about in the right place to do something exciting' (quoted in Apted, 1997).

The idea that there are absolutes – there's an absolute church, an absolute art system, an absolute politic, doesn't seem to make any sense now, as we pull back the covers of our reality and find that chaos is a far more accurate picture of what we are, and how we live.

– Bowie (CBC News 1995)

In *Man's Rage for Chaos*, Morse Peckham notes that art can function like a safe zone to explore the dangerous and disconcerting aspects of existence: 'Art is the exposure to the tensions and problems of the false world such that man may endure exposing himself to the tensions and problems of the real world' (1967, 314). Art that explores and maps out the dark territories can help us confront and understand the darkness in ourselves, with Jung's *The Red Book* providing many examples of how going through, handling and coming to terms with darkness, guilt, loss of control and chaos can help you to grow and understand yourself in the world. Disorder, uncertainty and randomness are written into our cellular structures; if a chaotic event doesn't get you first, then entropy definitely will. It is our birthright, as Lulu Miller states plainly: 'Chaos is the only sure thing in this world. The master that rules us all. Chaos will rot your plants and kill your dog and rust your bike. It will decay your most precious memories, topple your favourite cities, wreck any sanctuary you can ever build' (2020, 3).

But more than just a coping mechanism for dealing with the truth of cruel reality, chaos is also the seat of creativity. Gilles Deleuze defined chaos as an infinity of potentials, 'containing all possible particles and drawing out all possible forms ... chaos is an infinite speed of birth and disappearance' (1994, 118). And our ability to handle and process chaos, in the words of Elizabeth Grosz, to 'elaborate an innovative and unpredictable response to stimuli, to react, or simply to act, to enfold matter into itself, to transform matter and life in unpredictable ways' ([2008] 2020, 6), is the basis of creativity and growth, the capacity for evolution encoded in even the simplest living cell. In the prologue to *Thus Spake Zarathustra* (1883–5), Nietzsche writes: 'One must still have chaos in oneself to be able to give birth to a dancing star.' Scholar Babette Babich explains what is meant here by the word *chaos*: '[It is] is a word for both nature and art. Nietzsche's creative conception of chaos equates it with the will to power: as the foundational essence of the world … also the stylistic prerequisite for creating oneself as a work of art' (2001). The creative potential of the simplest living cell, and the whole known universe. We can give birth to a star. The *dancing star* is spoken of as a lasting good, a unique contribution to the world. A newly created thing that shines light where there was none before, rooted in chaos and riding the 'waves of a vibratory universe without direction of purpose. In short, the capacity to enlarge the universe by enabling its potential to be otherwise' (Grosz [2008] 2020, 24).

10

Prodigal sons

Throughout the late period we have already noted some of the ways in which Bowie, at the end, has circled back to the start of things, connecting beginnings to conclusions and stitching the remaining dangling threads into a final tapestry. From 'Silly Boy Blue' miming the flight of Jetsun Milarepa to Newton's rebirth after his trial through the bardos, to charting the wormholes that allow us to slip through time between 1969 and 1975 and 2016. Long-running themes become enriched by complex intertextual details drawn to the surface of a body of ideas, artistry and myth some fifty years in the making. Archetypal characters – the outsized egos, vulnerable animas, tricksters, tyrants and shadows that lurk in the catalogue – are confronted. Karmic ledgers are balanced. The dead are taken for one last walk.

We've witnessed Major Tom's corpse, his headless body floating peculiarly in deep space. An image of Pierrot lying dead in the arms of the Thin White Duke, whose unsavoury shadow haunts the monsters and victims of *The Next Day*. The intrepid astral somnambulist from 1975, seen for the last time retreating into his wardrobe in the video for 'Lazarus'. And all of those other returns – working beside Visconti and exploring the communicative power of their shared musical legacies; returning to the fervours of his youth, the theatre and jazz; going back to the sound of his chosen childhood instrument, the saxophone, choosing it to act as his emotional-expressive avatar across his final artistic summation.

Just past the halfway point in ★, we are led through two compositions that appear to contain riddles. One has a lyric written in a mangled dialect consisting of English, a secret queer slang and a made-up language originating in dystopian fiction. The other

contains an elegantly dark pun in the chorus lyric, one that no-one
seemed to notice until it was too late – an admission from the artist
himself that he was dying, too. Both musical compositions, in their
own different ways, communicate extra-musical ideas from within
their harmonic and textural construction. They explore themes of
vulnerability and longing from very different perspectives. Again,
we sense the artist calling back to the start of things, pulling in the
direction of home.

'Girl Loves Me' (★ track 5)

Tempo: 68 bpm.
Tonalities: C major in the intro; Bb minor in the verses and
refrains; Db major in the bridge and breakdown.
Song form: AABABA variant (intro, verse/refrain (A1/A2),
bridge/breakdown (B1/B2)).

It's mostly two chords and a driving beat, yet this is far from a simple
composition. The harmonic territory is shrouded and ambiguous,
shifting between Gbmajor7/Bb and C; it is unclear which direction
'home' is, where the harmonic energy wants to go. When Bowie
opens the song by intoning on C, the song also leans towards C
major, suggesting a lydian modal effect between C and Gb (F#),
feeling bright, 'lifted' and open (a feeling supported by weightless
pads in the background). At the entrance of the beat (A1 at 0:28)
('Where the fuck did Monday go?'), Bowie's melody shifts to a Bb
minor broken chord shape and the track assumes a darker, more
uncertain alignment, losing the open lydian quality as the harmonic
energy pulls down to Bb minor. The bass line lingers across the bar
on Bb for two extra beats, clouding the change to C even further
(see Figure 10.1). The vocal is the force that tips the balance towards
light or dark; the mysterious energy of the track is partly due to the
way it teeters on this boundary.

   The reduction of the harmonic theme to two ethereal chords
stuck in limbo has precedent in the catalogue, notably with
Hours... B-side and *Omikron* soundtrack composition 'No One
Calls' (1999), which pivots on a similar movement from Eb minor
(melody suggesting Eb diminished) to F major.

FIGURE 10.1 *'Girl Loves Me', (from 0:21), showing the last two bars of the intro, where Bowie sings notes suggesting a resolution to C major, and the first two bars of verse 1, where Bowie sings notes that suggest Bb minor, casting darker colour over the song.*

The vocal writing in the verse (A1) sections exploits the break in Bowie's voice at the end of the phrase, flipping from chest voice to head voice with a yelp.[1] The singing is copied by a delay effect loosely aligned to the quarter note value (at around 68 bpm), tapping back copies of the sound in rhythm with up to four repetitions. In the first statement of the A section (0:28), the gaps in the vocal delivery are filled with repeating yelping echoes: 'Where the fuck did Monday go? *-day go, -day go, -day go, -day go'*. The effect creates a vocal cutup, splicing syllables together and overlapping words into rhythms that fuse with the groove; it portrays a sense that Bowie is stuck, not only in the weekly cycle of disorientation suggested by the lyric, but also trapped inside a strange reflecting environment – an unnatural echo chamber or hall of mirrors. This complexity of reflections is intensified in the return to the A section at 1:24 with the new background voice repeating a spoken 'go go go go go' on the eighth-note triplet rhythm; words that could be heard as a rally of encouragement or a warning to get out.

The chorus (A2) splits Bowie's voices into two factions – a single, distant, reverberated 'girl loves me' calls out and is responded to with a closer proximity group of high-and low-layered voices singing 'hey cheena' on the octave; the call-and-answer characterizations in this section recall similar moments in 'African Night Flight' (between the

---

[1] A vocal break is an abrupt change between vocal modes. A well-known example of a controlled vocal break is yodelling. This is a signature feature of Bowie's vocal style, heard all over the catalogue (choruses of 'Never Get Old' (*Reality*), 'Slow Burn' (*Heathen*), 'New Angels of Promise' (*Hours...*), 'DJ' (*Lodger*) and at the end of 'Because You're Young' (*Scary Monsters*).

voices of 'his burning eye' and 'one of these days', *Lodger* 1979) and something of the shape and colour of the 'oh by jingo' interjections from 'After All' (*The Man Who Sold the World*).

The bridge (B) sequence ('you viddy at the cheena') is only heard in full once (at 1:46) and is a moment of reprieve; the music steps upwards through changes that, for the first time, suggest a stable tonality of D♭ major. Later, at 3:09, elements of the bridge section appear once again, only in a more deconstructed way; unmoored from the discipline of the bass and beat, it floats up and away from any functional harmony, a ghostly cluster of D♭ and C diminished over an E♭ pedal point.

A dreamy-dark current with a stalking, hypnotic beat, Bowie's multitude voice spits bravado and lust, trapped inside its prism. The drumming was informed by Bowie's demo, which had two different rhythm loops laid on top of each other, making a 'very dense groove' which was impossible for Guiliana to perform all at once (Micallef 2016), inspiring him to break it into a heavy half-time beat with complex rhythmic ghost notes on the hat and snare. Approaching the end of the track the arrangement becomes more insistent and agitated, with fidgety snare and tom fills, the guitar and bass stubbornly poking at the same spot; the music breaks to a stop, leaving only the sound of James Murphy's synths fizzing into vapour. Taken together, the elements of the composition and its arrangement, performance and production suggest notions of uncertainty and frustration (in the harmonic movement), entrapment, bewilderment and drudgery (in the use of effects, rhythm and repetition).

The focus on intricate and specific rhythms in the beat and vocal delivery, not to mention the hard-hitting bottom-heavy production, are elements that flirt with the aesthetics of hip hop, making 'Girl Loves Me' arguably the most contemporary-sounding track on ★ (and probably of the entire late period). On-trend and accessible in one sense, impenetrable in another. McCaslin recalled that there was a draft lyric being worked on in the studio ('he had a pen and paper in the studio while we were listening, he was moving words around') and a conversation went on about what an authentic 'slang' or street language might be for someone of Bowie's generation and background: 'He mentioned the *Clockwork Orange* language in the studio ... it was around the idea of spoken word and rap. I think he might have been looking for a spoken word [approach] that felt authentic to him. Instead of taking modern hip-hop language, [he was] looking for this older slang and drawing from it' (Mohammad 2020, part 2, 19:01).

The lyrics use vocabulary from two varieties of 'old slang' that have connections to Bowie's youth. Polari, a secret language used by gay men and drag performers in Britain during the first half of the twentieth century, when homosexuality was illegal and heavily stigmatized. A useful means of conducting conversations, flirtations and gossip in open spaces without giving yourself away, 'the language itself, full of camp, irony, innuendo and sarcasm, also helped its speakers to form a resilient worldview in the face of arrest, blackmail and physical violence' (Baker 2017). Bowie may have picked it up amongst queer circles in his youth; his ill-fated 1968 rock opera, *Ernie Johnson*, reportedly had a comedy song that used it, most likely inspired by the BBC Radio comedy show *Round the Horne* (1965–8), which popularized the lexicon with a straight audience as an introduction to camp comedy. A smattering of Polari appears in the verses of 'Girl Loves Me': 'dizzy'/silly, 'omeys'/men, 'nanti'/no. The rest of the non-English words featured in the lyric can be traced to Nadsat, the made-up street slang from Anthony Burgess's 1962 novel *A Clockwork Orange*. This cryptic slang is used throughout the novel by its delinquent narrator, Alex, and his gang of 'droogs' and was faithfully retained in the script of Stanley Kubrick's 1971 film adaptation.

Even with this knowledge, 'Girl Loves Me' is a challenge to translate. A basic summary might look like this: pretty girls expertly separating men from their money every day of the week, except for Monday, which is a blur. The bridge of 'Girl Loves Me' warns someone to watch this woman's balls ('devotchka watch her garbles'), you'll sleep in a police cell ('spatchko at the rozz-shop'), she'll relieve an old man of his money ('split a ded from his deng deng'), echoing the story of the fierce lady thief that punched like a dude in "Tis a Pity' back on track two. The prevailing lyrical image in a translation of 'Girl Loves Me' is one of strong women looking after themselves and men getting only what they deserve. That the message is coded within arcane vocabulary opens interesting possibilities for queer readings of the composition; a song about outsiders, to be understood by outsiders, thus the outsiders have become the exclusive inner circle. The provenance and design of the code itself, drawn from twentieth-century literature and counterculture, unlocks new layers of potential communicative intent.

A Clockwork Orange was a formative influence on Bowie's *Ziggy* period, his band of droogs being the Spiders, their looks inspired in part by the gang's costumes from Kubrick's film – the bowler hats, bovver boots and codpieces from designer Milena Canonero.[2] Bowie's attraction to fashionable and beautifully dressed street thugs and wild boys was a theme running from the Spiders through to *Diamond Dogs* and *The Gouster*, right up to the *Glass Spider Tour*, Tin Machine and *The Next Day*'s 'Dirty Boys'. *Peaky Blinders* (2013–present) also aligns with the theme here: a gang of pretty, well-dressed criminals are trapped in cycles of street violence and revenge, traumatized by war and suffering with PTSD and addiction; strong women, in their archetypically constrained roles, are the ones holding things together and surviving – matriarchs, wives, sex workers, and the spy that sociopathic gang leader Thomas Shelby (Cillian Murphy) falls in love with, who will inevitably betray and humiliate him (but whom he later marries).

O'Leary suggests even more literary references can be folded in; the 'chestnut tree' could be the Chestnut Tree Café, the symbolic location of betrayal where Winston sits after his release from being tortured at the Ministry of Love in Orwell's *Nineteen Eighty-Four*, or a nod towards a plot point in Gabriel García Márquez's 1967 novel *One Hundred Years of Solitude*, in which the family's patriarch goes mad, stuck in a time loop of perpetual Mondays, and is eventually tied to a chestnut tree by his family and left for dead (O'Leary 2019, 643). After the bookishness of *The Next Day*, for Bowie to reference Burgess, Orwell and Márquez in a single song doesn't seem to be a stretch; throw in a sprinkling of historical queer patois and what you get is not only a cypher that can be translated, but also a clutch of references of personal significance to Bowie, anchored to a specific time and place in his youth.

---

[2] Bowie in 1993: 'The idea was to hit a look somewhere between the Malcolm McDowell thing with the one mascaraed eyelash and insects. It was the era of *Wild Boys*, by William S. Burroughs. That was a really heavy book that had come out in about 1970 and it was a cross between that and *Clockwork Orange* that really started to put together the shape and the look of what Ziggy and the Spiders were going to become' (Sinclair 1993).

You can't go home again

Susan Sontag once described literature as a 'passport to enter a larger life', allowing a person to 'escape the prison of national vanity, of philistinism, of compulsory provincialism, of inane schooling, or imperfect destinies and bad luck' (2003). In the early 1970s, Bowie and his glittered droogs would come to symbolize a similar longing to escape the prison of ordinariness. As Thomas Jones notes, Ziggy and the Spiders made a 'spectacle of not-belonging' with alien decadence and glamour that also read as crude costume-box fantasy, 'outpourings of suburban yearning, describing the condition that they hold out the promise of escape from' (2012). London was the escape from suburbia and stardom was the escape from England. When asked by *Interview* magazine in 1973, 'What does imprisonment mean to you?' a young Bowie answered, 'I think I've been in prison for the last 24 years. I think coming to America has opened one door' (Salvo 1973). Within a year Bowie had left England for good. For the rest of his life, he would live abroad in Europe, the United States, even Australia, and presumably enjoyed the low-tax benefits of settling for stretches of time in Lausanne, Switzerland and the Caribbean island of Mustique, before setting up home with Iman in Manhattan. Maybe it was a lucky escape. Decades later, in 1991 on a Tin Machine tour bus en route to the Brixton Academy, Bowie asked the driver to take him through his childhood neighbourhood, with guitarist Eric Schermerhorn recalling a tearful and reflective Bowie saying, 'It's a miracle … I probably should have been an accountant. I don't know how this all happened' (Trynka 2011, 5).

Yet it seems apparent that David Jones held on to a vivid image of his English home and the idea of one day returning there. When visiting London, he made a point of revisiting the landmarks of his childhood and early career[3] and, with his involvement with the four-part BBC adaptation of Hanif Kureishi's 1990 semi-autobiographical

---

[3] In addition to the Brixton visit to Stansfield Road in 1991, there are other occasions that we know about: stopping by Haddon Hall in 1977 after Bolan's funeral; touring around Ziggy's London haunts with journalist David Sinclair for *Rolling Stone* in 1993; in 2013 taking his daughter Lexi to visit his childhood home in Plaistow Grove, Bromley, and also Foxgrove Road, in Beckenham, where he lived as a young man.

novel *The Buddha of Suburbia* (dir. Roger Michell 1993), via his
wistful and reflective 1993 LP of the same name, one can sense the
pulse of bittersweet nostalgia for his Brixton and Bromley roots.
He spent years designing and creating his dream home in London
(on Gilston Road in Chelsea) with interior designer and architect
Jonathan Reed, which was fully appointed with Japanese-inspired
minimalist detail and bespoke furnishings. In the end, he never lived
in the house and it was sold in 2009.

Over the years he collected mid-century British art by the likes
of David Bomberg, Leon Kossoff and Frank Auerbach, though it
surprised some to learn that Bowie was interested in more than
just dark and provocative pieces, as he sought out landscape
paintings by the likes of Wilhelmina Barns-Graham and Bryan
Wynter of England's blue-grey coastlines, much of it depicting St
Ives, Cornwall, and evergreen countryside. When Sotheby's staged
its *Bowie/Collector* sale of more than 350 artworks from David
Jones's private collection in 2016, art critic Jonathan Jones, with
characteristic hauteur, expressed his disappointment at the number
of 'unglamorous' artists represented, with 'paintings by Ivon
Hitchens, Winifred Nicholson, Peter Lanyon, Graham Sutherland
and their ilk ... a lot of the art in Bowie's collection wallows in
melancholy nostalgic idylls of Englishness, albeit with the lightest
dusting of abstraction' (Jones 2016).

The last time Bowie visited Europe was when he brought his
family to Venice for a working holiday (he was filming an opulent
ad for Louis Vuitton) then popped over to London to see *David
Bowie Is* at the V&A in the summer of 2013. They were treated
to an early morning private tour of the exhibit, which must have
felt like a surreal *This is Your Life* setup – rooms filled with
the objects that prove the miraculous story of how a boy from
Brixton escaped the prison of an ordinary life, and his plausible
destiny as an accountant, to become David Bowie. That final visit
also included a ride on the London Eye and a visit to St Paul's
Cathedral, and he got to show Lexi some special places, including
the houses and neighbourhoods where he grew up (Cadwalladr
2014).

Over lunch at the Savoy with Robert Fox, Bowie tells him that he
wants to begin working immediately on a new musical, according
to Fox, 'the story of a man from another planet stuck in New York,
desperately trying to get home' (Fox 2016). Newton's final plan
to return to the stars is impossible, as is any hope of Major Tom

returning to Earth; they've travelled too far, been gone too long. Theirs is the same challenge we all face as the world continues to turn even in the places we leave behind. A small bedroom in Brixton where a young boy dreamed of becoming a star is now a home office in someone else's house. A row of plain houses on a quiet Bromley street. A dream home standing in a neighbourhood of empty Chelsea mansions owned by rich Russians who only visit in the summer. Keep driving past, there's nothing to see. The sad truth that all prodigal children know: you can't ever go home again.

'Dollar Days' (★ track 6)

Tempo: 60/120 bpm.
Tonalities: G minor & B minor.
Song form: verse-chorus (intro/verse 1/chorus/verse 2/middle 8/ chorus/outro).

In this reading of 'Dollar Days', the chord progressions and shifting tonalities tell a story; the music hovers around, moves towards and suggests the idea of 'home', but it never finds its way there. To gain a better understanding of how music can suggest such things, we look to music theory and the idea of *cadence* – the configuration of harmonies (i.e. chords) in sequence that suggest movement towards a resolution. Cadence points are a characteristic embedded within the Western tonal tradition and they function as indicators of tonality and key – setting up a listener's expectations of where 'home' might be, where phrases might expect to find their final resolution, interruption or surprise. The quality and movement between chords and pitches within a tonal system are understood in relation to the 'tonic', root or 'home' note and its established key tonality (whether that be major, minor or another mode). A movement that resolves to the tonic (or establishes a new one) has a stabilizing finality – these are the full stops of Western musical grammar that most ears have been attuned to.[4] Movement in a

---

[4] You can probably hear these readily in your head; some common examples are the plagal cadence (IV-I), the 'amen' at the end of a hymn, and the perfect cadence (V-I), which is the finality you can sense in the last two words of the 'Happy Birthday' song.

different direction can create other effects: energies that lean, pull and push towards, or away from, what we expect; motion that can be ambiguous, become trapped and frustrated; resolutions denied and left as unfinished business.

'Dollar Days' starts with the sound of pages turning, or paper money being handled and counted out. The music begins with a gentle, stirring piano and bass hovering between E♭major7 and F6 (a similar movement to Fleetwood Mac's 'Dreams' (1977)); the presence of D across both chords adds colour, in addition to setting up an expectation that the tonality is going to be B♭ major.[5] Incidentally, that D note will serve as the connecting thread throughout the piece, the point from where the song hinges between two tonal territories, the pragmatism of the verses in G minor and the emotions of the choruses in B minor (Figure 10.2).

During the dreamy opening, the musical pulse suggests a tempo of 60 bpm, the relaxed patience of a ticking clock. Monder's guitar adorns the changes with atmospheric picking, McCaslin's saxophone wakes, yawns and stretches. A blink from the drums and the band snaps us out of the daydream and into G minor, drums and acoustic guitar quickening the pulse to 120 bpm. In the absence of a demo, the instrumental arrangement for 'Dollar Days' was developed on the spot in the studio; the basis of the groove in the verses was crafted by Guiliana with assistance on the day from James Murphy. The tom and strum patterns recall 'Days' (*Reality*), a delayed backbeat kicking on the 4. From a precarious D on top of G minor, Bowie's vocal is cradled aloft as the music steps carefully downwards through pastel chord changes. The lyrics of the first verse set out, at first, an image of mundane but pleasant existence ('cash girls suffer me… '), followed by a suggestion of longing ('if I never see the English evergreens… '), both punctuated by the repetition 'it's nothing to me/it's nothing to see', the faux-dismissive words betrayed by an upper vocal harmony that hits a tone of vulnerability at the top of his vocal register.

The chorus pivots swiftly to a new tonal area, strongly suggesting B minor, and returns again to the more dream-like 60 bpm pulse

---

[5] My interpretation is that this passage is *not* lydian (i.e. the first chord we hear is not the root chord, but chord IVmajor7, moving to V6), since the 'modal effect' of the raised 4th is not present and a resolution towards B♭ major is subtly suggested in Lindner's keyboard riffing.

FIGURE 10.2 *'Dollar Days', showing how each section in the song is connected by a D (pitch) running through it; on the top of the opening harmonies; leading from Bowie's vocal in both the verses in G minor (e.g. 0:40) and choruses in B minor (e.g. 1:10).*

of the intro, the busyness of the verse's toms and acoustic guitars collapsing into heavier, widescreen drama with expressive piano, lush strings, bass and cymbals crashing upon the beat in stubborn waves. The chord changes throughout the chorus remain pinned down by an E in the bass that never lets go, an anchoring tether that prevents all movement and resolution. The harmony starts on a dark but hopeful E minor7 and attempts to move to F#7/E, a dominant seventh energy that wants to rise, but is thwarted by its

stubborn bass note; A/E is more stable, but it's another dead end –
it can't provide a way to B minor, the resolution that the music is
pulling towards. Bowie's melody stays in place for the most part,
fidgeting against adjacent notes. The music in the chorus supports
the lyrical images of frustration and striving.

Snapping back to the carefully treading realities of G minor, verse
two builds on the structure established in the first; mundane allusive
imagery made more troubling this time around with alliterative
'dollar days' and 'survival sex', the replacement of 'walking
down' with 'falling down' (echoing an image from Newton's crisis
point in *Lazarus*, 'I'm falling man'). After a second mention (and
dismissal) of the English evergreens, McCaslin's solo in the middle
8 section (2:16) takes the song to its 'home' in B minor for the
first time, releasing all of the pent-up tension accumulated so far
from the carefully tethered harmonies and tight melodic range up
to this point. Comparable to the solo break in 'Lazarus' (track 3)
that seemed to dramatize a struggle to fly, this solo revels in its
temporary freedom – expressive and nimble, pulling contours that
dance up the walls, weightless yet surefooted. A short-lived reprieve,
as the chorus returns (2:48) to pin the rest of the song down as
firmly as before, now with ominous vocal textures lurching in the
shadows, reminiscent of the joining segue between sections A and
B of 'Blackstar'.

Across the outro (3:21 onwards), Bowie repeats the words 'I'm
trying to/I'm dying to' while the music struggles between two
stubborn major chords, a minor third apart (F# and A, both held
over an E bass). It's a similar chord relationship to the one that
supports the climactic 'You're not alone!' moment of 'Rock 'n' Roll
Suicide' (*Ziggy*) that was similarly teased in 'You Feel So Lonely
You Could Die' (*The Next Day*) and 'The Informer' (*The Next
Day Extra*). Here, the E in the bass prevents the build-up of any
momentum, it's all striving and heavy effort; locked in a futile tug
of war, pushing from F#/E and pulling from A/E, there is simply no
way home from here. The song never resolves; it slowly drowns. A
new shape emerges from the tension between these two oppositional
harmonic forces, climbing up from Monder's lead guitar a line that
feels Ronson-esque in shape (with similar angles and tone to the
segue and closing theme of 1970's 'Width of a Circle', the moment
in the song on stage when Ziggy would perform the 'flying eagle').
The line is traced by the strings with increasing width, height and

scope. As Bowie's voice and the thrashing drums are lost to the waves, this monolithic theme rises tall and triumphant out of the ocean. Like Newton trapped and dreaming himself a way out of his limbo, 'Dollar Days' dreams up its own ending and finds a different way home. It's not the resolution you thought you were running to. Instead, you find a way to transcend.

11

Blackstar theory

*I've now decided that my death should be very precious. I
really want to use it. I'd like my death to be as interesting as
my life has been and will be.*

– BOWIE (*PLAYBOY*, SEPTEMBER 1976)

The imagery that Jonathan Barnbrook devised for the ★ album
package is suggestive of space travel, tapping into Bowie's already-
established stellar mythologies – the deep-field Hubble photograph
gazing out into a star field, the atomic star-sustaining proton–proton
chain, the Pioneer plaques (designed by Carl Sagan and launched
on spacecraft leaving the solar system in 1972) and the track names
and sections of lyrics stylized as constellation maps. A black hole/
gravitational singularity is referenced in an image of interlacing
geometric lines that bend in the centre, suggesting an unseen mass
that alters space-time, the heavy non-presence also suggested by the
vinyl edition's star-shaped cutout on the front. Where *The Next Day*
obscured Bowie's star image, inviting projection from the outside,
★ replaces the artist's image with the symbol of a star. Barnbrook
developed the artwork independently, listening to the album as he
went along, and was unaware of Bowie's health situation. He told
me, 'I picked up on the images in terms of what Bowie was saying in
the songs and from the music's distinct atmosphere; obviously there
are directions toward mortality, but I really didn't see it in relation
to him dying. It's strange looking back on it, as the meaning is quite
clear now.'

The transformation of Bowie's image into the symbol of the
dead star resonates with the plot for his unfinished Ziggy Stardust

musical; the rock star that explodes and becomes the black hole. It also foregrounds the murky tensions that exist on the album, the haughty promises of immortality and specialness from 'Blackstar' against the frustrated longing of 'Dollar Days'. The concept seems to knowingly reference different levels of star identification; Bowie's obvious status as a rock star, the existential riddle couched in the Crowleyan promise of human potential ('every man and woman is a star') and Sagan's reassurance that we are actually the real thing (made of 'star stuff').

In *Stars* ([1979] 1998), Richard Dyer provided a conceptualization of the Hollywood film-star phenomenon of the twentieth century, explaining how 'star images' are constructed and circulated in culture – not just by products (film roles and, in Bowie's case, pop music), but also in their promotion and the press coverage and discourse around stars' public and private lives. As an academic discipline, star studies has grown from an initial emphasis on the function of film stars from the studio era to a wider-ranging application across different types of media, the various industries that produce 'stars' in our present celebrity culture (Holmes and Redmond 2007, Nayar 2009, Mendes and Perrott 2020). While the field of stardom has broadened and diversified as media landscapes have transformed, Dyer's theorization of star images, what they represent and what they do, remains relevant today (Shingler 2012). Star images continue to function as a way for people to define and explore social identities (theirs and others) by articulating and demonstrating ways to be human: 'We're fascinated by stars because they enact ways of making sense of the experience of being a person' (Dyer 1986, 17).

Dyer's Star Theory reveals to us how an individual performer can come to signify larger ideas and become representative of something else, something more. It could be a shorthand reference to a specific historical period (Charlie Chaplin and silent film), an aesthetic ideal (Marilyn Monroe and post-war glamour), an archetype (John Wayne as a figure of Wild West–inspired masculinity) and so on. An individual transformed into a symbol which 'can be seen variously to handle opposed, or uneasily related, notions' such as existing as both a constructed image and a real person at the same time, embodying a role, existing as a subject, being evoked as an essence (Dyer [1979] 1998, 161). Bowie's star image also straddles complex boundaries in the ordinary/extraordinary paradox: alien everyman, author and text, authenticity and artifice; a man stranded in space, an alien stranded on Earth, the boy in the Bromley 'burbs, the refugee in Berlin, the Englishman in New York. Bowie's star image exemplifies a social reality of self-actualization and demonstrates the creative plasticity of the performed self. And yet, in the rear view (and in spite of the mountains of discourse around Bowie's 'ch-changes' and radical reinventions), the full and complete body of work appears more notable for its cohesion and interconnectedness than for its randomness or changeability.

At the conclusion of *Stars*, Dyer suggests that a fruitful way to analyse a star would be to chart the ways in which these oppositional tensions are present, 'the ways that this crisis is articulated in, through and by them' (ibid.). Throughout his last works we can trace paratextual elements of construction that place Bowie (and David Jones) impossibly both inside and outside of the canon. *The Next Day* deliberately obscures the performing persona and speaks in a specialized language, inviting the listener to assemble and project the star image for themselves. *Lazarus* is enriched and complicated by the ways in which it connects to the artist's biography, blurring the boundaries between real and fictive selves from the past and the present.

★'s crisis is existential. As text on the page, the mortal themes seem to be no more pronounced than on other albums in the late period; in fact, ★ actually lacks the self-serious epitaphs of *Heathen*, *Reality* and *The Next Day*. As it progresses, we are served lyrical images of grifters, deluded fools, people rendered powerless by their circumstances, and yet from these songs many listeners have been able to unearth narratives of triumph. Simon Critchley found that 'within Bowie's negativity, beneath his apparent naysaying and gloom, one can hear a clear Yes, an absolute and unconditional affirmation of life in all of its chaotic complexity, but also its moment of transport and delight' (Critchley 2016, 107). For psychiatrist and writer Niall Boyce, the images of illness in the 'Blackstar' and 'Lazarus' videos function as hopeful symbols of exploration (Boyce 2016). Jake Cowan saw the final album as a 'rhetorical autobituary, as a writing-towards-death', that made space for communal mourning (Cowan 2018, 26) while Gareth Schott saw Bowie's songs addressing 'the existential isolation that so many individuals experience as they prepare for death' (Schott 2019, 171). Bowie's terminal condition unavoidably underwrites

★'s context, his death becoming one of the crucial puzzle pieces that completes the work. This creates new tensions between readings of what is apparent versus what is implied: what exists versus what is seen, heard and felt; what can be assembled from connecting fragments of knowledge together; what is projected through our participation as listeners, with our perceptions coloured by our own beliefs and anxieties about death. And reflecting back from ★ is an awareness of the tensions of our very existence – our in/significance demonstrated and disproven. We embody the most powerful and the most worthless, the eternal and the fleeting. Our materiality is made of stars and dust.

Star myths

The star symbol, embedded with consistency throughout his catalogue, subsumes Bowie's final form, capping off the mythological narrative of the oeuvre. In a Jungian sense, it could be said that the arc of this star illustrates the mythical 'hero's journey' in search of knowledge and perfection of the self. The start of Bowie's stardom was synchronized with a moment when global consciousness of space travel – as a symbol of our best human potential – was acute. Gene Roddenberry's original *Star Trek* series (1966–9) articulated the era's romanticism and humanistic ideals around space exploration. Arthur C. Clarke's *The Promise of Space* and Clarke and Kubrick's *2001: A Space Odyssey* (both 1968) possessed a similar optimism that was further embedded and inspirited in the consciousness by *Apollo 11*'s successful Moon landing in 1969. Apollo, god of oracles and leader of the Muses, became the namesake to the twentieth century's space-bound aspirations: that there exists a higher world full of mysteries and divine potentials above us, contrasting starkly with our ordinary, limiting lives on the ground. Erich von Däniken's *Chariots of the Gods?* (also 1968) helped popularize the hypothesis that extraterrestrial visitors may have influenced ancient human civilizations by sharing advanced technologies and religious philosophies, an idea that is also foundational to the plot of Tevis's *The Man Who Fell to Earth* (1963). UFOs and alien visitors descending to Earth represent a version of the arrival of the gods 'pressing in upon consciousness from a higher order of the archetypal consciousness' (Izod 2001, 188–9). The arrival of the 'Star Men' (the 'Infinites') is interpreted as such by Ziggy and his followers; the hubristic assumption that these higher-order beings would be benevolent is a warning that is echoed in other twentieth-century science fiction, from H. G. Wells's *War of the Worlds* and John Wyndham's *The Kraken Wakes* to Ridley Scott's *Alien* franchise. Countering these fears is the brave altruism of those special humans who go out to meet the unknown, becoming the alien explorers and benevolent god-visitors descending to other realms.

For both Dr Dave Bowman (*2001: A Space Odyssey*) and Major Tom, the heroic one-way journey to the over-world would see them surrendering to the control of unknown forces. The intelligence that Bowman eventually encounters in *2001*'s fourth act isn't even corporeal or humanoid, but rather some higher, all-knowing elemental consciousness that blesses him with knowledge and ascension. The fateful, consciousness-expanding discoveries of *2001* are underscored by Richard Strauss's tone poem *Also Sprach Zarathustra, Op. 30* (1896), its unsolvable 'world riddle' theme serving as a leitmotif for the mysteries whose revelations then serve as doorways to human advancement. Bowman's odyssey, symbolic of man's quest for enlightenment, was couched in imagery and language appropriate for its age. Bowie's star story provides a narrative that speaks optimistically to sensibilities in the early twenty-first century: with a fuller knowledge of the violence our existence brings to the world around us, and navigating our way through a chaotic godless reality, can we hope to find meaning and achieve wholeness?

Bowman and Bowie's mythic arcs start at a nearly synchronized point in history and both end with a depicted cosmic transformation. A notable difference in Bowie's version is the lack of any higher intelligence embedding consciousness-expanding moments into the timeline on his behalf – no monoliths buried in the past, no mysterious entity to seize control of his destiny. Bowman was always on a mission; Major Tom was cut adrift. Chaos energy is what propelled Bowie's star – the cut-ups, the happy accidents, the non/sense making refractions of life in the vortex. Chaos creates, destroys and recreates, and it is amoral; its gifts are the shooting star, the mountainscape, the cell mutation. According to Nietzsche, it's the necessary element for the creation of anything good and lasting in this universe, the *dancing star*, for we know that nothing new and surprising can ever arise from order. Innovation and evolution are brought about by disruption. This chaos creativity, which can be wielded to make, destroy and save your selves, is framed in Jung's *The Red Book* as meaning-making possibility: 'Events signify nothing, they signify only in us ... The meaning of events comes from the possibility of life in this world that you create' (2009, 152).

The *Red Book* and Nietzsche's *Thus Spake Zarathustra* ([1883–5] 1999) have a lot in common, both being 'visionary' texts concerned with the location of meaning in modern worlds which have outgrown their old traditions and belief systems. For Nietzsche, one conclusion (among others) was that 'God is dead' and there is no absolute source of morality: better get used to the idea of living according to your own set of values (Nietzsche [1881] 2011, 139). But for Jung, God could still be found alive in the recesses of the self, as an archetype encountered within the psyche. The abandonment of absolutes, with humans just as capable of the worst evil as the greatest good, is a risky proposition. To answer the challenge, both Nietzsche and Jung looked to the image of the ultimate self-created hero: the *Übermensch*, and the finally unified, individuated self.

Free to invent their own morality, the *Übermensch* unites conflicting tensions within themselves ([1901] 1968, 966) to 'overcome the opposites of good and evil from a standpoint that is beyond the opposites ... he symbolises the unification and synthesis of opposites that is appropriate to the further promotion of creativity' (Huskinson 2004, 30). Bowie read the translated versions of *Thus Spake Zarathustra* and Nietzsche's *Beyond Good and Evil* in the early 1970s, his interpretation of the *Übermensch*, such as it was at the time,[1] metabolizing into lyrical ideas that surfaced in songs like 'The Supermen' (*The Man Who Sold the World*) and *Hunky Dory*'s 'Oh! You Pretty Things' and 'Quicksand'.

---

[1] In a 1976 BBC interview with Stuart Grundy, Bowie confessed to not quite understanding the texts at the time: 'I was still going through the thing when I was pretending I understood Nietzsche... ' (Buckley 2012).

Who knows? Maybe I'm insane too, it runs in my family, but I always had a repulsive sort of need to be something more than human. I felt very, very puny as a human. I thought, 'Fuck that. I want to be a Superman'.

— Bowie (Crowe 1976a)

For a young man feeling puny and longing to feel powerful, the promise of the self-actualized *Übermensch* is a seductive thought experiment. Nietzsche's 'Will a "self", and thou shalt become a "self"' ([1879] 1996) could twist easily into Crowley's 'Do what thou wilt shall be the whole of the Law' (1904). If the laws of the land that govern our behaviour and the promise of heaven or hell were to suddenly disappear, if you found yourself in possession of power over others, would you become a monster? Nietzsche writes that the only genuine morality is found in the mastery of our selves, which can only be achieved through self-knowledge, self-cultivation and self-control. Confrontation with the dark side of the psyche can be terrifying but, as Jung persists, recognition and acceptance of this aspect of our selves is the path to wholeness. The *Übermensch*'s consolidation of 'all opposites fused together into a new unity' (Nietzsche [1888] 2009, 72) has the same healing energy of Jung's completely integrated *individual* (Cybulska 2012, Huskinson 2004). There is affinity between the hero-mythic worlds of *The Red Book* and *Zarathustra*, whereby the evil found within must be balanced and integrated so that it may be overcome. 'I teach you the Superman. Man is something that should be surpassed. What have ye done to surpass him?' (*Zarathustra*, Prologue)

The last works in Bowie's catalogue are rife with unpleasant characters and murky morality – the monsters and tyrants of *The Next Day*, Newton's embittered shadow, the trickster of 'Blackstar' and the would-be murderer in 'Sue'. The path to individuation and wholeness requires the necessary confrontation with the monstrous and frightening aspects of our selves. Man is the obstacle, the riddle at the heart of our predicament; that which drives us to transcend is what makes human existence *heroic* (Becker 1973, 33). As the ego progressively loses ground to chaos with each successive track on ★, the gradual process of becoming creates unification between impossible opposites – knowledge and mystery, logic and emotion, order and chaos, transience and immortality.

Death

All art gains intensity and force from the way it is experienced, and the facts of Bowie's serious illness and eventual death build new intuitive layers into ★. 'Sue' becomes elevated from its narrative about a confused and murderous lover as its visceral liveness comes to the fore. His whooping affirmations, egging the band on, in "'Tis a Pity' feels more about the intensity and sensation of the moment rather than illustrating the context of an emasculating mugging incident. Elsewhere, constellations of ideas wait behind curtains, begging to be discovered and connected: Bowie's biting guitar ($\flat$VII-i/G-A minor) figure from 'Lazarus' points back to 2013's 'Plan', then further back to 1977 when Marc Bolan gifted Bowie that very guitar, mere days before his fatal car accident. Another line threads 'Plan' to 'No Plan' (2016), as they bookend the period of Bowie's last works, his final season of creativity and chaos; 'No Plan' to Newton and his revelation of nowness and back to *Lazarus*. For any meaningful configuration you might build, the dead star at the centre provides a crucial context. Without it, the album is opaque and mysterious; once Bowie's death is revealed, it gains translucence and new coherence.[2]

★ brings the intangible to the sensory realm; transforming abstract, even metaphysical, notions into physical material that can be heard, seen and felt. We recognize not only Bowie's voice but also, for the first time, his breathing, his fingers and hands rustling paper, the materiality of his performing body at the edge of its existence. Intimate, tactile sounds that do not suggest the polished star image of 'Bowie' as much as reveal something of the dying man behind the mask. The expiring spark at the centre of it all now frozen immortal in sound.

And yet, in spite of these ways in which Bowie/Jones's non-absence is preserved, his non-presence is also keenly felt, especially in Barnbrook's design concept. The ★ symbol that replaces the album

---

[2] Scholar Claude Chastagner (2018) surveyed a number of reviews of ★ that were published before and after the announcement of Bowie's death, noting how the news had changed critical appreciation of the work. Simon Critchley also reflects on how his appreciation of the album dramatically altered after learning of Bowie's death (2016, 107).

title in discourse and the artist's own image on the front cover has a mystifying function. Signifying not only death and nothingness (as Barnbrook explained, 'the black hole sucking in everything') but also mysterious cycles of life and everythingness ('the Big Bang, the start of the universe') (Howarth 2016). 'On the edge of silence' is how Barnbrook would later describe the symbolism to me, a stubborn absence that interrupts and insists whenever the ★ symbol punctuates a block of text. A vanishing point.

I got to meet William Burroughs when I was a student, and I asked him about the future of typography. He told me, 'It's in between pictograms and Egyptian hieroglyphs' – he basically predicted emojis. Our approach to ★ was sort of like an emoji, but more serious. Also, a bit like the monolith in *2001*. It had to be beyond language.
– Barnbrook (interview with the author, 2020)

Even though Bowie had been singing about death in some form or another since the very start, the compositions on his final album seem to possess a unique quality by virtue of their genuine proximity to Bowie's real death. Pegg describes this difference as 'a new kind of serenity' (2016, 478). Not as angry as *The Next Day* or as traumatized as *Lazarus*. The elegiac seriousness of *Heathen* can't be found here, nor the melancholy and worry of *Reality*'s loneliest guys and disco kings. The mortal obsessions of *1. Outside* are abstract fantasy, a solvable mystery; ★'s death is much closer, inscrutable, unresolvable. It's a quality that Boyce identifies as a new development in the long history of Bowie's handling of mortal themes; in the light of his serious illness, 'death is now literal rather than metaphorical' (2016). This proximity is what many great thinkers have argued opens up possible connections to the divine, a sense of fulfilment as a *being* in the Heideggan sense – if human life is finite, then finitude defines it; therefore, ultimate meaning and true authentic life can only be experienced in confrontation with our own deaths (Heidegger [1927] 2008; also see Kovacs 1981, Scheler 1987).

That ★ is Bowie's last album invests the project with inescapable gravity that may or may not have been intended. The material was developed quickly in late 2014, during what seems to have been a challenging period in Bowie's illness progression – when *Lazarus* workshops necessitated his participation via video link and sessions with McCaslin and his band had to be postponed. It's plausible that ★ was conceived as a farewell message from a seriously ill artist who recognized that he was dying. Then again, Visconti told *Rolling Stone* that at some point in mid-2015 Bowie's prognosis improved (Hiatt 2016a), while both he and McCaslin recalled conversations with him about new music ideas, more studio sessions and even potential gigs in 2016.[3] I apologize to any reader who has made it this far looking for a firm answer about whether the uncannily consummate execution of ★ was by accident or design. If Bowie meant for these to be his last words to the world, then the answer you're looking for is both 'no' and 'yes'. Sometimes it's more wonderful to be left wondering.

'I Can't Give Everything Away' (★ track 7)

Tempo: 120 bpm.
Tonality: F major.
Song form: binary (verses and refrains/solo sections).

'I Can't Give Everything Away' is announced by an electronic drum loop that emerges and pulls focus from the thrashing turmoil and transcendence at the end of 'Dollar Days'. While the ear holds on to the towering E note high in the strings, we are swiftly plopped down in the unexpected territory of F major.

The musical elements that are the basis of the track are simple and repetitious. Harmony is grounded more or less in a basic movement of I – vi – IV (F, D minor, B♭), but with added keyboard warmth and a rhythmic hook that provides forward momentum, teasing gentle dissonance against the underlying chords. The structure cycles between two defined sections of different phrase lengths – one a triangle (three chords in the progression), the other a square (four chords). The introduction and refrains are twelve bars long, rolling around in an effortless spiral. The verses and

---

[3] McCaslin, as far as he was aware: 'We were going to record again in January … everything was still moving ahead creatively, despite him being realistic, I think, about what he was dealing with' (Mohammad 2020, part 3, 39:27).

solo sections are sixteen bars, with an extra four bars of #ivø7
(B half diminished seventh) inserted between vi (D minor) and IV
(B♭), adding drama at the peak of the melodic climb through the
verses.

The verse melody begins on C, casting familiar shapes and
climbing over similar chord changes that recall the verse sections
of 'Soul Love' (*Ziggy*). This sequence is matched with confessional-
style couplets that are interrupted before they can reveal too much –
a sudden 'I can't *give*... ' leaping dramatically to high E. 'Give'
is the expressive melodic limit of the song, repeating resolutely
against changing harmonic colours: at first, creating a surprising
dissonance over #ivø7 then again with more open-sounding lydian
effect over IVmaj7, Bowie's voice jumping between major 7ths
before resolving on C ('away'). The refrain keeps this pattern going,
the word positioned over different chords, his high E sounding
less alarmed now, casting more tender colours over the spiralling
progression (see Figure 11.1). The effect of this device is the feeling
that, after we hit the blockage that interrupts Bowie's confessional

FIGURE 11.1 *'I Can't Give Everything Away', changing harmonic
colour against repeating vocal notes (0:39–1:20).*

flow in the verses, the limit itself becomes the source of beauty in the song, from every angle the enduring musical theme and central point of fascination.

'I Can't Give Everything Away' was tracked in the last week of recording at the Magic Shop in March 2015. The drum loop that opens the piece was retained from Bowie's demo, as was his harmonica performance – a detail that many commentators observed as redolent of similar harmonica parts from 'A New Career in a New Town' (*Low*), calling up ideas of transition and frontiersmanship, and also the opening strains of 'Never Let Me Down' (from the 1987 album of the same name), a candid and emotionally genuine expression of gratitude (Critchley 2016, 117; Pegg 2016, 118; Kardos 2017). Around these elements McCaslin and his band construct a thickly layered 'wall of sound', with stacked saxophones, flutes and synth pads (Lindner's Prophet 12) holding on long tones. The texture is almost monolithic, if not for the two moments where the arrangement reacts dynamically to the song: the repetition of the first verse (at 3:12) temporarily halts to expose Bowie's vocal harmonies, and a moment at 4:28 when the synth pads drop out of the mix ahead of the final refrain. Further layers of synthetic strings in the refrain sections smother the sound with presence and warmth. The mix sounds notably different to the tracks which precede it, it's saturated, with a sibilant brightness and harmonic distortion in the low-mid range frequencies. With its blown-out tones and sizzling, extended high end (a shelf boost from 10kHz and above), the sound of 'I Can't Give Everything Away' has enhanced weight and altered air. Heavy and ethereal, huge and effortless.

According to McCaslin, Bowie's demo had spaces earmarked for solos; his saxophone first enters the background of Bowie's refrain at 1:52, then steps forward into the spotlight for an impressively virtuosic, utterly joyous solo that dances deliriously across a sixteen-bar, then a twelve-bar, section (starting at 2:15), lingering thereafter. Monder's solo (4:08) is similarly sparkling and playful, at times edging on slightly manic, evoking something of the spirit of Robert Fripp's soloing over Bowie's big major-key anthems '"Heroes"' ("*Heroes*") and 'Teenage Wildlife' (*Scary Monsters*).

The rolling repetition of verses, refrains and solos lend the track an affectionate, lingering quality, like it doesn't quite want to leave yet. Let's go round again. When it does finally come to a stopping point it lands unexpectedly on D minor with a dark puff that dissipates into a more open and mysterious figure built from superimposed perfect 5ths on D and G. Monder's guitar traces intervals high up the harmonic series, echoing Ronson's similar gesture in the first verse of 'Soul Love' and resonating pleasingly with the 'world riddle' theme of Strauss's *Zarathustra* (the musical leitmotif for *2001*), another composition with a notable 'question mark' ending that hints at the metaphysical possibilities of being.

'I Can't Give Everything Away' became ★'s third single, released posthumously on 6 April 2016. The release was accompanied by a music video created by Barnbrook, featuring animated imagery from his album design and synchronized lyrics. The animation depicts space flight with stars, symbols, constellations and words appearing, spinning, whizzing past the viewer's point of view. It starts in monochrome, eventually moving into wild technicolour for the final refrain, with kaleidoscopic colours and shapes that bring to mind the Star Gate sequence from *2001*. At the end, as the word 'everything' pulses on the screen, a figure of an astronaut vanishes into the vortex of coloured nebulae.

These lyrics, the last words of the songbook, have rare and unusual candour. Here is no apparent obscuring language, no character mask. The mood is lovingly withholding. Seeming to personally address the listener, in one respect gently asserting boundaries of personal privacy, in another way signalling a shared understanding between artist and audience: he knows, he knows we will know, he knows we will have so many questions; we know that he wanted us to know only so much. And we both know it's better this way, because knowing too much spoils the magic trick.[4] This is the moment in ★ when the listening audience might feel seen and embraced. The lyric twirls on its logical incoherence, bringing

---

[4] 'The magician takes the ordinary something and makes it do something extraordinary. Now you're looking for the secret... but you won't find it, because of course you're not really looking. You don't really want to know. You want to be fooled. But you wouldn't clap yet. Because making something disappear isn't enough; you have to bring it back. That's why every magic trick has a third act, the hardest part, the part we call "The Prestige"' (*The Prestige* 2006).

together those impossible oppositional tensions into something reassuring, affirming and possible: everything and more, nothing and less; no and yes. Everything and nothing is all he ever meant.

The radical potential of ★

Bowie's death on 10 January 2016 instigated a global outpouring of public grief and hastened a dramatic contextual shift in his stardom and surviving star image. Bowie became transformed, his image adopting new signification in the dominant popular culture. Birth and death days marked with celebrations, release anniversaries commemorated, sins forgiven, and poorly appraised work revisited and critically re-evaluated. Bowie's image is now redefined as a signifier of restless originality, singular artistic vision and 'genius'. A hungry market emerged for posthumous products, trinkets and tributes.

This phenomenon is a form of life-beyond-death that is powered in part by the continuing relevance of the body of work and in part by our active, collective rites of remembrance. Zygmunt Bauman would describe this as a mutually beneficial suspension of death's finality, separating 'bodily death' from 'social death', only granting true finality to the social kind, thereby constructing a loophole that, with an amount of participatory effort, can (at least temporarily) fix the problem of transience (1992, 52–3). Wearing a T-shirt that says 'Bowie forever'; the certainty of fiftieth-, sixtieth- and seventieth-anniversary collectible reissues up until the point when/if the appetite disappears. In this way our capitalist death industries keep our stars alive.

The human obsession with immortality is fed by the cognitive impossibility of us imagining our own non-existence. The notion of living forever is an increasingly aspirational idea, with the medicalization of death deconstructed into a series of specific afflictions and problems that can be logically treated and solved, making victims of anyone who loses the 'fight'. In defiance of our mortal limitations, some of us work hard to construct what we intend to be our everlasting legacies, hoarding wealth, collecting objects or creating culture that survives beyond our consciousness in the memory of others. Yet 'being remembered' can only be a temporary fix. Time remains the prime antagonist of both the living and those reanimated by memory; it takes a cigarette and puts it in your mouth, then it waits in the wings. Time ensures the constant burn through life – quickly at first, and then the slow burn through living and historical memory. In time, the Earth will assuredly forget us, we can achieve no immortality here. We must return to the stars.

Dyer's Star Theory investigates the ways stars articulate ideas about personhood and potential, and it is ★'s radical articulation of human potential that enriches and elevates its message and aspiration above simply wishing to be adored and remembered after death. The blackstar is not a filmstar, not a pop star, it's something more. As tempting as it is to pull at every affordance to learn 'what [black]star-dom means', it's more useful to instead ask 'what does [black]star-dom do?' (Dyer [1979] 1998, 200). How does the blackstar foreground and transgress stereotypes and archetypes, articulate contradictions and embody oppositional identifications (ibid., 162)? How can Bowie's final star image operate as a site for visualizing and working through issues around the construction of (his and our) identity? How can it help us better understand our selves?

As outlined earlier in this chapter, ★ provides the final piece of Bowie's star-mythic narrative, the heroic odyssey from lift-off in 1969 to 2016's transformative cosmic ascension. The album caps off Bowie's last period of creativity where he was actively exploring the dynamics of opposing forces in his work: light and shadow, immortality and transience, order and chaos, everything and nothing, endings and beginnings. ★ begins with troubled supplication and ends with a joyous harmony of dissonances; embrace and consolidation of the selves, individuation for the mortal with potential of a superman. This hero's journey to the edges of existence, consciousness and the cosmos offers us the boon of enhanced self-understanding. The unfathomable scale between the atomic and the galactic that is the scope of our existence; our eyes the lens of perception that separates outer and inner space, infinite and immeasurable adventure in either direction.

Bowie's star image and mythic narratives demonstrate interconnectedness between texts, dreams, fictions and realities. Of music, sound, imagery, idea, author and audience. The ways that all of these things connect to and construct identity. ★'s imagery also points towards an inlying connectedness and unified understanding about the universe and our place within it, what Jeremy Lent describes as the great cosmic 'web of meaning', the possibility of 'finding meaning ultimately through connectedness within ourselves, to each other, and to the natural world' (Lent 2017, 440). It makes way for a new cosmic romanticism, a philosophy of some hopeful substance, one which recognizes opportunities to overcome the most troubling aspects of ourselves within phenomenological and universal truths.

The blackstar is a symbol of a powerful, mysterious no/thing. An impossible void, all paths lead from and to it: 'Black holes are our history and our future. Black holes may have precipitated out of the primordial soup of a baby universe first and may inhabit the dying universe last' (Levin 2020, 138). You are doomed and you are born. The singularity that can bend the very things that constrain us – space and time. It shares this ability with music, an art form that also permits time to be bent and stretched, compressed and elongated, battered and caressed. Intensified and eternalized (Grosz [2008] 2020, 4). Music manipulates time energy; through it we can alter the speed of life. And artful record production can discover new kinds of space, new soundings from alien landscapes that bear the uncanny physics of impossible architecture, reflections and surfaces. The interconnectedness of music, sound and memory acts as a signifying language that allows for stitches in time and wormholes that can connect thoughts across history, time and space. In *Mortality, Immortality and Other Life Strategies* (1992), Bauman suggests that immortality can exist, echoing Buddhist ideas around the decomposition of eternity into a single frozen 'now' as a means of claiming immortality through impermanence: 'Now one moment is no different from another. Each moment, or no moment, is immortal. Immortality is here – but not here to stay. Immortality is as transient and evanescent as the rest of things' (ibid., 168). Forever contained in the blossomest blossom, the essence of everything that you are in the place without a plan. A triumph over time.

★ ends joyfully with an unresolved question, one that stands in the centre of these absurd impossibilities, in the face of mortal limits. In her *Black Hole Survival Guide* (2020), Janna Levin explains that impossibilities are the very things that guide us towards unimaginable breakthroughs, the 'visionary creativity that explodes in the face of fundamental limits':

We rewrote reality in an astonishing new language ... The limits are the scaffolding enabling creativity. Limits can be worthy adversaries that galvanise our best, most inventive, most agile natures. Before I succumbed to the seduction of the elegance and transcendence of limits, I did not understand the thrill of imagination crashing into truth. (Ibid., 3)

The radical potential of [black]stardom says that, even within the limits of what we're given, we may still be able to expand consciousness and penetrate the mysteries of the unknown, for the self (the life's work) and what lies beyond the edge of existence (death's work).

Epilogue: Legacies and voids

Bowie's death, on 10 January 2016, seemed to usher in a year of notable mortalities, with many cultural figures passing away over the course of the following eleven months – music stars like Prince, Leonard Cohen, George Martin, Merle Haggard and George Michael; film legends like Alan Rickman, Gene Wilder and Carrie Fisher, and many more across diverse spheres of cultural influence (Muhammad Ali, Victoria Wood, Harper Lee and Pierre Boulez). It was a year when public grieving and shared rites of remembrance took on a new kind of participatory energy, aided by the internet and social media, with their quick access to streamable media archives that let people share, remember and celebrate. It was not only fans who were mourning the loss of their favourites. The loss of these stars was felt in the most ordinary corners of many lives – via the memories of records our parents played; loving *Star Wars* or *Labyrinth* or the *Harry Potter* films as children; a song on the radio when we drove alone on the motorway for the first time; the soundtracks of our formative first gigs, first kisses, dance parties, breakups, house moves. The medal ceremony in 2012 when Mo Farah won gold at the London Olympics and '"Heroes"' rang out. The cultural moments that become the textures of our life stories.

When our heroes die, we feel the loss in ourselves where we hold on to those formative moments. We mourn the loss of stars who were our teachers and mentors, who opened our eyes to new philosophies, art and literature, who taught us about sexuality and gender and fashion, about different places and people. They taught us something valuable about being human and their art enriched our experience of living. Bowie's death, in particular, left behind an impossible void, supermassive and silent – a still powerful gravitational force drawing new discourse and products and meanings into its orbit.

When I set out to write this book, my plan was that it was going to be about 'death art'. Not quite in the sense of work made by artists who knew they were dying (Freddie Mercury, Warren Zevon, Derek Jarman), or those artists who use death to comment on or teach us about life (Damien Hirst, Hermann Nitsch), or even artists whose very manner of death could be considered as art pieces (Yukio Mishima, Mark Rothko). But rather the artist who incorporates their life story and death event *into* the piece, where the death is artfully rendered and becomes the key to unlocking and understanding the work. Something clever and elaborate, like what Dennis Potter had achieved with *Karaoke* and *Cold Lazarus*. This is what I believed Bowie's last work was, and the idea of it soothed my grieving: *what an artiste! Using his death to forge his last masterpiece!* It made everything easier to take. However, I soon realized that such matters are never so clear-cut and easy. From speaking with collaborators from the period, it seemed clear that Bowie was fighting to live and wished to carry on working. He was experiencing creative momentum that was tragically cut short by his circumstances. If Bowie had been given time to release more work, would that diminish the power of ★ and *Lazarus*? Does the last work need to be the 'last' in order to 'work'? And if he had happened to die after any of his other late-period projects, couldn't we just as easily read the closing tracks of *Heathen*, *Reality* and *The Next Day* as calculated epitaphs and spin entirely different books that try to analyse and explain why they hold such power? Yes, my 'death art' plan fell to pieces. That is not to suggest ★ isn't the 'parting gift' that Visconti said it was; part of me still hangs on to the idea that the immaculate construction and timing of Bowie's final works were conceived with a degree of intuition. What I realized from working on this book was that in Bowie's characteristically complex style, there's always more than one meaning to be found. Everything and nothing *is* all he ever meant. And it's better to talk about what the last work *does*, rather than assume its intentions. What does the music say and make happen? What do these ideas connect to? What constellations can be seen? I set out looking for evidence of Bowie's morbid artistry, but what I found was something far more affirming, drawing upon more than five decades of creativity and becoming: *life art*.

There is comfort to be found here. The themes that Bowie weaves into these works – transcendence and unification of the self, a cosmic return – speak hopefully about existence, offering us a way to better understand and cherish our transience. In 1997, Bowie spoke about the continuous themes of his work, what he called a search for 'spiritual sustenance':

> Everything that I seem to have written, in some way or other, keeps refocusing on the idea that, in the late twentieth century, we are without our God ... We really have to reinvent God. I think that our religious philosophies trail so far behind the way that we actually live today that we find ourselves in a spiritual void.
>
> – Bowie (Ill 1997)

The spiritual desolation of *Heathen*'s endemic godlessness is resolved in the last works by the continuation and completion of a new myth, a theodicy rooted in the natural world, in the mysteries of the cosmos and of science. These ideas don't stand alone but are shared and emergent from our present collective consciousness. When Nick Cave wrote the song 'Fireflies' (*Ghosteen* 2019), he was working through his grief at the death of his son. Drawn to the imagery of a cosmic return for all existence, he sings about bodies – ours, his teenage son's, Jesus being held by his mother, all just 'photons released from a dying star'. He describes how we 'lie among our atoms' and attempt to communicate with those that are gone, as if we know deep down that we are, as Carl Sagan said, 'a way for the universe to know itself. Some part of our being knows this is where we came from. We long to return' (Sagan 1980). Actor and comedian Rob Delaney deployed similar concepts when he spoke with BBC Radio 4 about the tragic death of his young son:

> I don't know if Henry's death made me love his brothers more, but it certainly made me love them better, because when I hold them now, I know what they really are. They're temporary gatherings of stardust, just like Henry. I'm here now, but one day I'll be wherever Henry is. I'll have to die to get there, but that's okay with me.
>
> – Delaney (2020)

We all needed to draw ourselves back to a state of wonder. My
way was to write myself there … and in doing so I found a way
back, or at least a way through the veil of grief, to the other
side … It became clear that as human beings we have enormous
capabilities that allow us to rise above our suffering – that we are
hardwired for transcendence. This was an acute realisation that
changed the nature of our relationship to everything.

                                                        – Cave (2018)

From grief to wonder, suffering to transcendence. Look up at
the stars and recognize yourself reflected. Nick Cave was correct
when he said that we contain photon particles from the stars. A
Japanese study from 2009 found that 'the human body literally
glimmers' with photon emissions; it may be at a lower level
than can be seen with the naked eye, but our bodies pulse with
rhythmic bioluminescence, nonetheless (Kobayashi et al. 2009).
In 2013, scientist Julian Heeck conducted an experiment to try to
determine the minimum lifetime of photons; using observations
collected by NASA satellites, he studied data on the oldest light
in the universe. He found that very few photons, if any, have
decayed since the Big Bang. That makes the minimum lifetime of
a photon about $10,^{18}$ or one billion billion years (Heeck 2013).
I know, some things are so big they make no sense. But it's a
comfort all the same and, in a Jungian sense, the science that
supports these ideas allows them to function perfectly as modern
myth: something to believe in that relates to the transcendent and
the infinite (Hollis 1995, 15) that can help us make sense of life
and prepare for death.

I was incredibly fortunate to be able to interview a number of
people who collaborated with Bowie on these last works. I asked
them about the legacy of their shared creative experience and what
feelings they carry about the work now (which, at the time we
spoke, was almost five years after Bowie's death).

For Henry Hey, *Lazarus* still holds on to its complex mysteries:

I've now seen the piece so many times, over and over. And I've
thought about it over and over. And even now, I'm still making
new discoveries about it. There are some people who would
presume to say 'this is what he meant', but I still hold that he
means many things and nothing, all at the same time. That's

what makes it a really great piece of art. I get rewarded by it every new time that I see it.

– Hey (interview with the author, 2020)

Jonathan Barnbrook, reflecting on a collaborative design partnership going all the way back to *Heathen*, the beginning of the late period, said 'I feel very lucky to have known him, and to have experienced his trust,' adding that 'I just hope I did a good job, that it was worthy of the man.' At his own expense, Barnbrook still maintains the Bowieblackstar.net domain, which houses downloadable versions of the ★ design assets. The experience of fans engaging with the white square element of *The Next Day* (using it to obscure social media profile photos, for example) showed him the value of there being symbols that everyone can use, share and be a part of: 'I discussed it with Bowie at the time, who thought it was a nice idea ... Fans could use it in their own art or for tattoos. That was absolutely part of the design.'

I was given the chance to converse with Donny McCaslin over a three-part podcast series (Mohammad 2020), and he talked not only about how the collaborative experience of ★ made him feel ('one of the most special things I've been involved with in my life') but also how the effects of this experience were seen in his subsequent work, such as the atmospheric *Beyond Now* (2016) and the sonically daring, art-rock inspired *Blow.* (2018). 'Of course [Bowie] affected my music, I did a record not too long after ★ came out that that was influenced by him for sure. *Blow.* has a deeper connection ... "Tiny Kingdom", for example, really feels like it has some hues from ★.' The folding of jazz, pop, art-rock and sonic/electronic experimentation into a new hybrid sound is something he credits to his time working with Bowie: 'How to mix these elements together, that comes from ★. I feel like David laid that out' (ibid., part 2, 19:05).

Tantalizingly, there were conversations between McCaslin and Bowie about plans to record together again in early 2016 and, if he was well enough, join Donny and his band on stage during his Village Vanguard residency in January ('We were going to do "'Tis a Pity" and "Lazarus" ... I can't imagine it, it would have been insane!'). Similar accounts from Visconti about new music being in the works paints a picture of ongoing creative momentum throughout Bowie's final weeks. The place without a plan, the not-quite-yet.

The legacy of the Magic Shop, Bowie's preferred recording studio, lives on even though the premises was closed down and sold in 2016. The vintage 1970 Neve 80 series custom wrap-around console that Bowie tracked *The Next Day*, ★ and what became the *No Plan* EP on was purchased in the sale, along with other key pieces of outboard equipment, and painstakingly refurbished. Currently the equipment is housed in the Magic Barn, a new studio facility in Solon, Iowa. The first track recorded there was a cover of '"Heroes"' (Little Village 2017).

Erin Tonkon remembers feeling embraced, invited in on the process and nurtured:

> For women, a lot of bad stuff can happen when you work in studios, times when you have to smile and put on a happy face and put up with things, but working with David was the opposite of that. I was able to learn so much from him – creative lessons, life lessons ... I learned an incredible amount. He was a good person, and I'm proud to be a small part of remembering him and speaking to his legacy.
>
> – Tonkon (interview with the author, 2020)

For Visconti, after more than five decades of friendship and collaboration, his relationship with David Bowie is still alive:

> Five years on, I still feel so privileged to have worked with him on so many projects. It was a friendship till the end, and a strong one for sure. And this might sound a bit eerie, but I've got a portrait of my parents over my doorway in my flat ... I have been talking to them in my mind since they passed away, and now in a similar way I talk to David. It's almost like, you know, 'What would Jesus do?'; I go 'What would David do?' And in my studio I've got a portrait of him over my right shoulder (that a friend of mine, Tina Weatherby, did, a hand drawing of him which is so beautiful), and I look over my shoulder while I'm doing a mix – even when I was remixing *Lodger* and *The Man Who Sold the World* – and I turn around to say 'What do you think?' So he is very much with me, he's alive within me as my parents are alive within me. I'll remember him as long as I live, and before I take my final breath I know I will think of him.
>
> – Visconti (interview with the author, 2020)

In multiple realities, Bowie gets to live on. The estate continues to release new music and new versions of old music. *Lazarus* continues to be staged throughout the world and streamed across the globe. Bowie lives in the memories of his friends and creative partners and in the imaginations of his audience. As Paul Morley's catch-all 'David Bowie Is... ?' provocation demonstrated, Bowie can exist in multiple forms beyond mortal limits because Bowie is a construction. He never legally changed his name from David Jones. The idea that the public-facing 'Bowie' that we know was something of an extended performance by Jones is supported by statements made by people close to him. Comedian Ricky Gervais, a lifelong Bowie fan who became friends with the star during the late period, explained that he would never get starstruck because 'David Bowie doesn't really exist. I saw Mr. Jones. Mr. Jones was my mate, and Mr. Bowie was my hero and you don't equate the two' (Radio X 2018).

The suggestion that Jones was haunted and sometimes troubled by his rock-star doppelgänger is threaded right through the Bowie star narrative, but in the last works the opposite feels more accurate: Bowie is all we can see, a vast star image completely remystified, and haunting the scene is a guy called David Jones, the artist who was ill and we didn't know. The one whose time was running out. Who loved to read and paint, and maybe dreamed about returning to England one day. We are left to wonder about this quiet, intelligent man, and why he chose to do it this way. There might yet emerge more music for us to discover from this last period. 'Blaze', the only unreleased finished track from the ★ sessions (we assume), and other bits and pieces lost in the creative whirlwind of 2015, who knows if they will ever see the light of day? If my quest to find meaning in the last works has led me to any conclusions, it's that it's better to not give everything away. I'm perfectly content for any private secrets and sketches to remain stashed in Davy Jones's locker, with the rest of the drowned sailors.

Ideas are powerful, potentially life-changing and world-altering on their own, even more so when they connect and combine and become tangible as art. Bowie's last works tackle the biggest of ideas – life, death, what we are and who we can be – through the artistic depiction of the process of individuation. Upon reflection, researching this book has felt very much like observing the night sky;

locating the constellations, tracing the connecting lines, zooming in on the blank spaces to discover exquisite depths where mysteries reside – elemental chaos creativity, black hole singularities, the everything and nothing at the end of time itself. The late works are a postmodern performance of identity, a dense barrage of juxtaposing images spun through the vortex and emerging as new kinds of sense. They might help us better understand and appreciate the chaos of life, the nature of our mortality and immortal legacies, and maybe even help us become less afraid of our inescapable destiny as corpses and everlasting traces.

REFERENCES

Art pieces, plays, poems and exhibitions

Auden, W. H. (1938) 1991. 'Musée des Beaux Arts'. In *Collected Poems*, ed. Edward Mendelson, 179. New York: Vintage International.

Bowie, David, and Brian Eno. 1995. 'Manuscript Notes on 1. Outside.' The David Bowie Archive.

Bowie, David. 2013–18. *David Bowie Is*.

Bruegel, Pieter. c. 1560. *Landscape with the Fall of Icarus*.

Burden, Chris. 1974. *Trans-Fixed*. Performance.

Coleridge, Samuel Taylor. (1816) 2004. 'Kubla Khan.' In *Coleridge's Poetry and Prose*, ed. Nicholas Halmi, 182. New York: Norton.

Da Messina, Antonello. 1475. *Saint Jerome in his Study*.

Duchamp, Marcel. 1913. *Bicycle Wheel*. Metal wheel mounted.

Dürer, Albrecht. 1514. *Saint Jerome in his Study*.

Dylan, Bob. The Bob Dylan Center. Tulsa, Oklahoma. https://www.bobdylancenter.com.

Emin, Tracey. 1998. *My Bed*. Box frame, mattress, linens, pillows and various objects.

Heckel, Erich. 1917. *Roquairol*.

Ingrassia, Anthony (dir.). 1971. *Andy Warhol's Pork*.

Jung, C. G. 2009–10. *The Red Book of C.G. Jung: Creation of a New Cosmology*. Rubin Museum of Art.

Klinko, Markus. 2002. *Heathen* session. https://www.markusklinkostudio.com/markus_klinko_bowie.

Lazarus, Emma. (1883) 2002. 'The New Colossus.' In *Emma Lazarus: Selected Poems and Other Writings*, ed. Gregory Eiselein, 233. Peterborough (Ontario): Broadview Press.

Malevich, Kazimir. 1915. *Black Square*.

Malevich, Kazimir. 1918. *White on White*.

McPherson, Conor (dir.). 2017. *Girl from the North Country*. Old Vic.

No artist. c. 540–515 BC. *Kroisos Kouros*.

Plath, Sylvia. (1965) 1981. 'Lady Lazarus'. In *The Collected Poems*, Ted Hughes (ed.), 244–7. New York: Harper & Row.

Saar, Betye. 1998. *The Fragility of Smiles (of Strangers Lost at Sea)*. Screenprint and rubber stamp.
Schwarzkogler, Rudolf. 1965. *3rd Action*.
Tharp, Twyla. 2006. *The Times They Are a-Changin'*. Brooks Atkinson Theatre.
Van Cleve, Joos. 1528. *Saint Jerome in his Study*.
Van Hove, Ivo. 2015–16. *Lazarus*. New York Theatre Workshop.
Warhol, Andy. 1976. *Skulls*.
Williams, William Carlos. (1960) 1962. 'Landscape with the Fall of Icarus.' In *Pictures from Brueghel and Other Poems: Collected Poems 1950–1962*, 4. New York: New Directions.

Books and short stories

Adorno, Theodor W. 2002. *Essays on Music*. Translated by Susan H. Gillespie. Berkeley: University of California Press.
Adorno, Theodor W. (1964) 2017. *Moments Musicaux*. Translated by Martin Kaltenecker. Geneva: Éditions Contrechamps.
Barthes, Roland. 1967. *The Death of the Author [La Mort de L'auteur]*. Paris: Mantéia V.
Bauman, Zygmunt. 1992. *Mortality, Immortality and Other Life Strategies*. Cambridge: Polity Press.
Becker, Ernest. 1973. *The Denial of Death*. New York: Free Press.
Bowie, David, and Enda Walsh. 2016. *Lazarus: The Complete Book and Lyrics*. London: Nick Hern Books.
Buckley, David. (2005) 2012. *Strange Fascination*. New York: Random House.
Buckley, David. 2015. *David Bowie: The Music and the Changes*. London: Omnibus Press.
Burgess, Anthony. 1962. *A Clockwork Orange*. London: William Heinemann.
Burroughs, William S. 1959. *Naked Lunch*. New York: Grove Press.
Burroughs, William S. 1961–4. *The Nova Trilogy*. Paris: Olympia Press and New York: Grove Press.
Burroughs, William S. 1971. *The Wild Boys*. New York: Grove Press.
Burroughs, William S., and Brion Gysin.1978. *The Third Mind*. New York: Viking.
Carrington, Leonora. 1941. *White Rabbits*. In Carrington, Leonora. 2018. *The Skeleton's Holiday*. London: Penguin.
Charles, Alec. 2021. 'Lady Lazarus: The Death (and Rebirth) of a Gender Revolutionary.' In Fosbraey, Glenn, and Nicola Puckey (eds.) *Misogyny, Toxic Masculinity, and Heteronormativity in Post-2000 Popular Music*, 233–51. London: Palgrave Macmillan.

Clarke, Arthur C. 1968. *The Promise of Space*. New York: Harper and Row.
Clarke, Eric. 2011. *Ways of Listening: An Ecological Approach to the Perception of Musical Meaning*. New York: Oxford University Press.
Critchley, Simon. (2014) 2016. *Bowie*. New York: OR Books.
Crookall, Robert. 1981. *The Techniques of Astral Projection*. London: Harper Collins Distribution.
Crowley, Aleister. (1904) 1976. *The Book of the Law*. Yorke Beach, Maine: Weiser Books.
Crowley, Aleister (as Khaled Khan). 1938. *The Heart of the Master*. Order Templi Orientis Brighton: Booklegger/Albion: (OTO Private Press). Booklegger/Albion.
De Quincey, Thomas. 1822. *Confessions of an English Opium-Eater*. London: Taylor & Hessey.
Deleuze, Gilles, and Félix Guattari. 1994. *What Is Philosophy?* Translated by Burchell, Graham and Hugh Tomlinson. London: Verso.
Di Pirajno, Alberto Denti. 1956. *A Grave for a Dolphin*. London: Andre Deutsch Ltd.
Dimery, Robert. 2014. *1001 Albums You Must Hear Before You Die*. Sydney: Murdoch Books.
Dyer, Richard. 1986. *Heavenly Bodies: Film Stars and Society*. Basingstoke: Macmillan.
Dyer, Richard. (1979) 1998. *Stars*. London: British Film Institute. Citations refer to the newer edition, 1998.
Dyer, Richard. 2007. *Pastiche*. London: Routledge.
Dylan, Bob. 2004. *Chronicles, Vol 1*. New York: Simon & Schuster.
Elliott, Richard. 2015. *The Late Voice: Time, Age and Experience in Popular Music*. London: Bloomsbury Academic.
Eno, Brian. (1996) 2020. *A Year with Swollen Appendices*. London: Faber & Faber.
Evans-Wentz, W. Y. (1927) 2000. *The Tibetan Book of the Dead*. Oxford: Oxford University Press.
Ford, John. 1633. *'Tis Pity She's a Whore*. London: Richard Collins.
Fremaux, Stephanie and Bethany Usher. 2015. 'Turn Myself to Face Me: David Bowie in the 1990s and Discovery of Authentic Self.' In Devereaux, Eoin, Dillane, Aileen, and Martin J. Power (eds). *David Bowie: Critical Perspectives*, 56–81. London: Routledge.
Grosz, Elizabeth. (2008) 2020. *Chaos, Territory, Art: Deleuze and the Framing of the Earth*. New York: Columbia University Press.
Gysin, Brion. 1982. *Beat Museum/Bardo Hotel Ch. 2*. Berkeley, California: Inkblot Publications.
Hall, Manly P. (1928) 2011. *The Secret Teachings of All Ages*. USA: Pacific Publishing Studio.

Halliwell, Leslie and Walker, David. 2003. *Halliwell's Who's Who in the Movies*. London: Harper Collins.

Heidegger, Martin. (1927) 2008. *Being and Time*. Translated by John Macquarrie and Edward Robinson. London: Harper Perennial Modern Thought.

Heylin, Clinton. (1991) 2011. *Bob Dylan: Behind the Shades*. London: Faber & Faber.

Hollis, James. 1995. *Tracking the Gods: The Place of Myth in Modern Life*. Scarborough, Ontario: Inner City Books.

Holocek, Andrew. 2013. *Preparing to Die: Practical Advice and Spiritual Wisdom from the Tibetan Buddhist Tradition*. Ithaca, New York: Snow Lion Publications.

Holmes, Su and Redmond, Sean. (eds.) 2007. *Stardom and Celebrity: A Reader*. London: SAGE.

Hopkins, Jerry. 1985. *Bowie*. New York: Prentice Hall & IBD.

Huskinson, Lucy. 2004. *Nietzsche and Jung: The Whole Self in the Union of Opposites*. Hove, Sussex: Routledge.

Izod, John. 1992. *The Films of Nicolas Roeg: Myth and Mind*. London: Palgrave Macmillan.

Izod, John. 2001. *Myth, Mind and the Screen*. Cambridge: Cambridge University Press.

Jung, C. G. 1933. *Modern Man in Search of a Soul*. Translated by Cary F. Baynes with William Stanley Dell. San Diego: Harcourt, Brace & Co.

Jung, C. G. 1951. *Aion - Researches into the Phenomenology of the Self*. Translated by R. F. C. Hull. Princeton, N.J.: Bollingen.

Jung, C. G. 1963. *Memories, Dreams, Reflections*. Translated by Richard and Clara Winston. New York: Pantheon Books.

Jung, C. G. 1970. *Mysterium Coniunctionis*. Translated by R. F. C. Hull. Princeton, N.J.: Bollingen.

Jung, C. G. 1981. *Part 1: Archetypes and the Collective Unconscious*. 2nd ed. Translated by Adler, Gerhard and R. F. C. Hull. Princeton, N.J.: Bollingen.

Jung, C. G. 2009 (Shamdasani, Sonu, ed.). *The Red Book: Liber Novus*. Translated by Kyburz, Mark, Peck, John and Sonu Shamdasani. New York: W. W. Norton & Co.

Kureishi, Hanif. 1990. *The Buddha of Suburbia*. London: Faber & Faber.

Leary, Timothy. (1964) 2007. *The Psychedelic Experience*. New York: Citadel Press.

Leary, Timothy, Metzner, Ralph and Richard Alpert. (1964). 2008. *The Psychedelic Experience: A Manual Based on the Tibetan Book of the Dead*. London: Penguin Classics.

Lent, Jeremy R. 2017. *The Patterning Instinct: A Cultural History of Humanity's Search for Meaning*. Buffalo, New York: Prometheus Books.

Leorne, Ana. 2015. 'Dear Dr. Freud - David Bowie Hits the Couch.' In Devereaux, Eoin, Dillane, Aileen, and Martin J. Power (eds). *David Bowie: Critical Perspectives*, 111–27. New York: Routledge.

Levin, Janna. 2020. *Black Hole Survival Guide*. New York: Random House.

Márquez, Gabriel Garcia. 1967. *One Hundred Years of Solitude*. Translated by Gregory Rabassa. Buenos Aires, Argentina: Editorial Sudamericana.

Mendes, Ana Christina and Perrott, Lisa. 2020. *David Bowie and Transmedia Stardom*. London: Routledge.

Miller, Lulu. 2020. *Why Fish Don't Exist: A Story of Loss, Love, and the Hidden Order of Life*. New York: Simon & Schuster.

Morrissey. 2013. *Autobiography*. London: Penguin Classics.

Naiman, Tiffany. 2015. 'Art's Filthy Lesson.' In Devereaux, Eoin, Dillane, Aileen, and Martin J. Power (eds). *David Bowie: Critical Perspectives*, 178–95. New York: Routledge.

Nayar, Pramod K. 2009. *Seeing Stars: Spectacle, Society and Celebrity Culture*. London: SAGE.

Nietzsche, Friedrich Wilhelm. (1879) 1996. *Assorted Opinions and Maxims*. Translated by Marion Faber and R. J. Hollingdale. Cambridge: Cambridge University Press.

Nietzsche, Friedrich Wilhelm. (1881) 2011. *Dawn: Thoughts on the Prejudices of Morality*. Translated by Brittain Smith. Stanford, Connecticut: Stanford University Press.

Nietzsche, Friedrich Wilhelm. (1882) 1974. *The Gay Science*. Translated by Walter Kaufmann. New York: Vintage.

Nietzsche, Friedrich Wilhelm. (1883–5) 1999. *Thus Spake Zarathustra*. Translated by Anthony Common. Ware, Hertfordshire: Wordsworth Editions.

Nietzsche, Friedrich Wilhelm. (1888) 2009. *Ecce Homo: How to Become What You Are*. Translation by Duncan Large. New York: Oxford University Press.

Nietzsche, Friedrich Wilhelm. (1901) 1968. *The Will to Power*. Translated by Walter Kaufmann and R. J. Hollingdale. New York: Vintage.

O'Connell, John. 2019. *Bowie's Books: The Hundred Literary Heroes Who Changed His Life*. London: Bloomsbury Publishing.

O'Leary, Chris. 2019. *Ashes to Ashes*. London: Repeater.

Orwell, George. 1949. *Nineteen Eighty-Four: A Novel*. London: Secker & Warburg.

Peckham, Morse. 1967. *Man's Rage for Chaos: Biology, Behaviour and the Arts*. New York: Schocken Books.

Pegg, Nicholas. 2016. *The Complete David Bowie*. London: Titan Books.

Pitt, Kenneth. 1983. *David Bowie: The Pitt Report*. London: Lume Books.

Priest, Christopher. 1995. *The Prestige*. New York: St. Martin's Press.
Sagan, Carl. 1980. *Cosmos*. New York: Random House.
Said, Edward. 2006. *On Late Style*. London: Bloomsbury Publishing.
Sarabyanov, Dmitri. 1990. *Russian Art from Neoclassicism to the Avant-Garde: 1800–1917*. New York: Harry N. Abrams, Inc., Publishers.
Schapiro, Steve. 2016. *Bowie*. Brooklyn, New York: Powerhouse Books.
Scheler, Max. 1987. *Schriften aus dem Nachlass: Vol. 3 Philosophische Anthropologie. Gesammelte Werke*, vol. 12. Ed. M. S. Frings. Bonn: Bouvier Verlag.
Sedgwick, Eve Kosofsky. 2003. *Touching Feeling: Affect, Pedagogy, Performativity*. Durham, North Carolina: Duke University Press Books.
Seitz, William Chapin. 1989. 'The Realism and Poetry of Assemblage.' In *The Art of Assemblage*, 81–92. New York: Museum of Modern Art.
Shingler, Martin. 2012. *Star Studies: A Critical Guide*. London: Palgrave Macmillan.
Sontag, Susan. 2005. *Regarding the Pain of Others*. London: Penguin Books Limited (UK).
Stark, Tanja. 2015. 'Confronting Bowie's Mysterious Corpses.' In Cinque, Toija, Moore, Christopher and Sean Redmond (eds.). *Enchanting David Bowie: Space Time Body Memory*, 61–77. New York and London: Bloomsbury.
Tevis, Walter S. (1963) 2016. *The Man Who Fell to Earth*. London: Gollancz.
Tinker, Chris. 2005. *Georges Brassens and Jacques Brel: Personal and Social Narratives in Post-War Chanson*. Liverpool: Liverpool University Press.
Trynka, Paul. 2011. *Starman*. London: Hachette UK.
Von Däniken, Erich. (1968) 1970. *Chariots of the Gods*. Translated by Michael Heron. New York: G. P. Putnam & Sons.
Young, Rob. 2012. *No Regrets: Writings on Scott Walker*. London: Orion Publishing Company.
Young, Rob. 2013. *No Regrets*. London: Orion Publishing Company.
Waldrep, Shelton. 2015. *Future Nostalgia: Performing David Bowie*. New York and London: Bloomsbury.
Wilson, Scott. 2019. *Scott Walker and the Song of the One-All-Alone*. New York: Bloomsbury Academic.

Films, TV shows, plays and games

30 Century Man. 2006. Directed by Stephen Kijak. Verve Pictures.
2001: A Space Odyssey. 1968. Directed by Stanley Kubrick. MGM.
A Clockwork Orange. 1971. Directed by Stanley Kubrick. Hawk Films.
All That Jazz. 1979. Directed by Bob Fosse. 20th Century Fox.

An Interview with Dennis Potter. 1994. Directed by Tom Poole. LWT for Channel 4.
Baal. 1982. Directed by Alan Clarke. BBC.
Blade Runner. 1982. Directed by Ridley Scott. Warner Bros. Pictures.
Blade Runner 2049. 2017. Directed by Denis Villeneuve. Warner Bros. Pictures.
CBC News. 1995. 'David Bowie on Death, Violence and Chaos in "Outside".' YouTube. https://www.youtube.com/watch?v=-R9W2fUddiE.
Cold Lazarus. 1996. Directed by Renny Rye. Channel 4.
Cracked Actor. 1975. Directed by Alan Yentob. BBC.
David Bowie: Five Years. 2013. *David Bowie: The Last Five Years.* 2017. *David Bowie: Finding Fame.* 2019. All directed by Francis Whately. BBC.
Flaming Star. 1960. Directed by Don Siegel. 20th Century Fox.
Friday Night with Jonathan Ross. 2004. Directed by Mick Thomas. Series 6, episode 10. BBC.
Inspirations. 1997. Directed by Michael Apted. Argo Films.
Karaoke. 1996. Directed by Renny Rye. BBC.
La Jetée. 1962. Directed by Chris Marker. Argos Films.
Metropolis. 1927. Directed by Fritz Lang. UFA.
Mister Ed. 1961. Directed by Rod Amateau. 'The First Meeting', season 1, episode 1. CBS.
Moon. 2009. Directed by Duncan Jones. Sony Pictures Classics.
MTV. 1983. Interviewed by Mark Goodman. YouTube. https://www.youtube.com/watch?v=XZGiVzIr8Qg.
MTV. 1987. Interviewed by Linda Corradina. YouTube. https://www.youtube.com/watch?v=Dvx2p5-3uIc.
Peaky Blinders. 2013–present. BBC Studios.
Song of Norway. 1970. Directed by Andrew L. Stone. ABC Pictures.
Star Trek. 1966–9. Created by Gene Roddenberry. Desilu Productions & Paramount.
The Buddha of Suburbia. 1993. Directed by Roger Michell. BBC.
The Cabinet of Dr. Caligari. 1920. Directed by Robert Wiene. Decla Film.
The Hunger. 1983. Directed by Tony Scott. MGM.
The Importance of Being Morrissey. 2002. Directed by Tina Flintoff and Ricky Kelehar. Chrysalis Television/Channel 4.
The Last Panthers. 2015–6. Directed by Johan Renck. +Canal and Sky Atlantic.
The Man Who Fell to Earth. 1976. Directed by Nicolas Roeg. British Lion Films.
The Nomad Soul (Omikron: The Nomad Soul in the US). 1999. Directed by David Cage. Quantic Dream.
The Prestige. 2006. Directed by Christopher Nolan. Warner Bros Pictures.

The Rugrats Movie. 1998. Directed by Igor Kovalyov. Klasky Csupo.
The Singing Detective. 1986. Directed by Jon Amiel. BBC.
VH1's Storytellers. 1999. Directed by Michael Simon. Viacom.

Magazines, newspapers and journal articles

Adetula, Elizabeth. 2017. 'Blade Runner 2049 Director Reveals David
    Bowie Was Meant to Star in the Film.' *Metro*, July 23. Accessed 1 July
    2020. https://metro.co.uk/2017/07/23/blade-runner-2049-director-
    reveals-david-bowie-was-meant-to-star-in-the-film-6800450.
Babich, Babette E. 2001. 'Nietzsche's Chaos Sive Natura: Evening Gold
    and the Dancing Star.' *Revista Portuguesa De Filosofia* 57(2): 225–45.
Barceló, Carlos, Liberati, Stefano, Sonego, Sebastiano and Matt
    Visser. 2009. 'Black Stars, Not Black Holes.' *Scientific American*
    301(4): 38–45. Accessed 7 July 2020. https://www.researchgate.net/
    publication/26837333_Black_Stars_Not_Holes.
Bowie, David. 1994. 'The Last Legendary Painter (Balthus with David
    Bowie).' *Modern Painters* 7(3): 14–33.
Bowie, David. 1996. 'Basquiat's Wave.' *Modern Painters* 9(1): 46–7.
    Accessed 1 August 2020. http://www.bowiewonderworld.com/
    ownword.htm#JMBasq.
Boyce, Niall. 2016. 'Strangers When We Meet: David Bowie, Mortality,
    and Metamorphosis.' *The Lancet* 387(10018): 528–9. Accessed 12
    August 2020. https://www.thelancet.com/journals/lancet/article/
    PIIS0140-6736(16)00226-9/fulltext.
Brantley, Ben. 2015. 'Review: David Bowie Songs and a Familiar Alien in
    "Lazarus".' *The New York Times*, December 7. Accessed 17 August 2020.
    https://www.nytimes.com/2015/12/08/theater/review-david-bowie-songs-
    and-a-familiar-alien-in-lazarus.html.
Brown, Mick. 1974. 'Lindsay Kemp: the Man Who Taught Bowie His
    Moves.' *Crawdaddy!*, September. Accessed 8 July 2020. http://www.
    bowiewonderworld.com/press/70/7409lkemp.htm.
Brown, Tina. 1975. 'The Bowie Odyssey.' *The Sunday Times Magazine*,
    July 20. Accessed 8 July 2020. http://www.bowiegoldenyears.com/
    press/75-07-20-sunday-times.html.
Bury, Liz. 2013. 'David Bowie's Top 100 Must-read Books.' *The Guardian*,
    October 1. Accessed 14 July 2020. https://www.theguardian.com/
    books/2013/oct/01/david-bowie-books-kerouac-milligan.
Buskin, Richard. 2003. 'David Bowie and Tony Visconti: Recording
    Reality.' *Sound On Sound*, October. Accessed 18 July 2020. https://
    www.soundonsound.com/techniques/david-bowie-tony-visconti.

Butler, Don. 2016. 'David Bowie: Integrating the Alien.' *Journal of Analytical Psychology* 61(5): 708–11. Accessed 21 July 2020. https:// onlinelibrary.wiley.com/doi/abs/10.1111/1468-5922.12266.

Cadwalladr, Carole. 2014. 'Iman: "I Am the Face of a Refugee".' *The Guardian*, June 29. Accessed 8 August 2020. https://www.theguardian. com/fashion/2014/jun/29/iman-i-am-the-face-of-a-refugee.

Cavanagh, David. 1997. 'Changes Fifty Bowie.' *Q*, February. In Sean Egan (ed.). *Bowie on Bowie: Interviews and Encounters*, Chicago: Chicago Review Press, 2015, 323.

Chastagner, Claude. 2018. 'Modern Death. La Critique Rock Face à Blackstar.' *Miranda* 17(17). Accessed 12 August 2020. https://www. researchgate.net/publication/328203850_Modern_Death_La_critique_ rock_face_a_Blackstar.

Copetas, Craig. 1974. 'Beat Godfather Meets Glitter Mainman: William Burroughs Interviews David Bowie.' *Rolling Stone*, February 28. Accessed 8 August 2020. https://www.rollingstone.com/feature/beat-godfather-meets-glitter-mainman-william-burroughs-interviews-david-bowie-92508/.

Cowan, Jake. 2018. 'Autobituary: The Life and/as Death of David Bowie and the Specters from Mourning.' *Miranda* 17. Accessed 11 August 2020. https://journals.openedition.org/miranda/13374.

Crowe, Cameron. 1976a. 'David Bowie: Ground Control to Davy Jones.' *Rolling Stone*, February 12. Accessed 13 July 2020. https://www. rollingstone.com/music/music-news/david-bowie-ground-control-to-davy-jones-77059/.

Crowe, Cameron. 1976b. 'The Playboy Interview with David Bowie.' *Playboy*, September. Accessed 13 July 2020. https://www.playboy. com/read/playboy-interview-david-bowie. [republished on January 11, 2016].

Cunningham, Michael. 2017. 'Stage Oddity: The Story of David Bowie's Secret Final Project.' *GQ*, January 9. Accessed 15 July 2020. https:// www.gq.com/story/david-bowie-musical.

Cybulska, Eva. 2012. 'Nietzsche's Übermensch: A Hero of Our Time?' *Philosophy Now* 93. Accessed 17 July 2020. https://philosophynow. org/issues/93/Nietzsches_Ubermensch_A_Hero_of_Our_Time.

Dean, Jonathan. 2020. 'He Fell to Earth: How David Bowie Dealt with a Decade of Obscurity.' *The Sunday Times Magazine*, August 16. Accessed 18 July 2020. https://www.thetimes.co.uk/article/ he-fell-to-earth-how-david-bowie-dealt-with-a-decade-of-obscurity-xzk9mwmdq.

Doggett, Peter. 1995. 'David Bowie's Lost Rock Opera.' *Record Collector*, June, 92.

Du Noyer, Paul. 2002. 'Contact.' *Mojo*, July. Accessed 1 August 2020. https://www.pauldunoyer.com/david-bowie-interview-2002/.

Du Noyer, Paul. 2003. 'I Could Thank God. Yeah. But Which One?' *The Word*, November. Accessed 3 August 2020. https://www.vice.com/en/article/rb8b8q/an-interview-with-david-bowie-2003. [republished on January 11, 2016].

Eager, Gerald. 1961. 'The Missing and the Mutilated Eye in Contemporary Art.' *The Journal of Aesthetics and Art Criticism* 20(1): 49. Accessed 15 August 2020. https://www.jstor.org/stable/i217774.

Einav, Dan. 2018. 'America - Simon & Garfunkel's 1968 Anthem is Steeped in National Mythology.' *Financial Times*, November 19. Accessed 7 August 2020. https://ig.ft.com/life-of-a-song/america.html.

Empire, Kitty. 2013. 'David Bowie: The Next Day - Review.' *The Observer*, March 10. Accessed 8 August 2020. https://www.theguardian.com/music/2013/mar/10/david-bowie-next-day-review.

Fear, David. 2011. 'Nicolas Roeg on The Man Who Fell to Earth.' *Time Out New York*, June 21, 43.

Fox, Robert. 2016. 'Remembering David Bowie.' *Vogue*, January 11. Accessed 15 August 2020. https://www.vogue.co.uk/article/david-bowie-a-tribute-robert-fox-lazarus-new-york-stage-production.

Furby, Jacqueline. 2018. 'New Killer Star.' *Cinema Journal* 57(3): 167–74.

Gerard, Jeremy. 2015. 'David Bowie's Searing "Lazarus" Brings The Man Who Fell to Earth Back from the Dead - Review.' Deadline, December 7. Accessed 1 July 2020. https://deadline.com/2015/12/david-bowie-lazarus-review-1201658036/.

Gilmore, Mikal. 2012. 'David Bowie: How Ziggy Stardust Fell to Earth.' *Rolling Stone*, February 2. Accessed 17 July 2020. https://www.rollingstone.com/feature/david-bowie-how-ziggy-stardust-fell-to-earth-183340/#ixzz3xKmR59dw.

Graff, Gary. 2013. 'Inside David Bowie's Stealth Comeback: Q&A with Producer Tony Visconti.' *Billboard*, January 13. Accessed 3 July 2020. https://assets.billboard.com/articles//1484319/inside-david-bowies-stealth-comeback-qa-with-producer-tony.

Greene, Andy. 2013a. 'David Bowie "Likes the Struggle" of Winning Fans, Says Drummer.' *Rolling Stone*, February 1. Accessed 4 July 2020. https://www.rollingstone.com/music/music-news/david-bowie-likes-the-struggle-of-winning-fans-244410/.

Greene, Andy. 2013b. 'Flashback: David Bowie Faces Heat on Glass Spider Tour.' *Rolling Stone*, August 1. Accessed 6 April 2021. https://www.rollingstone.com/music/music-news/flashback-david-bowie-faces-heat-on-glass-spider-tour-89166/.

Greene, Andy. 2015. 'The Inside Story of David Bowie's Stunning New Album.' *Rolling Stone*, November 23. Accessed 4 July 2020. https://www.rollingstone.com/music/music-features/the-inside-story-of-david-bowies-stunning-new-album-blackstar-231351/.

Greene, Andy. 2016a. "Inside David Bowie's Pioneering Internet-Age LP 'Hours…'." *Rolling Stone*, September 26. Accessed 2 April 2021. https://www.rollingstone.com/music/music-news/inside-david-bowies-pioneering-internet-age-lp-hours-122392/.

Greene, Andy. 2016b. 'David Bowie's Parting Gift: Inside New "Lazarus" Soundtrack.' *Rolling Stone*, October 10. Accessed 4 July 2020. https://www.rollingstone.com/music/music-features/david-bowies-parting-gift-inside-new-lazarus-soundtrack-117676/

Grow, Kory. 2015. 'David Bowie's "Lazarus" is Surrealistic Tour de Force.' *Rolling Stone*, December 8. Accessed 5 July 2020. https://www.rollingstone.com/culture/culture-news/david-bowies-lazarus-is-surrealistic-tour-de-force-59085.

Halperin, Shirley. 2013. 'David Bowie Producer Talks New Music, Health Scare: "Album Is Physical Evidence That He's Fine" (Q&A).' *The Hollywood Reporter*, January 11. Accessed 13 July 2020. https://www.hollywoodreporter.com/news/david-bowie-producer-new-album-411233.

Hart, Ron. 2016. 'What It Was Like Recording "Blackstar" With David Bowie.' *Observer*, January 10. Accessed 8 July 2020. https://observer.com/2016/01/what-it-was-like-recording-blackstar-with-david-bowie/.

Hayman, Martin.1973. 'Outside David Bowie is… the Closest You're Gonna Get.' *Rock Magazine*, October 8. Accessed 7 February 2021. http://www.5years.com/outside.htm.

Heeck, Julian. 2013. 'How Stable Is the Photon?' *Physical Review Letters* 111(2). Accessed 11 July 2020. https://journals.aps.org/prl/abstract/10.1103/PhysRevLett.111.021801.

Heller, Jason. 2017. 'David Bowie's 1978 Slump Held Its Own Weird Magic.' *The Atlantic*, April 27. Accessed 6 April 2021. https://www.theatlantic.com/entertainment/archive/2017/04/david-bowies-1987-slump-held-its-own-weird-magic/524295/.

Hiatt, Brian. 2016a. 'David Bowie Planned Post-"Blackstar" Album, "Thought He Had Few More Months".' *Rolling Stone*, January 14. Accessed 11 July 2020. https://www.rollingstone.com/music/music-news/david-bowie-planned-post-blackstar-album-thought-he-had-few-more-months-37095/.

Hiatt, Brian. 2016b. 'Inside David Bowie's Final Years.' *Rolling Stone*, January 27. Accessed 13 July 2020. https://www.rollingstone.com/feature/inside-david-bowies-final-years-237314.

Howarth, Dan. 2016. 'David Bowie Was "Facing His Own Mortality" Says Barnbrook.' *Dezeen*, January 20. Accessed 3 August 2020. https://www.dezeen.com/2016/01/20/david-bowie-blackstar-album-cover-designer-jonathan-barnbrook-facing-his-own-mortality/.

Hughes, Rob. 2019. 'A Garage Band with a Budget!' *Uncut*, July, 86.

Hunter-Tilney, Ludovic. 2016. '"Lazarus" Playwright Enda Walsh on Working with David Bowie on His Final Project.' *Financial Times*, October 21. Accessed 3 August 2020. https://www.ft.com/content/5fbe4602-9553-11e6-a1dc-bdf38d484582.

Ill, Paul. 1997. 'David Bowie: Maintaining the Vision in a World of Change.' *The Music Paper*, March, n.p.

Irvin, Jim. 1995. 'Scott Walker: "That Francis Bacon, In-The-Face Whoops Factor…".' *Mojo*, May, 12.

Jones, Thomas. 2012. 'So Ordinary, So Glamorous.' *London Review of Books* 34(7). Accessed 2 August 2020. https://www.lrb.co.uk/the-paper/v34/n07/thomas-jones/so-ordinary-so-glamorous.

Jones, Jonathan. 2016. 'David Bowie's Sombre Art Collection Needs More Space Oddities.' *The Guardian*, October 11. Accessed 3 August 2020. https://www.theguardian.com/artanddesign/2016/oct/11/david-bowie-art-collection-sothebys.

Kardos, Leah. 2017. 'Bowie Musicology: Mapping Bowie's Sound and Music Language across the Catalogue.' *Continuum* 31(4): 552–63.

Kellaway, Kate. 2016. 'Ivo van Hove: "I Give It All as Bowie Gave It All - in a Masked Way".' *The Guardian*, November 6. Accessed 2 July 2020. https://www.theguardian.com/stage/2016/nov/06/ivo-van-hove-i-give-it-all-like-bowie-gave-it-all-in-a-masked-way-lazarus-interview.

Kobayashi, Masaki, Kikuchi, Daisuke and Hitoshi Okamura. 2009. 'Imaging of Ultraweak Spontaneous Photon Emission from Human Body Displaying Diurnal Rhythm.' *PLOS One* 4(7):e6256. Accessed 22 April 2021. https://pubmed.ncbi.nlm.nih.gov/19606225/.

Kornhaber, Spencer. 2016. 'What Is David Bowie's "Blackstar" Really About?' *The Atlantic*, January 7. Accessed 4 July 2020. https://www.theatlantic.com/entertainment/archive/2016/01/blackstar-david-bowie-review-interpretation-isis-ego-stardom/422928/

Kovacs, George. 1981. 'Death and the Question of Immortality.' *Death Education* 5(1): 15–24. Accessed 4 July 2020. https://www.tandfonline.com/doi/abs/10.1080/07481188108252073.

Kurutz, Steven. 2016. 'David Bowie: Invisible New Yorker.' *The New York Times*, January 16. Accessed 5 July 2020. https://www.nytimes.com/2016/01/17/fashion/david-bowie-invisible-new-yorker.html.

Lewis, Wyndham. 1914. 'Long Live the Vortex!' *Blast*, June. Accessed 5 August 2020. https://www.poetryfoundation.org/articles/69478/long-live-the-vortex-and-our-vortex.

Little Village. 2017. 'Maiden Voyage: Collective of Iowa City Musicians Celebrates the Local Rebirth of Revered NYC Recording Studio with Salute to David Bowie's "Heroes".' *Little Village*, January 8. Accessed 5 September 2020. https://littlevillagemag.com/magic-shop-nyc-iowa-barn-recording-studio/.

Loder, Kurt. 1987. 'David Bowie: Stardust Memories.' *Rolling Stone*, April 23. Accessed 7 August 2020. https://www.rollingstone.com/music/music-news/david-bowie-stardust-memories-105451/.

Lynch, Joe. 2015. 'David Bowie's "Blackstar" Single/Short Film Debuts, Director Explains "Popeye" Influence.' *Billboard*, November 19. Accessed August 27 2020. https://www.billboard.com/articles/news/6770048/david-bowie-blackstar-video-debut-popeye.

Maruffa, Luca. 2015. 'I Was Born with the Gift of a Golden Voice.' *L'aperitivo Illustrato* 68(15). Accessed 7 August 2020. https://lucamaruffa.medium.com/i-was-born-with-the-gift-of-a-golden-voice-about-leonard-cohen-e3b7aa102519.

McCormick, Neil. 2013. 'David Bowie, The Next Day, Album Review.' *The Daily Telegraph*, February 25. Accessed 8 August 2020. https://www.telegraph.co.uk/culture/music/cdreviews/9888192/David-Bowie-The-Next-Day-album-review.html.

McGeorge, Alistair. 2015. 'David Bowie's New Song Blackstar Was "Inspired By ISIS".' *The Mirror*, November 25. Accessed August 17 2020. https://www.mirror.co.uk/3am/celebrity-news/david-bowiedenies-claims-new-6899451.

Mercurio, Gianni. 2016. 'Interview with Tony Oursler.' *Open Obscura*, December 21. Accessed 8 August 2020. https://issuu.com/tonyoursler/docs/open_obscura_book.

Micallef. Ken. 2016. 'Track by Track: Mark Guiliana on David Bowie's Blackstar.' *Modern Drummer*, February. Accessed 2 September 2020. https://www.moderndrummer.com/2016/02/track-by-track-mark-guiliana-on-david-bowies-blackstar/.

Morley, Paul. 2016. 'Dalí, Duchamp and Dr Caligari: The Surrealism That Inspired David Bowie.' *The Guardian*, July 22. Accessed 12 August 2020. https://www.theguardian.com/books/2016/jul/22/david-bowie-surrealist-inspired-dali-duchamp-dr-caligari.

Nelson, Jim. 2004. 'Morrissey Returns!' *GQ*, April. Accessed 19 September 2020. https://www.gq.com/story/morrissey-interview-jim-nelson.

Orshoski, Wes. 2003. 'Never Get Old.' *Steinway*. Accessed 18 August 2020. https://www.steinway.com/news/features/never-get-old-david-bowie.

Oursler, Tony. 2016. 'David Bowie.' *Art Forum* 54(7), March. Accessed 17 July 2020. https://www.artforum.com/print/201603/david-bowie-58102.

Palmer, Landon. 2013. 'Re-collecting David Bowie: *The Next Day* and Late-Career Stardom.' *Celebrity Studies* 4 (3), 384–6. Accessed 17 July 2020. https://www.tandfonline.com/doi/abs/10.1080/19392397.2013.831628.

Pareles, Jon. 2016. 'David Bowie Dies at 69; Star Transcended Music, Art and Fashion.' *The New York Times*, January 11. Accessed 17 June 2020. https://www.nytimes.com/2016/01/12/arts/music/david-bowie-dies-at-69.html.

Penman, Ian. 1995. 'The Resurrection of Saint Dave.' *Esquire*, October, 59–64.
Perkins, Zelda. 2019. 'David Bowie: The Final Bow.' *The New European*, November 28. Accessed 28 July 2020. https://www.theneweuropean. co.uk/brexit-news/david-bowies-final-bow-63706.
Perrott, Lisa. 2017. 'Bowie the Cultural Alchemist: Performing Gender, Synthesizing Gesture and Liberating Identity.' *Continuum* 31(4): 528–41. Accessed 28 August 2020. https://www.tandfonline.com/doi/ abs/10.1080/10304312.2017.1334380.
Perrott, Lisa. 2019. 'Time is Out of Joint: The Transmedial Hauntology of David Bowie.' *Celebrity Studies* 10(1): 119–39. Accessed 2 July 2020. https://www.tandfonline.com/doi/abs/10.1080/19392397.2018.1559125.
Petridis, Alexis. 2013. 'David Bowie: The Next Day - Review.' *The Guardian*, February 25. Accessed 27 June 2020. https://www. theguardian.com/music/2013/feb/25/david-bowie-next-day-review.
Petridis, Alexis. 2020. "David Bowie's 50 Greatest Songs – Ranked!" *The Guardian*, March 19. Accessed 5 April 2021. https://www.theguardian. com/music/2020/mar/19/david-bowie-50-greatest-songs-ranked.
Power, Ed. 2020. 'Bass Oddity: Why David Bowie's "Jungle Nuttah" D'n'B Phase Is Worth Rediscovering.' *The Independent*, April 15. Accessed 2 September 2020. https://www.independent.co.uk/arts- entertainment/music/features/david-bowie-dnb-earthling-tour-jugle- nuttah-space-oddity-ziggy-stardust-a9465931.html.
Roberts, Chris. 1999. 'David Bowie: "I'm Hungry for Reality!"' *Uncut*, October. Accessed 2 August 2020. https://www.uncut.co.uk/features/ david-bowie-i-m-hungry-for-reality-part-2-27235.
Rogers, Jude. 2016. 'The Final Mysteries of David Bowie's Blackstar - Elvis, Crowley and the Villa of Ormen.' *The Guardian*, January 21. Accessed 2 September 2020. https://www.theguardian.com/ music/2016/jan/21/final-mysteries-david-bowie-blackstar-elvis-crowley- villa-of-ormen.
Rook, Jean. 1976. 'Waiting for Bowie.' *Daily Express*, May 5. Accessed 12 August 2020. http://www.bowiegoldenyears.com/press/76-05-05-daily- express.html.
Saal, Hubert. 1972. 'The Stardust Kid.' *Newsweek*, October 9. Accessed 2 August 2020. http://www.5years.com/tsk.htm.
Salvo, Patrick. 1973. 'New Again, David Bowie.' *Interview*, March. Accessed 8 September 2020. https://www.interviewmagazine.com/ music/new-again-david-bowie.
Schjeldahl, Peter. 2011. 'Shapes of Things: After Kazimir Malevich.' *The New Yorker*, March 6. Accessed 2 July 2020. https://www.newyorker. com/magazine/2011/03/14/shapes-of-things.
Schott, Gareth. 2019. '"Look Up Here, I'm in Heaven": How Visual and Performance Artist David Jones Called Attention to His Physical Death.'

Celebrity Studies 10(1): 140–52. Accessed 2 September 2020. https:// www.tandfonline.com/doi/abs/10.1080/19392397.2018.1559126.

Shaar Murray, Charles. 1972. 'Bowie - Dry Ice, Nice Legs and Absolute Ascendency.' *New Musical Express*, August 26, 24.

Simpson, Dave. 2002. 'Ground Control.' *The Guardian*, June 5. Accessed 2 August 2020. https://www.theguardian.com/culture/2002/jun/05/ artsfeatures.shopping.

Sinclair, David. 1993. 'Station to Station.' *Rolling Stone*, June 10. Accessed 2 July 2020. https://www.rocksbackpages.com/Library/Article/david-bowie-station-to-station-2.

Sischy, Ingrid. 2002. 'Is There No Reason?' *Interview*, June, 23.

Sloan, Billy. 2003. 'I Missed My Son Growing Up... I'm Not Going to Make the Same Mistake with My Daughter.' *Scottish Sunday Mail*, November 23. Accessed 5 July 2020. http://www.bowiewonderworld. com/press/00/031123imissedscottish.htm.

Soloski, Alexis. 2015a. 'A Visit to the Strange, Secretive World of David Bowie's "Lazarus".' *The New York Times*, November 10. Accessed 2 August 2020. https://www.nytimes.com/2015/11/15/theater/a-visit-to-the-strange-secretive-world-of-david-bowies-lazarus.html.

Soloski, Alexis. 2015b. 'Lazarus Review - Bowie's Baffling Starman Lands Off-Broadway.' *The Guardian*, December 8. Accessed 12 July 2020. https://www.theguardian.com/stage/2015/dec/08/lazarus-review-david-bowie-jukebox-musical-off-broadway-new-york.

Sontag, Susan. 2003. 'Literature as Freedom.' *Irish Pages* 2(1): 175–85. Accessed 2 September 2020. https://www.jstor.org/stable/i30057234.

Stanford, Peter. 2016. 'Lazarus Co-Author Enda Walsh: "David Bowie Had So Much More He Wanted to Do".' *The Daily Telegraph*, October 24. Accessed 23 July 2020. https://www.telegraph.co.uk/ men/thinking-man/lazarus-co-author-enda-walsh-david-bowie-had-so-much-more-he-wan/.

Sweeney, Ken. 2013. 'Irish Guitarist Reveals Secret Role in New Bowie Album.' *Irish Independent*, March 2. Accessed 2 July 2020. https:// www.independent.ie/entertainment/music/irish-guitarist-reveals-secret-role-in-new-bowie-album-29104394.html.

Tolstaya, Tatyana. 2015. 'The Square.' *The New Yorker*, June 12. Accessed 2 April 2021. https://www.newyorker.com/culture/cultural-comment/ the-square.

Trynka, Paul. 2016. 'David Bowie's Lazarus.' *Mojo*, October. Accessed 21 June 2020. https://www.pressreader.com/uk/mojo-uk/20161025/284541587640948.

Vengerova, Zinaida. 1915. 'Angliiski Futuristy', in Belenson, Alexander (ed). *Strelets: Sbornik Pervyi*. January. Reproduced in *Paideuma: Modern and Contemporary Poetry and Poetics* 11(3): 473–86. https:// www.jstor.org/stable/i24722370.

Von Bader, David. 2016. 'David Bowie's Ben Monder and Tim Lefebvre: Just Like That Bluebird.' *Premier Guitar*, January 15. Accessed 23 June 2020. https://www.premierguitar.com/artists/david-bowies-ben-monder-and-tim-lefebvre-just-like-that-bluebird.

Wells, Steven. 1995. 'The Artful Codger.' *NME*, November 25, 20.

Whitaker, Ashley. 2016. 'David Bowie: Transience and Potentiality.' *NeuroQuantology* 14(2): 427–32. Accessed 24 April 2021. https://manwithoutqualities.files.wordpress.com/2017/07/955-2550-1-pb.pdf.

White, Ethan Doyle. 2019. '"One Magical Movement from Kether to Malkuth": Occultism in the Work of David Bowie.' *Correspondences* 7(2): 367–409. Accessed 24 April 2021. https://correspondencesjournal.com/ojs/ojs/index.php/home/article/view/84.

Wild, David. 1993. 'Bowie's Wedding Album.' *Rolling Stone*, January 21, 14.

Zollo, Paul. 2017. 'Remembering Blackstar: Bowie's Final Studio "Experiment".' Grammy.com, May 15. Accessed 21 July 2021.

Music (artists other than Bowie)

Berlioz, Hector. 1830. *Symphonie Fantastique Op. 14*.

Cave, Nick. 2019. *Ghosteen*. Ghosteen/Bad Seed.

Cohen, Leonard. *You Want It Darker*, 2016; *Thanks for the Dance*, 2019 (both Columbia).

Dylan, Bob. *Infidels*, 1983; *Time Out of Mind*, 1997; *Christmas in the Heart*, 2009; *Shadows in the Night*, 2015; *Fallen Angels*, 2016; *Triplicate*, 2017; *Rough and Rowdy Ways*, 2020 (all Columbia).

McCaslin, Donny. *Casting for Gravity*, 2012; *Fast Future*, 2015 (both Greenleaf); *Beyond Now*, 2016; *Blow.*, 2018 (both Motéma).

Schneider, Maria. *Sky Blue*, 2007; *The Thompson Fields*, 2015 (both ArtistShare).

Strauss, Richard. 1896. *Also Sprach Zarathustra, Op. 30*.

Strauss, Richard. 1948. *Four Last Songs*.

Walker, Scott. *Tilt*, 1995 (Fontana); *The Drift*, 2006; *Bish Bosch*, 2012; *Soused*, 2014 (with Sunn O)))) (all 4AD).

Music videos/short films

Bayer, Samuel (dir.). 1995. 'Strangers When We Meet'.

Bowie, David (dir.). 2013. 'Love Is Lost.'

Buñuel, Luis (dir.). 1929. *Un Chien Andalou*. Les Grands Films Classiques.

Gavras, Romain (dir.). 2013. 'I'd Rather Be High (Venetian Mix)' (Vuitton ad version).
Hingston, Tom (dir.). 2013. 'I'd Rather Be High (Venetian Mix)'.
Hingston, Tom (dir.). 2017. 'No Plan.' Hingston Studio.
Koepke, Gary (dir.). 2002. 'Slow Burn'.
Mallet, David (dir.). 1980. 'Ashes to Ashes'.
Oursler, Tony (dir.). 2013. 'Where Are We Now?'
Renck, Johan (dir.). 2015. 'Blackstar', 'Lazarus'.
Rock, Mick (dir.). 1972. 'Space Oddity'.
Roper, Barnaby (dir.). 2013. 'Love Is Lost'.
Sigismondi, Floria (dir.). 1996, 1997, 2013. 'Little Wonder', 'Dead Man Walking', 'The Next Day', 'The Stars (Are Out Tonight)'.
Thomson, Malcolm J (dir.). 1969. *Love You Till Tuesday*. Polygram.
Van Sant, Gus (dir.). 1990. 'Fame '90'.

Online

Associated Press. 2011. 'Militant Caught in Afghanistan Dressed as Woman.' CBS News, July. Accessed July 7 2020. https://www.cbsnews.com/news/militant-caught-in-afghanistan-dressed-as-woman/.
Baker, Paul. 2017. 'A Brief History of Polari: the Curious After-life of the Dead Language for Gay Men.' The Conversation, February 8. Accessed July 7 2020. https://theconversation.com/a-brief-history-of-polari-the-curious-after-life-of-the-dead-language-for-gay-men-72599.
BBC. 2016a. 'David Bowie's Love Affair with Japanese Style.' BBC News, January 12. Accessed July 8 2020. https://www.bbc.co.uk/news/world-asia-35278488.
BBC. 2016b. 'David Bowie "a Big Fan" of Peaky Blinders Show.' BBC News, April 26. Accessed July 8 2020. https://www.bbc.co.uk/news/entertainment-arts-36132905.
Bowie, David. 2019. 'Annotated Sketch for "Lazarus" Music Video.' The David Bowie Archive. Accessed August 7 2020. https://davidbowieisreal.com/.
Cave, Nick. 2018. 'Issue #1.' The Red Hand Files, September. Accessed August 7 2020. https://www.theredhandfiles.com/writing-challenge-skeleton-tree/.
Earls, John. 2019. 'Bowie '69: How Everything Changed for Bowie.' *Long Live Vinyl*, August 1. Accessed August 19 2020. https://longlivevinyl.net/2019/08/01/bowie-69-how-everything-changed-for-bowie/.

Fuller, Graham. 2015. 'The Singing Detective: 25 Years On.' British Film
Institute, June 22. Accessed September 7 2020. https://www2.bfi.org.uk/
news-opinion/sight-sound-magazine/features/singing-detective-25-years.

Johnson, Justin (interviewer). 2016a. 'Q&A with Robert Fox and Michael
C. Hall.' BFI, London. September 18. Accessed August 27 2020.
https://www.youtube.com/watch?v=-pa9xTfxCLU.

Johnson, Kevin. 2016b. 'Let Me Get By: An Interview with Tim Lefebvre.'
No Treble, January 14. Accessed July 27 2020. https://www.notreble.
com/buzz/2016/01/14/let-me-get-by-an-interview-with-tim-lefebvre.

Kachka, Boris. 2016. 'Bowie Collaborator Tony Oursler on the Icon's Art-
World Ties, Generosity, and Final Years.' Vulture, February 1. Accessed
July 27 2020. https://www.vulture.com/2016/02/tony-oursler-on-
david-bowies-art-world-ties.html.

Kogan, Judith. 2017. 'The Unsettling Sound of Tritones, the Devil's
Interval.' NPR, October 31. Accessed July 27 2020. https://www.npr.
org/2017/10/31/560843189/the-unsettling-sound-of-tritones-the-
devils-interval?t=1613715930591.

Line 6. 2013. 'Line 6 Artist Gerry Leonard Helps Make Rock History on
David Bowie's "The Next Day".' Line6.Com, July 19. Accessed July 15
2020. https://nl.line6.com/news/general/1459/.

McCarthy, Keiran. 2017. 'An Evening with Enda Walsh Q&A - The Sugar
Club Dublin.' YouTube, January 7. Accessed August 16 2020. https://
www.youtube.com/watch?v=SRLj18GjJVE.

Moody, Rick. 2013. 'Swinging Modern Sounds #44: And Another Day.'
The Rumpus, April 25. Accessed August 27 2020. https://therumpus.
net/2013/04/swinging-modern-sounds-44-and-another-day.

O'Leary, Chris. 2011. '"Heroes".' Pushing Ahead of the Dame, May 11.
Accessed July 19 2020. https://bowiesongs.wordpress.com/2011/05/11/
heroes.

O'Leary, Chris. 2016. 'Heat.' Pushing Ahead of the Dame, October 12.
Accessed July 19 2020. https://bowiesongs.wordpress.com/2016/10/12/
heat.

Roberts, Chris. 2013. 'Great Dame: David Bowie's The Next Day
Reviewed.' The Quietus, February 26. Accessed July 29 2020. https://
thequietus.com/articles/11500-david-bowie-the-next-day-review.

Sandberg, Marian. 2010. 'David Bowie Glass Spider (1987) - Top
Concert Tour Design of All Time.' Live Design, August 1. Accessed 6
April 2021. Accessed July 22 2020. https://www.livedesignonline.com/
projects/david-bowie-glass-spider-1987-top-concert-tour-design-all-
time.

Santos, Juan Jose. 2013. 'Putting Video to David Bowie's Music: A
Conversation with Artist Tony Oursler.' TonyOursler.com, February
7. Accessed July 9 2020. https://tonyoursler.com/putting-video-to-

david-bowies-music-a-conversation-with-artist-tony-oursler-by-juan-jose-santos.

Sequential. 2016. 'Featured artist: Jason Lindner.' July 12. https://www.sequential.com/artists/jason-lindner.

Smith, Clyde. 2013. 'Ty Roberts: From Working with David Bowie to Co-founding Gracenote.' Hypebot, March 8. Accessed 6 April 2021. http://www.hypebot.com/hypebot/2013/03/ty-roberts-on-the-trail-from-working-with-david-bowie-to-co-founding-gracenote.html.

Trendell, Andrew. 2018. 'Glastonbury 2000: The Night Bowie Reclaimed His Legend.' *NME*, December 4. https://www.nme.com/reviews/glastonbury-2000-night-bowie-reclaimed-legend-2414842.

Troncale, Joseph. 2020. 'From Kazimir Malevich's *Black Square* to the *Midnight Sun* of Adi Da Samraj.' Daplastique.com, November 9. Accessed 6 April 2021. https://www.daplastique.com/essay/from-kazimir-malevichs-black-square-to-the-midnight-sun-of-adi-da-samraj/.

Tuffrey, Laurie. 2013. 'Jonathan Barnbrook Talks Bowie Artwork.' The Quietus, January 8. Accessed 6 August 2020. https://thequietus.com/articles/11062-david-bowie-the-next-day-jonathan-barnbrook-cover-artwork.

Trynka, Paul. 2017. 'Lazarus: A Trilogy of Memories.' Trynka.net, January 7. Accessed 16 August 2020. http://trynka.net/2017/01/lazarus-a-trilogy-of-memories/.

United Nations. 2021. 'Refugees.' Accessed 6 August 2020. https://www.un.org/en/sections/issues-depth/refugees/.

Wilson, Carl. 2020. 'Bob Dylan's New Album Is His Best in Many Years, Maybe Decades.' Slate, June 18. Accessed 20 June 2020. https://slate.com/culture/2020/06/bob-dylan-rough-rowdy-ways-album-review.html.

Yahoo! 2000. 'Halloween chat.' BowieWonderworld, Oct 31. Accessed 26 August 2020. http://www.bowiewonderworld.com/chats/dbyahoo311000.htm.

Yakas, Ben. 2010. 'Anti-Semitic Driver Drops "Kill Jews" Notes Around NY.' Gothamist, November 3. Accessed 16 July 2020. https://gothamist.com/news/anti-semitic-driver-drops-kill-jews-notes-around-ny.

Podcasts, talks and radio shows

Delaney, Rob. 2020. BBC Radio 4 Today, December 8. Accessed 6 August 2020. https://www.bbc.co.uk/programmes/p06lp2h5.

Dylan, Bob. 2006–15, 2020. Theme Time Radio Hour. Sirius/XM/Deep Tracks. https://www.themetimeradio.com/.

Koenig, Peter-Robert. 1996. 'Ecstatic Creation of Culture.' Lecture.
C.E.S.N.U.R., University of Montreal, August. Accessed 19 February
2021. https://www.pararreligion.ch/ecstasy.htm.
Leonard, Gerry. 2013. Mouthcast, March 4. Accessed 18 February 2021.
https://themouthmagazine.com/2013/03/04/gerry-leonard-mouthcast.
Mohammad, Arsalan. 2020. 'Donny McCaslin and Leah Kardos on ★.'
David Bowie: Album to Album. Acast, June 21, July 6, August 9.
Accessed 9 February 2021. https://play.acast.com/s/davidbowie-
albumtoalbum.
Radio X. 2018. 'Ricky Gervais: "David Bowie Doesn't Really Exist".' Radio
X, March 13. Accessed 21 February 2021. https://www.radiox.co.uk/
artists/david-bowie/ricky-gervais-bowie-doesnt-exist-normal-bloke/.
Stark, Tanja. 2016. 'David Bowie and Carl Jung: Creativity and Catharsis,
Dreaming and Death.' Lecture. C. G. Jung Society of Queensland, July 7.
Visconti Studio. 2020. 'Tape Is a Beast - Tony Visconti, Chris Kimsey,
Martin Terefe, George Murphy and Andy Cook.' SoundCloud, August
8. Accessed 6 August 2020. https://soundcloud.com/viscontistudio/
tape-is-a-beast-tony-visconti-chris-kimsey-martin-terefe-george-
murphy-and-andy-cook.
Wilson, John. 2002. 'John Wilson talks to David Bowie in New York, in
2002.' Front Row, BBC Radio 4. Accessed 11 August 2021. https://
www.bbc.co.uk/news/av/entertainment-arts-35278805.

Bibliography

Bataille, Georges. 2004. *On Nietzsche*. Translated by Bruce Boone.
London: A&C Black.
Battistini, Matilde. 2005. *Symbols and Allegories in Art*. Translated by
Stephen Sartarelli. Los Angeles: Getty Publications.
Baudrillard, Jean. 2016. *Symbolic Exchange and Death*. Translated by
Iain Hamilton Grant. California: Sage.
Brackett, David. 2000. *Interpreting Popular Music*. Berkeley: University of
California Press.
Bradley, Ben, Feldman, Fred and Jens Johansson, eds. 2015. *Oxford
Handbook of Philosophy of Death*. Oxford: Oxford University Press.
Campbell, Joseph. 1949. *The Hero with a Thousand Faces*. New York:
Pantheon Books.
Cook, Nicholas. 1994. *A Guide to Musical Analysis*. Oxford: Oxford
University Press.
Curcio, James. 2019. *Masks*. Bristol: Intellect Books.

Drob, Sanford L. 1999. *Symbols of the Kabbalah*. Lanham, Maryland: Jason Aronson, Inc.

Egan, Sean. 2015. *Bowie on Bowie: Interviews and Encounters with David Bowie*. Chicago: Chicago Review Press.

Elferen, Isabella van. 2012. *Gothic Music*. Cardiff: University of Wales Press.

Elmhirst, Tom. 2019. 'Inside the Track #21 "Lazarus".' Mix with the Masters, April 23. https://mixwiththemasters.com/itt21.

Fisher, Mark. 2017. *The Weird and the Eerie*. London: Repeater.

Frith, Simon. 1998. *Performing Rites*. Cambridge, MA: Harvard University Press.

Hall, James A. 1989. *Hall's Dictionary of Subjects and Symbols in Art*. London: John Murray.

Hallam, Elizabeth. 2001. *Death, Memory and Material Culture (Materializing Culture)*. London: Bloomsbury Academic.

Hanh, Thich Nhat. 1999. *The Heart of the Buddha's Teaching*. New York: Random House.

Hillman, James. 1990. *The Essential James Hillman: A Blue Fire*. London: Routledge.

Huron, David. 2006. *Sweet Anticipation*. Cambridge, Mass: MIT Press.

Lachman, Gary. 2014. *Aleister Crowley*. New York: TarcherPerigee.

Levitin, Daniel J. 2011. *This Is Your Brain On Music*. London: Atlantic Books Ltd.

Moore, Allan F. 2016. *Song Means: Analysing and Interpreting Recorded Popular Song*. London: Routledge.

Partridge, Christopher. 2017. *Mortality and Music*. London: Bloomsbury.

Pascale, Enrico De. 2009. *Death and Resurrection in Art*. Los Angeles: Getty Publications.

Patel, Aniruddh D. 2010. *Music, Language, and the Brain*. Oxford: Oxford University Press.

Penfold-Mounce, Ruth. 2018. *Death, the Dead and Popular Culture*. Bingley, West Yorkshire: Emerald Group Publishing.

Roth, Martin (ed). 2013. *David Bowie Is the Subject*. London: Victoria & Albert Museum.

Schumacher, Bernard N. 2010. *Death and Mortality in Contemporary Philosophy*. Cambridge: Cambridge University Press.

Strong, Catherine. 2015. *Death and the Rock Star*. Farnham, Surrey: Ashgate Publishing Ltd.

Tagg, Philip. 2013. *Music's Meanings*. Larchmont, New York: Mass Media Music Scholar's Press.

Townsend, Chris. 2008. *Art and Death*. London: Bloomsbury Publishing.

Visconti, Tony. 2008. *Tony Visconti: The Autobiography: Bowie, Bolan and the Brooklyn Boy*. London: Harper Collins UK.

INDEX